VISUAL QUICKSTART GUIDE

RAY DREAM STUDIO 5

FOR WINDOWS AND MACINTOSH

RICHARD KAHN
ANDRE PERSIDSKY

Peachpit Press

Visual QuickStart Guide
Ray Dream Studio 5 for Windows and Macintosh
Richard Kahn and Andre Persidsky

Peachpit Press
1249 Eighth Street
Berkeley, CA 94710
510/524-2178
800/283-9444
510/524-2221 (fax)

Find us on the World Wide Web at: http://www.peachpit.com
Peachpit Press is a division of Addison Wesley Longman

Copyright © 1998 by Richard Kahn & Andre Persidsky
Cover design: The Visual Group

Notice of Rights

Notice of Liability

ISBN 0-201-69671-1

9 8 7 6 5 4 3 2 1

Printed and bound in the United States

TABLE OF CONTENTS

Chapter 5: **Introducing the Free Form Modeler** 61

Chapter 6: **Working with Points and Axes** 73

Chapter 7: **Mastering the Free Form Modeler** 85

Table of Contents

PART III: FINISHING 3D OBJECTS 165

Chapter 11: **Using Deformers**...193

Table of Contents

PART IV: PRODUCING SCENES 219

Chapter 14: **Action!** 249

Chapter 15: **Rendering Stills and Movies** 267

Table of Contents

PREFACE

WHAT IS RAY DREAM STUDIO 5?
Ray Dream Studio 5 is easily the most powerful, affordable and comprehensive 3D graphics modeling, rendering, and animation package available today.

WHO SHOULD BUY THIS BOOK?
Although Ray Dream Studio 5 is sleek and efficient, its breadth and depth can make it as challenging for trainers and educators to teach as it is for users and students to learn.

We carefully designed this book to be a valuable addition to the library of every member of the Ray Dream community.

- Beginning users will be brought up to speed quickly within the first few chapters.
- Intermediate users will quickly locate and master the specific concepts, tools, and techniques needed to become experts.
- Advanced users will appreciate the many nuances and insights that can only come from hundreds of hours of poking, prodding, and probing the program to push it to its limits.
- Trainers and educators will appreciate both the conceptual framework and the fully illustrated step-by-step instructions.

WHAT DOES THIS BOOK COVER?
This book is presented in four parts containing 15 chapters:

PART I: GETTING STARTED

will get you oriented and operational as quickly as possible.

Chapter 1: **Jump-Starting Ray Dream Studio 5** gets you up and running instantly! In just a few pages, you'll create a complete indoor scene, modify it, animate it, render it as a still image, and render it again as a movie, using Ray Dream's advanced wizards, stock objects, and other powerful features.

Chapter 2: **How Ray Dream Studio 5** Works provides a comprehensive guide to both the organization and utilization of all of the program's major housekeeping, file-management, object modeling, and scene lighting, photographing, animating, and rendering features. Every major window, menu, tabbed dialog box, and other feature is presented in the order in which it is normally used, and described in a commentary that spans the entire chapter.

Chapter 3: **Managing The Scene** shows you how to manage and navigate a scene visually with the Perspective Window and logically with the Time Line Window. Key concepts like the scene's universe, the Perspective window's working box, and an object's bounding box are explained and related.

PART II: MODELING 3D OBJECTS

provides complete coverage of Ray Dream's Primitives and it's Free Form and Mesh Form modeling tools.

Chapter 4: **Using Primitives** teaches you how to add a primitive 3D object, such as a cube, cone, sphere, text, or infinite plane, to your scene. It also shows you how to align objects in the scene so that they touch, contain, or support each other.

Chapter 5: **Introducing the Free Form Modeler** teaches you how to define 2D shapes and how to extrude and lathe them into 3D objects.

Chapter 6: **Working with Points and Axes** explains Ray Dream's 3D coordinate system and teaches you how to manipulate points, lines, segments, Bezier curves, and 2D shapes to model 3D objects and events.

Chapter 7: **Mastering the Free Form Modeler** helps you harness the full power of the Free Form Modeler. It shows you how to work with multiple 2D shapes and cross sections; how to define the sweep path, the extrusion envelope, and the lathing profile; and how to extrude shapes along those paths.

Chapter 8: **Introducing the Mesh Form Modeler** illustrates key Mesh Form concepts such as vertices, edges, polygons, polylines, and polymeshes with a brief hands-on exercise. It concludes with a functional classification of the Mesh Form Modeler's various tools and techniques.

Chapter 9: **Mastering the Mesh Form Modeler** builds on the classification set out in Chapter 8. The Mesh Form Modeler's use of polylines, extrusions, sweeps, and lathes, and its non-use of Bezier curves, are covered in detail.

PART III: FINISHING 3D OBJECTS

shows you how to customize the appearance of the different types of 3D objects that appear in your scene.

Chapter 10: **Using Shaders and 3D Paint** teaches you how to apply Ray Dream's innovative shaders to objects to give their surfaces color, texture, highlights, shininess, transparency, texture, and even images and video clips. It also teaches you how to create, edit, recycle, preview, and manage shaders with the Browser palette, the Shader Document window, the Shading tab of the Properties palette, and the Current Shader Editor window.

Chapter 11: **Using Deformers** shows you how to customize the volumetric appearance of objects by applying deformers to their surfaces. It also teaches you how to create, edit, recycle, preview, and manage deformers with the Browser palette, the Deformer Document window, and the Deformer tab of the Properties palette.

PART IV: PRODUCING SCENES

shows you how to deploy lights and cameras, how to choreograph animations, and how to render still images and movie files for use by themselves or with all popular post-production tools.

Chapter 12: **Lights!** teaches you how to select, insert, place, configure, aim, and control lights and cameras to enhance the impact of every scene you build.

Chapter 13: **Cameras!** teaches you how to select, insert, place, configure, aim, and control single and multiple cameras to capture the still and movie renders you need. Special attention is paid to working with multiple Perspective windows and cameras simultaneously, and to the intricacies of pan, track, and dolly camera movements.

Chapter 14: **Action!** covers both the fundamental principles of animation and the details of Ray Dream Studio 5 animation and behaviors. It teaches you how to animate a scene's 3D objects, lights, and cameras by populating the scene's Time Axis with key events and tweener transition effects.

Chapter 15: **Rendering Stills and Movies** teaches you how to render still images and movies from your scene. It further teaches you how to select and configure the different rendering features and attributes. Step-by-step instructions show you how to select and configure the Adaptive, Draft Z-Buffer, NaturalMedia ThinkFish, and Ray Tracer rendering engines; the output file format and other options; and the stock render effects and filters. It shows how to use Ray Dream's Image and Movie Viewer tools to review your renders. And it provides in-depth instruction on how to save, load, and override render settings; how to launch a single render with a single mouse click; and how to define, launch, and manage multiple renders with the batch queue dialog box.

HOW IS THE MATERIAL PRESENTED?

This book is designed to flatten the Ray Dream learning curve: A consistent, top-down approach leads you naturally from the conceptual to the practical, and from the general to the specific. Dozens of vital concepts and mini-tutorials, consisting of hundreds of numbered steps and bulleted tips, and over one thousand numbered and captioned screen shots and illustrations, will provide you with the most painless and efficient Ray Dream Studio 5 learning experience that money can buy.

HOW SHOULD THIS BOOK BE USED?

Chapters and sections may be used in or out of sequence. We have tried hard not to make an island out of any individual topic. We hope that both the sequential reader and the skip-and-skim reader will benefit from the frequent comparisons of previously presented and subsequently covered concepts and techniques.

THANK YOU!

We thank you for purchasing our work and wish you many contented hours of 3D modeling, shading, deforming, lighting, photographing, animating, and rendering with Ray Dream Studio 5!

ACKNOWLEDGMENTS

We thank Jeanne Woodward, Editor, and Kenneth R. Berri, Ph.D., for their invaluable editorial assistance.

DEDICATION

For my Great Uncle, Philip Capece—R. K.
For my inspiration, Dzhennet Eschekova—A. P.

Part I:
Getting Started

JUMP-STARTING RAY DREAM STUDIO 5

Figure 1. One of Ray Dream's powerful features is its ability to render photorealistic still images of your scene.

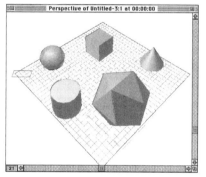

Figure 2. Ray Dream's Primitive tools allow you easily to create the basic geometric forms.

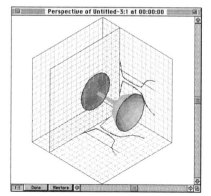

Figure 3. The Free Form Modeler allows you to "extrude" simple 2D shapes into complex 3D forms.

Mastering Ray Dream Studio 5 can be a very challenging journey. Our mission is to ease that journey as much as possible.

In this chapter you will learn:

- What Ray Dream can do—and what it cannot.

- How to construct a scene with the Scene Wizard, modify the shading of one of the scene's objects, render a photorealistic still image of the scene **(Figure 1)**, add a behavior to an object, preview the spinning behavior, and render a movie of the animation.

SCOPING OUT RAY DREAM STUDIO 5

Ray Dream Studio 5 is a powerful, comprehensive, and complex application that combines sophisticated modeling, finishing, production, and animation tools within a single integrated environment.

What Ray Dream Studio can do

Ray Dream Studio excels at the following tasks:

- Creating and managing scenes comprised of 3D objects, lights, cameras, behaviors, and key-frame animations.

- Modeling 3D objects with:
  - Primitive tools like cubes, cones, cylinders, spheres **(Figure 2)**, and text strings.
  - An extrusion tool called the Free Form Modeler that extrudes 2D shapes along simple or complex sweep paths and extrusion envelopes **(Figure 3)**.

- A sculpting tool called the Mesh Form Modeler **(Figure 4)**.
- A set of grouping, arranging, aligning and positioning tools that let you manage objects easily, efficiently and intuitively.
- Customizing the surface characteristics of 3D objects with:
  - Shader and 3D Paint tools that apply single or multiple layers of colors, patterns **(Figure 5)**, textures, and even bitmaps and video clips to the surfaces of 3D objects.
  - Deformer tools that apply single or double deformations, such as dents, bends, twists, and spikes **(Figure 6)**, to the surfaces of 3D objects.
  - Rendering still images and movies from a scene one at a time or, using the batch queue, several at a time.
  - Importing and exporting scenes and animations to and from a wide variety of 2D and 3D graphics file formats for deployment across a wide variety of media types, such as print publications, CD-ROMs, and the Internet.

Because Ray Dream Studio excels at each of these tasks, it is a favorite tool in the toolbox of graphics designers, multimedia producers, fine art artists, and the academic community.

What Ray Dream Studio can't do

As complete as Ray Dream Studio 5 is, it doesn't do everything. Other programs, such as Sonic Foundry's Sound Forge, or Adobe's Premiere and After Effects, are routinely used by Ray Dream users to add sound tracks and composite video clips, and to perform other audio and video effects in the post-production phase.

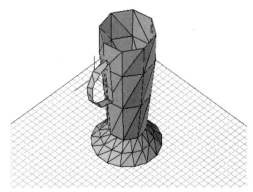

Figure 4. The Mesh Form Modeler allows you to create objects by directly manipulating their vertices, edges, and polygons.

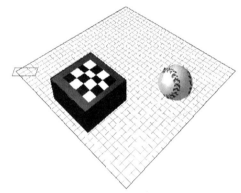

Figure 5. Ray Dream's 3D paint and shader tools allow you to apply textures and shaders to the surface of objects.

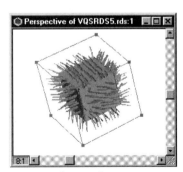

Figure 6. Deformers allow you to create complex predefined deformation patterns such as twists, spikes, and dents on the surfaces of your 3D objects.

Figure 7. Ray Dream's Browser palette offers many preset "drag and drop" items like shaders and behaviors.

Figure 8. You can use the Scene Wizard to generate complete scenes quickly.

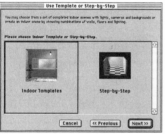

Figure 9. The Scene Wizard offers two types of scenes: completed templates and step-by-step component scenes.

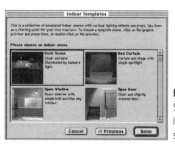

Figure 10. The Scene Wizard's Indoor Template scenes.

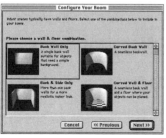

Figure 11. The Scene Wizard's Indoor Step-by-Step scenes.

Cross-platform support

Another reason for Ray Dream Studio's popularity is its availability and file compatibility across today's most powerful and popular computing platforms: the Macintosh Power Mac series, Windows 95, and Windows NT.

BLASTING OFF WITH RAY DREAM STUDIO 5

Ray Dream beginners will be delighted to learn that there is a quick, easy, and fun way to start using this powerful and complex program.

Three of Ray Dream's many state-of-the art features—the Browser palette that brims with prebuilt shaders **(Figure 7)**, the Scene Wizard that builds complete scenes in seconds **(Figure 8)**, and the preconfigured rendering engine—let you build, light, customize, and render an intriguing scene, all within minutes.

Creating, modifying, and rendering your first scene

The first task is to select and create a new scene with the Scene Wizard.

A Scene Wizard is an automated method for building, lighting, populating, and arranging a scene. After obtaining your answers to various questions that are presented in a series of dialog boxes, Ray Dream builds the scene for you in just a few seconds.

There are two types of Scene Wizards **(Figures 9–11)**: completed templates and step-by-step component-based scenes.

In the next couple of pages, you will create an interior tabletop scene with a Scene Wizard, change the table's finish, render a photorealistic image, apply a spinning behavior to a cup positioned on the table, and render an AVI or QuickTime movie of the cup spinning around the tabletop.

Create, Modify, Render Your First Scene

To use the Scene Wizard:

1. Choose New from the File menu **(Figure 12)**.

2. In the New dialog box, click the Use Scene Wizard button **(Figure 13)**.

3. The Scene Wizard dialog box presents the following options **(Figure 14)**:

- Logo Templates

- Indoor Scenes

- Photo Studio

- Outdoor Scenes

4. Select Indoor Scenes by double-clicking it or by clicking it once and then clicking the Next button at the bottom of the dialog box.

5. Select the Indoor Templates option by double-clicking its button.

6. Double-click the Desk Scene option.

7. Choose Workspace from the Windows menu **(Figure 15)**, and select 800x600 Animation to configure the Ray Dream windows and toolbars in an appropriate arrangement.

✔ Tips

■ If the New dialog box containing the Use Scene Wizard button does not open when you choose New from the File menu, close the new scene that is created without saving it, and enable the Scene Wizard as follows:

- Choose Preferences from the file menu.

- If the currently selected Preference is not already sent to General, set it now.

- In the Scene Wizard area of the dialog box, place a checkmark in the checkbox labeled "Use Scene Wizard on new" **(Figure 16)**.

Figure 12. Choose **New** from the **File** menu.

Figure 13. Click the Use Scene Wizard button in the **New** dialog box.

Figure 14. The **Scene Wizard** dialog box.

Figure 15. Choose **Workspace** from the **Windows** menu, and select **800x600 Animation**.

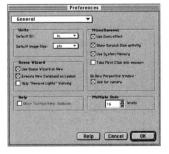

Figure 16. Check the "Use Scene Wizard" option in the **Preferences** dialog box for the **General** setting.

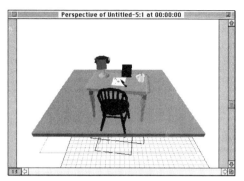

Figure 17. Click the title bar of the Perspective window to make it the current window.

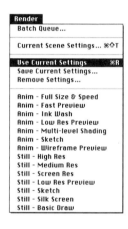

Figure 18. Choose **Use Current Settings** from the **Render** menu.

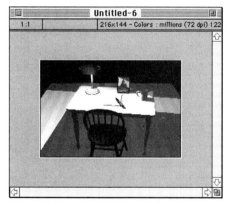

Figure 19. When the render is complete, the rendered image appears in the Render Document window.

■ If, at any time before you have clicked the Done button, you wish to change an answer to a previous question, click the Previous button as often as needed to return to dialog box that presented the question, give your new answer, and click the Next button to step through each subsequent dialog box.

Rendering a still image from the scene

The second task is to get a sneak preview of what the table will "really " look like by rendering it as a still image. The default render settings will yield an image that is large enough to give you an idea of what the scene will actually look like but small enough to render quickly.

To render the scene:

1. Make the Perspective window the current window by clicking its title bar **(Figure 17)**.

2. Choose Use Current Settings from the Render menu **(Figure 18)**.

3. In a moment, a Render Document window is opened **(Figure 19)**.

4. Scroll and resize the window as desired.

5. To zoom in, position the magnifying glass cursor in the render and click the image.

6. To zoom out, position the pointer, hold the Alt/Option key down and click the image.

7. Minimize or close the Render Document window, and save or discard the image.

Render the Scene

Applying a shader to a 3D object

The third task is to refinish the table by replacing its shader.

To apply a different shader to the table:

1. Click the Selection tool.

2. Click the table and hold the mouse down to display a pop-up list of objects **(Figure 20)**.

3. Drag the mouse over Table 3D to highlight it, and release the mouse button to select it **(Figure 21)**.

4. Confirm that the table has been selected by verifying that its bounding box is now visible.

5. Move the Browser palette into view.

6. Use the arrow keys of the Browser palette to navigate the tabs so that the Shaders tab comes into view.

7. Click the Shaders tab of the Browser palette.

8. Click the icon for the Blue Glow shader, and release the mouse **(Figure22)**.

9. Click the icon again, and without releasing the mouse, drag the icon to a position within the table's bounding box and release the mouse.

10. Repeat the render process outlined above to see what the table looks like with its new finish **(Figure 23)**.

Applying a behavior to a 3D object

The fourth task is to apply a spin behavior to the cup on the table and the pen that it holds.

To apply a spin behavior to a group of objects:

1. Click the Selection tool.

2. Click the table and hold the mouse to display a pop-up list of objects.

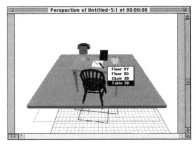

Figure 20. Click the table and hold the mouse down to display a pop-up menu.

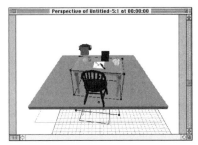

Figure 21. Choose **Table3D** from the pop-up menu to select the table.

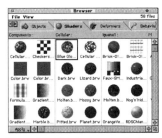

Figure 22. Click the icon for the Blue Glow shader in the Broswer palette.

Figure 23. Repeat the render process to view the table with its new shader surface.

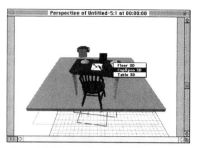

Figure 24. Choose **Cup&pen 3D** from the pop-up menu.

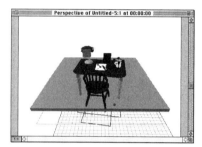

Figure 25. Confirm that the cup has been selected.

Figure 26. Click the Spin Behavior icon in the Behaviors tab of the Browser palette.

3. Drag the mouse over Cup&pen 3D to highlight it, and release the mouse button to select it **(Figure 24)**.

4. Confirm that the object group has been selected by verifying that its bounding box is now visible **(Figure 25)**.

5. Move the Browser palette into view.

6. Use the arrow keys of the Browser palette to navigate the tabs so that the Behaviors tab comes into view.

7. Click the Behaviors tab of the Browser palette.

8. Click the icon for the Spin behavior and release the mouse **(Figure 26)**.

9. Click the icon again, and without releasing the mouse, drag the icon to a position within the pen and cup group's bounding box and release the mouse.

Previewing behaviors

The fifth task is to preview the behavior in the Perspective window.

To preview an object's behavior in the Perspective window:

1. Make the Perspective Window the current window.

2. Click the Loop button on the Time Controller toolbar to toggle it into its "on" position **(Figure 27)**.

3. Click the Play button in the Controller toolbar.

4. Observe the motion of the cup and pen group.

Rendering a movie from the scene

The sixth and final task is to render a movie of the spinning cup scene.

Play button   Loop button

Figure 27. The Time Controller toolbar.

To render a movie from the scene:

1. Make the Perspective window the current window by clicking its title bar.

2. Choose Use Current Settings from the Render menu **(Figure 28)**.

3. In a moment, a render document window is opened **(Figure 29)**.

4. Resize the window as desired.

5. To play the movie, click the Play button.

6. To loop the movie continuously, press the Loop button.

7. To stop the movie, click the Stop button.

8. Minimize or close the Render Document window, and save or discard the image, as you choose.

Looking ahead: recycling and revising scenes and objects

You can, of course, dissect, modify, and reuse the scene and objects that you have just built. The remainder of this book will show how!

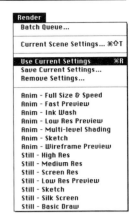

Figure 28. Choose **Use Current Settings** from the **Render** menu.

Figure 29. To play your rendered movie, click the Play button at the bottom-left corner of the Render Document window.

Render a Movie

HOW RAY DREAM STUDIO 5 WORKS

THE RAY DREAM STUDIO INTERFACE: AN OVERVIEW

Ray Dream Studio 5 is an advanced graphics suite that integrates 3D modeling, animating, and rendering within a single environment.

This chapter provides you with a walk-through of all of Ray Dream Studio's major windows, menus, dialog boxes, and other features.

The topics are covered in the following order:

- Ray Dream Studio main windows
- Menus
- General program operation
- Object management
- Scene creation and management
- 3D object modeling
- 3D object finishing
- Lights and cameras
- Animation
- Rendering

Ray Dream Studio Overview

Ray Dream Studio 5 main windows

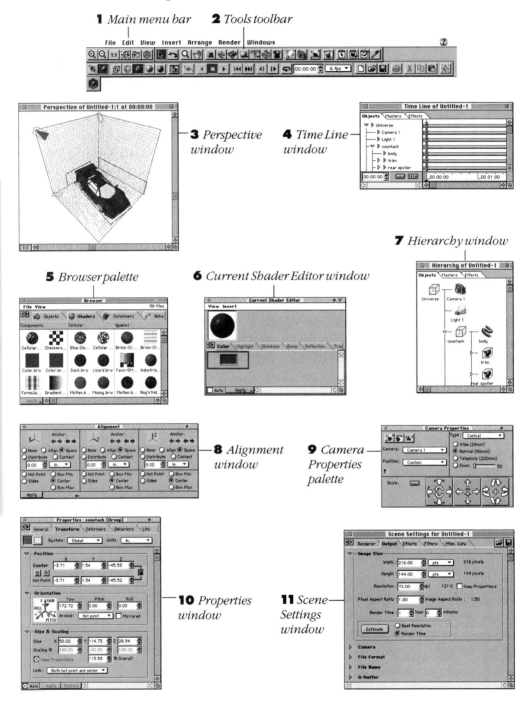

1 *Main menu bar* **2** *Tools toolbar*

3 *Perspective window*

4 *Time Line window*

7 *Hierarchy window*

5 *Browser palette*

6 *Current Shader Editor window*

8 *Alignment window*

9 *Camera Properties palette*

10 *Properties window*

11 *Scene Settings window*

Ray Dream Studio 5 Main Windows

Key to Ray Dream Studio 5 main windows

1. *Main Menu bar*

This is Ray Dream Studio's standard menu bar, which appears when the program starts up and whenever the Perspective window is active. The selection of menus is different when either the Mesh Form Modeler or the Free Form Modeler is active.

2. *Tools toolbar*

The Tools toolbar is shown for the Perspective window. The selection of tools in the Tools toolbar changes depending on whether the Perspective window, the Mesh Form Modeler, or the Free Form Modeler is active.

3. *Perspective window*

The Perspective window is where you arrange the 3D objects, lights, and cameras that populate the scene. Animation is achieved by changing the arrangement of the scene, and the position, orientation, or other characteristics of its objects, lights, and cameras at different points in time along the timeline.

4. *Time Line window*

The Time Line window displays a hierarchical list of all the objects in your scene, which includes all 3D objects, cameras, and lights. The Time Line window also shows the events, transitions, and length of your animation.

5. *Browser palette*

The Browser Palette is a tabbed dialog box that contains stored objects grouped by type, such as shaders and deformers. These objects can be edited, duplicated, and reused in as many scenes as you like.

6. *Current Shader Editor window*

The Current Shader Editor window displays Ray Dream's current shader and is used to edit, apply, and create shaders.

7. *Hierarchy window*

Like the Time Line window, the Hierarchy window displays the hierarchical relationships of objects in your scenes, but does so through icons rather than a text list. Unlike the Time Line window, the Hierarchy window does not display information concerning your animation.

8. *Alignment window*

The Alignment window is used to align two or more objects together in the Perspective window. For example, you can use this window to position objects precisely so that they rest on the same plane or so that they are stacked on top of each other.

9. *Camera Properties palette*

The Camera Properties palette lets you access several advanced tools and features, such as pan, track, and dolly tools, that apply specifically to cameras.

10. *Properties window*

The Properties window is used to display and edit the settings of the currently selected object in a scene.

11. *Scene Settings window*

The Scene Settings window is used to specify a wide variety of parameters that affect the appearance and output format of your scene.

Use this window to select the type of renderer used to render your scene, to set the output file format of your animation, and to include a backdrop image.

Main menu bar

File Edit View Insert Arrange Render Windows

The File menu selections such as Save, Open, Import, and Preferences apply to your Ray Dream Studio scene file as a whole.

The Edit menu provides standard editing commands such as Copy and Paste, which are used in the Perspective window as well as in the Mesh Form Modeler and the Free Form Modeler.

The Jump In Another Modeler command, also located under the Edit menu, allows you to specify the Ray Dream modeler you wish to use to edit a 3D object.

File	
New...	⌘N
Open...	⌘O
Close	⌘W
Save	⌘S
Save As...	
Import...	
Export...	
Print...	⌘P
Page Setup...	
Apply Scene Wizard...	
Preferences...	⌘⇧P
Posim:...:rendcar	
Posim:...:Ch1Tiff1	
Posim:...:ch1Tiff1	
Posim:Ray Dream Studio™:test1	
Quit	⌘Q

Edit	
Undo Jump Out	⌘Z
Can't Redo	⌘Y
Cut	⌘X
Copy	⌘C
Paste	⌘V
Delete	
Duplicate	⌘D
Duplicate with Symmetry	⌘opt D
Select All	⌘A
Select All Objects	⌘opt A
Find...	⌘F
Jump In	
Jump In New Window	
Jump In Another Modeler...	
Jump Out	

The View menu contains the various Preview Quality commands, such as Shaded Preview, used to view objects in the Perspective window.

The Insert menu is used to insert geometric and environmental primitives into your scene, such as a Cube and Fountain primitive. You can also insert a new camera or light via this menu.

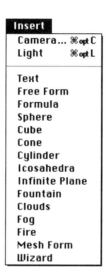

The Arrange menu commands, such as Align Objects and Center Hot Point, generally deal with arranging and aligning 3D objects in your scene.

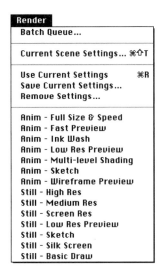

Use the Render menu to set Current Scene Settings, as well as to choose a renderer with which to render your current scene or animation.

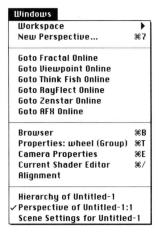

The Windows menu is used to open the various windows that are available in Ray Dream Studio, such as the Perspective and Hierarchy windows. The Workspace command, which allows you to quickly optimize your window workspace arrangement, is also found under the Windows menu.

Menu bar for the Free Form Modeler

File   Edit   View   Sections   Arrange   Geometry   Render   Windows

The menus listed below are those that are different from or unavailable in the main menu bar.

The View menu for the Free Form Modeler is used to set the Preview Quality for displaying objects in the modeler. You can also set the Modeling Box size from this menu.

The Sections menu generally deals with creating and managing the cross sections that compose the free form object in the Free Form Modeler.

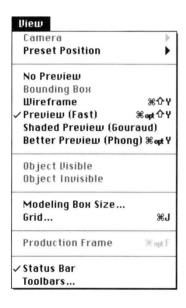

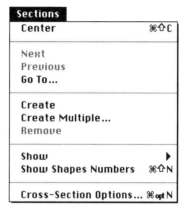

The Arrange menu for the Free Form Modeler generally deals with combining and grouping shapes located on a cross section.

The Geometry menu for the Free Form Modeler allows you to select the Extrusion Method used to extrude cross sections, to show or hide the extrusion envelope, and to scale and rotate shapes on cross sections.

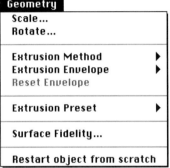

Menu bar for the Mesh Form Modeler

File   Edit   View   Selection   PolyMesh   Render   Windows

The menus listed below are those that are different
from or unavailable in the main menu bar.

The View menu for the Mesh Form
Modeler allows you to change the position of the current drawing plane, and to
change the viewpoint of the modeling
box to a Preset Position.

You can also set the Preview Quality of
objects in the Mesh Form Modeler through
the View menu.

The Selection menu for the Mesh Form
Modeler allows you to apply various functions such as Welding, Rotating,
Flattening, and Subdividing to the different types of possible selections you can
make in the modeler, such as vertices,
polylines, polygons, and polymeshes.

The Polymesh menu for the Mesh Form Modeler allows
you to perform Boolean operations on selected objects, as
well as to specify whether edges on your objects should
appear sharp or smooth.

View, Selection, Polymesh Menus

General program operation

Standard toolbar

Tools toolbar

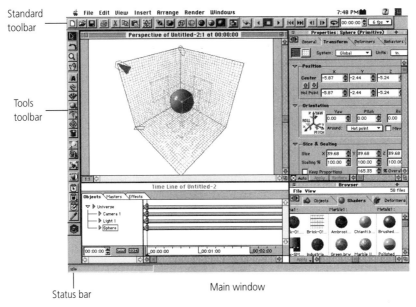

Status bar

Main window

Workspace configuration is vital to using Ray Dream efficiently. The **Workspace** command and its submenu let you choose from a list of prebuilt arrangements of windows and toolbars for a variety of different tasks. You can also save new workspace layouts.

The **Toolbars** dialog box shows the list of available toolbars. A check mark beside a name means that the toolbar is visible in the main window.

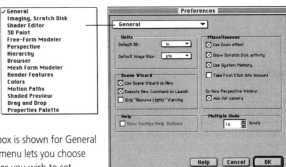

The **Preferences** dialog box is shown for General Preferences. The pop-up menu lets you choose which program preferences you wish to set.

Object management

Ray Dream excels at managing and reusing every conceivable kind of object, from 3D objects to shaders and deformers to behaviors and render settings.

The **Browser palette menu** is used to register and display the directories which contain disk files that hold information about the stored objects, to display icons or text for objects, and to enable or disable the float feature.

The **Browser palette** is a tabbed dialog box that contains stored objects grouped by type. These objects can be edited, duplicated, and reused in as many scenes as you like.

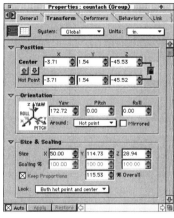

The **Properties Palette** is used to display and edit the settings of the object in a scene that is currently selected in either the Perspective window or the Time Line window. These settings can also be applied to other objects, or stored in the Browser palette, with a simple drag and drop movement. The Properties palette is opened by choosing Properties from the Windows menu.

The **Object Document** windows for a shader, a deformer, and a behavior are shown. Documents are disk files that contain the settings for a stored object, such as the various channels that describe a shader.

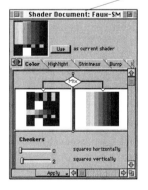

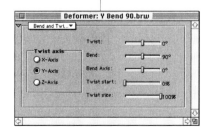

Object Management

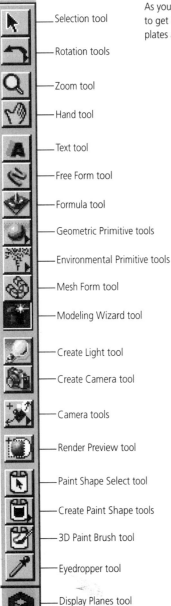

Selection tool

Rotation tools

Zoom tool

Hand tool

Text tool

Free Form tool

Formula tool

Geometric Primitive tools

Environmental Primitive tools

Mesh Form tool

Modeling Wizard tool

Create Light tool

Create Camera tool

Camera tools

Render Preview tool

Paint Shape Select tool

Create Paint Shape tools

3D Paint Brush tool

Eyedropper tool

Display Planes tool

Tools toolbar for the Perspective window. The tools in the Tools toolbar vary according to what part of the program is being used.

Scene creation and management

As you learned in the first chapter, Ray Dream makes it easy to get a scene up and running quickly and easily, with templates and scene wizards.

Zoom In

Zoom Out

Actual Size

Zoom to Select

Zoom to All Objects

Zoom to Working Box

The **Zoom toolbar** enables you to zoom in or out from a specific point in the Perspective window, or all objects in a scene, or the currently selected object.

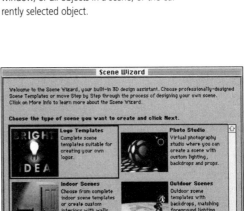

The **Scene Wizard**, which is launched using the **File/New** command, lets you create either a template scene or a scene that is built with components that you select by making a series of choices.

3D object modeling

3D object modeling is the process of building and refining discrete objects that can be named, positioned, scaled, shaded, painted, deformed, merged, linked, cloaked, animated, or otherwise manipulated with various parts of the program. Ray Dream Studio 5 features two object modelers: the Free Form Modeler and Mesh Form Modeler.

Free Form Modeler

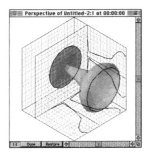

The Free Form Modeler lets you draw 2D shapes on cross sections and extrude them along simple or complex sweep paths to create a 3D shape.

Mesh Form Modeler

The Mesh Form Modeler allows you to create 3D objects by directly manipulating the vertices, edges, polylines, and polygons that form your objects.

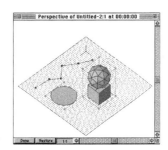

The Free Form Modeler window opens when you drag the **Free Form** tool on the Tools toolbar into the Perspective window. The Tools toolbar then changes to the toolbar on the left.

The Mesh Form Modeler window opens when you drag the **Mesh Form** tool on the Tools toolbar into the Perspective window. The Tools toolbar then changes to the toolbar on the right.

Tools toolbar for the Free Form Modeler

— Selection
— Rotation
— Zoom
— Hand
— Pen
— Point tools
— Draw tools
— Text
— Render Area
— Paint Shape Selection
— Paint Shape tools
— 3D Paint Brush
— Eyedropper

Tools toolbar for the Mesh Form Modeler

The **Primitive** tools on the Tools toolbar for the Perspective window (and their corresponding commands on the Insert menu) let you add true 3D spheres, cubes, cylinders, cones, infinite plane fields, and text to the scene with a simple click and drag. These objects can, of course, be refined, finished, or manipulated with other parts of the program, such as the Mesh Form Modeler by using the **Jump In Another Modeler** command in the **Edit** menu.

Selection —
Marquee —
3D Rotation —
2D Rotation —
Sphere of Attraction —
Zoom —
Hand —
Camera Dolly —
Polyline —
Vertex tools —
Create Primitive tools —
Sweep —
Extrude —
Lathe —
Loft —
Last Action —
Modifiers —

3D Object Modeling

3D object finishing

3D object finishing is the process of customizing the surface characteristics of a 3D object. Ray Dream provides two principal finishing tools: shaders and deformers.

Shaders

Shaders are a set of color, texture, and other surface characteristics that can be blended together in order to simulate any imaginable finish, ranging from chrome to stucco to a video clip.

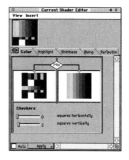

The **Shaders** tab of the Browser palette contains "stored shaders" that you can apply to objects in your scene.

The **Current Shader Editor** window is another window that can be used to edit, apply, and create shaders.

The **Shader Document** window is used to inspect and edit the settings of a stored shader.

The **Shading** tab of the Properties palette for the 3D object that is currently selected in the scene contains the shader that is currently applied to that object.

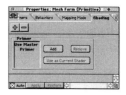

Deformers

Deformers are a set of surface characteristics that appear to alter the shape of a 3D object.

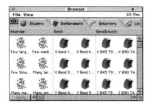

The **Deformers** tab of the Browser palette contains "stored deformers" that you can apply to objects in your scene.

The **Deformer Document** window is used to inspect and edit the settings of a stored deformer.

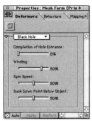

The **Deformers** tab of the Properties palette for the 3D object that is currently selected in the scene contains the deformer that is currently applied to that object.

3D Object Finishing

Lights and cameras

A Ray Dream scene can be configured with as much detail as any movie or theatrical set by adding, customizing, and positioning lights, cameras, and associated effects.

Lights

Lights can be augmented with a wide range of gels and can be animated to move to different positions in the scene. For example, a spotlight can be configured to track the movement of another object in the scene.

Lights are stored in the **Lights** tab of the Browser palette.

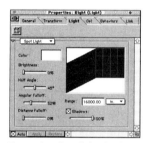

The settings for a light that has been placed in a scene can be inspected and edited in the Light tab of its **Properties** Palette.

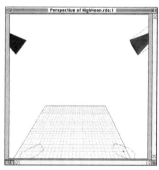

Double-click a light in the **Browser** palette to open the Perspective window for the specific light arrangement.

Cameras

Cameras play a crucial role in Ray Dream Studio: they "capture" the frame that is ultimately to be rendered as a still, or the sequence of images that will ultimately be rendered as a movie. Like lights, cameras come in different types and can be positioned, oriented, and configured in any number of different ways.

Cameras are stored in the **Cameras** tab of the Browser palette.

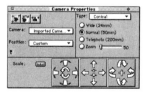

The **Camera Properties** window is a special window that lets you access several advanced tools and features, such as pan, track, and dolly tools, that apply specifically to cameras. This window is opened by choosing Camera Properties from the Windows menu.

Double-click a camera in the Browser palette to open the Perspective window for the specific camera viewpoint.

Lights and Cameras

Animation

Animation brings scenes to life. Ray Dream Studio uses traditional animation techniques to capture individual pictures, or "frames," of the scene at different points in time. When these frames are played back at a certain speed, they give the appearance that the 3D objects, lights, and cameras in the scene are moving and/or changing.

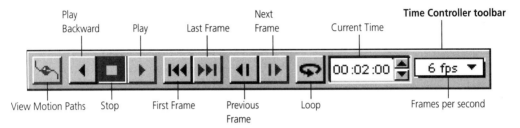

Play Backward · Play · Last Frame · Next Frame · Current Time · **Time Controller toolbar**

View Motion Paths · Stop · First Frame · Previous Frame · Loop · Frames per second

Tracks · Key event marker

The **Current Time** of the scene, as depicted in the Time Line window, can be set in several different ways. One easy way is to drag the Current Time bar to a desired position. If no key event marker already exists at that time, and if you change the position or property of any item in the scene, a new key event will automatically be created, and a new key event marker will be added to the track corresponds to the property that was changed.

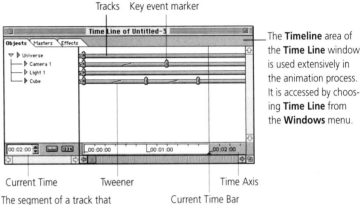

Current Time · Tweener · Time Axis

Current Time Bar

The **Timeline** area of the **Time Line** window is used extensively in the animation process. It is accessed by choosing **Time Line** from the **Windows** menu.

The segment of a track that falls between two key events is called a **tweener**. Ray Dream automatically generates the tweener frames for you.

You can control the speed, smoothness, and other qualities of the transition that occurs along the tweeners between two key events. Simply double-click the animated track on any empty location between the two key events to open the **Transition Options** dialog box. It allows you to select, configure, and apply a transition to the tweeners.

Another kind of movement that can be used to add realism or impact to a scene is called a **behavior**. Behaviors are stored in the Behaviors tab of the Browser palette.

Links specify how two connected objects move in concert. Like behaviors, they are stored in the Browser palette, applied to objects in a scene, and further edited in the Link tab of the object's Properties palette.

Rendering

Rendering a still image or a movie is almost always the goal of modeling objects and building scenes with Ray Dream Studio.

Stock renders that are suitable to a wide variety of render needs are provided in the **Render** menu.

Similarly, the **Render Area** tool on the Tools toolbar lets you draw a marquee around an area of the Perspective window that you would like to see rendered at the current frame. Like the Rendering toolbar's five preview quality toggle buttons, the Render Area tool is a visualization tool that plays no role in the rendering of still images and movies.

For custom renders, the various settings contained in the five tabs of the **Current Scene Settings** window determine the appearance and performance of the final render.

One of the render settings, called the **Filters** setting, can be saved to the Browser palette. Render Filter Documents can be opened, edited, applied, and resaved like other objects that are stored in the Browser palette.

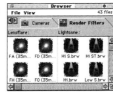

Rendering toolbar

— Collision Tracking

— Interactivity

— Bounding Box Quality

— Wireframe Quality

— Preview Quality

— Shaded Preview Quality

— Better Preview Quality

— Render

The five **Preview** buttons affect only the current display of the scene in the Perspective window, and not any still image or movie render that you may perform. The **Render** button starts a render.

When you render a single still image (as opposed to a batch queue rendering several images), and after Ray Dream has completed the render, the **Image Viewer** window opens automatically to let you review and save or discard the results.

Because rendering is frequently very time consuming, Ray Dream lets you define and perform multiple stills and movie renders in the **Batch Queue window** that is accessed with the **Batch Queue** command from the **Render** menu.

Similarly, when you render a single movie (as opposed to a batch queue rendering several movies), and after Ray Dream has completed the render, the **Movie Viewer** window opens automatically to let you review and save or discard the results.

MANAGING THE SCENE

Figure 1. Scenes you build with Ray Dream Studio 5 consists of 3D objects, lights, cameras, and a range of other subsidiary objects such as shaders and deformers.

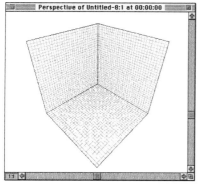

Figure 2. The Perspective window's working box.

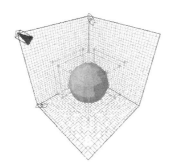

Figure 3. A bounding box is shown for a sphere primitive object.

As you have already learned, the scenes you build with Ray Dream Studio 5 consist of 3D objects, lights, cameras, and a host of subsidiary objects, such as shaders, deformers, behaviors, and external support files **(Figure 1)**.

In this chapter you will learn about the different tools and techniques that are provided by the Perspective window and the Time Line window to help you build and manage your objects, scenes, and productions.

The Perspective window is where you give birth to primitive objects, initiate the modeling of other objects, conduct the shading and deforming of all objects, and choreograph and orchestrate the entire scene and the entire production.

LOOKING THROUGH THE PERSPECTIVE WINDOW

To use the Perspective window efficiently, it is helpful to understand the definitions, uses, and relationships of five key concepts:

- The universe.
- The Perspective window's working box **(Figure 2)**.
- The bounding box that is displayed for a selected object, light, camera, or group of two or more such items **(Figure 3)**.
- The hot point of an object, light, camera, or group.
- Projections of a bounding box and its hot point.

Understanding the universe

A Ray Dream Studio scene comprises its own separate universe. The Perspective window is the window through which you view the scene's universe.

You can place objects, cameras, and lights anywhere in the universe. The maximum volume of a universe is a 3.32 kilometer cube.

The X,Y, and Z axes of the universe are fixed. The intersection of these axes—i.e., the position whose coordinate values are X = 0, Y = 0, and Z = 0, is called the point of origin **(Figure 4)**. The significance of the universal axes, planes, and origin are fixed and therefore can, but need not, be used as positional references for other Perspective window items, such as the working box and object, camera, and light bounding boxes.

Understanding the working box

The working box is the dominant feature of the Perspective window **(Figure 5)**. It is a working area that consists of three intersecting planes. The space within the working box is, of course, a subset of the space of the scene's entire universe.

You can size, position, and orient the working box anywhere you want to within the universe. You can also size, position, and orient objects, cameras and lights within the working box. Thus, the working box serves as a local universe, or a local reference cube, within which various objects, lights, and cameras can be positioned.

Understanding the bounding box

The bounding box is a hypothetical box frame that is just large enough to envelop an object, a light, or a camera **(Figure 6)**. It can, but doesn't have to, be a cube.

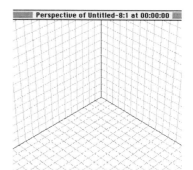

Figure 4. The point of origin is at the position where X=0, Y=0, and Z=0.

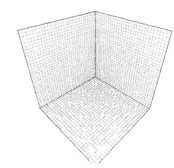

Figure 5. The working box consists of three orthogonal planes.

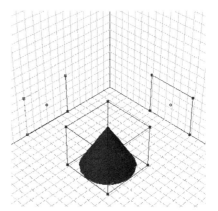

Figure 6. When you select an object in the Perspective window, a bounding box appears.

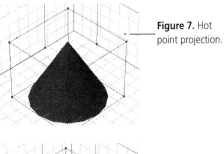

Figure 7. Hot point projection.

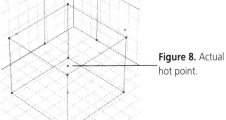

Figure 8. Actual hot point.

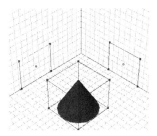

Figure 9. Shadows of the bounding box for this selected object are visible on the planes.

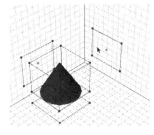

Figure 10. You can reposition an object by dragging its shadow on one of the planes.

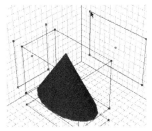

Figure 11. You can resize an object by dragging the handles on one of its shadows.

Depending on how fast your computer is, how complex your scene is, and what task you are trying to perform, it might take too much time to display fully rendered objects at all times. As detailed later in this chapter, Ray Dream lets you select from a range of preview qualities.

The next to lowest preview quality is the Bounding Box quality. In this preview mode, each visible object is represented in the scene by its bounding box. Because the bounding box is just a simple box frame, it can be drawn and redrawn very quickly.

Understanding the hot point

The hot point is a point in 3D space around which an object, light, or camera can be rotated **(Figures 7–8)**. Normally the hot point is located within the center of the item's bounding box; but as you will learn in subsequent chapters, you can reposition the hot point to effect a desired rotation or for other purposes.

Understanding bounding box and hot point projections

Ray Dream projects an imaginary "shadow" of the bounding box and the hot point for each visible object, light and camera against the interior of each working box plane that is visible **(Figure 9)**. You can select or position an object, light, camera, or hot point by clicking or dragging its projection along the plane on which it falls **(Figure 10)**. You can also resize an object by dragging the handles on its projection **(Figure 11)**.

With this background you are now ready to learn how to prepare and navigate the Perspective window.

Hot Point, Bounding Box Projections

ADJUSTING THE PERSPECTIVE WINDOW

You can prepare the Perspective window by:

- Selecting a preview quality mode.
- Setting the view.
- Configuring the working box.

Setting the preview quality mode

The speed with which Ray Dream can redraw the Perspective window depends largely upon the preview quality specified in the View menu.

✔ Tip

■ You can save a great deal of time by judiciously using the lowest preview quality necessary to perform a specific operation.

To set the preview quality:

1. Choose one of the following settings from the View menu **(Figure 12)**:

- No Preview displays only a 2D shape to indicate the relative position and size of objects **(Figure 13)**.

- Bounding Box displays a 3D rectangular frame around objects to indicate their relative position and volume **(Figure 14)**.

- Wireframe displays skeletal views of objects to indicate their 3D shape, volumetric size, and position **(Figure 15)**.

- Preview (Fast) displays objects as colored volumes without shadows **(Figure 16)**.

- Shaded Preview displays objects as colored volumes with shapes **(Figure 17)**.

- Better Preview displays objects as colored, shaded shapes with some texture detail **(Figure 18)**.

Figure 12. Choose a preview quality from the **View** menu.

Figure 13. No Preview view.

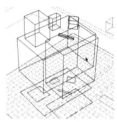

Figure 14. Bounding Box view.

Figure 15. Wireframe view.

Figure 16. Preview (Fast) view.

Figure 17. Shaded Preview view.

Figure 18. Better Preview view.

Set the Preview Quality

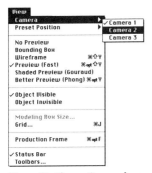

Figure 19. Choose **Camera** from the **View** menu, and select a camera from the pop-up menu.

Figure 20. Choose **Preset Position** from the **View** menu, and select a setting from the pop-up menu.

Figure 21. The **Preset Position Top** view is selected.

Setting the view

The Perspective window lets you view a scene from the vantage of a default camera, a custom camera, or one of many different Preset Positions.

A Preset Position view called the Reference View is the default view and the most useful view for getting a good feel of the shapes and relative positions of objects in your scene. The other Preset Position views help you view the scene from alternate angles.

To set the view from a camera:

1. Choose Camera from the View menu **(Figure 19)**.

2. Select the camera with which to view the frame from the pop-up menu.

To set the view to a preset position:

1. Choose Preset Position from the View menu, and select one of the following settings from the pop-up menu **(Figure 20)**:

   • Reference

   • Top **(Figure 21)**, Bottom

   • Left, Right

   • Front, Back

CONFIGURING THE WORKING BOX

The working box consists of three intersecting planes that resemble the interior of a cube. Ray Dream lets you display, hide, size, and orient the working box itself, display or hide each of its planes, and display, hide, and customize its grid lines.

Configure the working box by:

   • Toggling its view.

   • Setting preferences.

   • Fine-tuning grid settings.

   • Setting its properties.

Toggling your view of the working box:

1. If the Display Planes tool is invisible, choose Toolbars from the View menu.

and

In the Toolbars dialog box, click Tools in the list of toolbars to place a check next to it.

and

Click OK.

2. Toggle the visibility of each of the working box's three planes by clicking the corresponding region on the Display Planes tool **(Figures 22–24)**.

3. Toggle the visibility of the objects contained in the working box by clicking the cube in the center of the Display Planes tool.

Setting the active plane

The active plane of the working box is the plane along which objects are moved when you drag them with the mouse. Thus, if the ground plane is the active plane, dragging an object "up" the screen moves the object to the right along the X axis and to the rear along the Y axis, but not upward along the Z axis **(Figures 25–26)**.

To set the active plane:

1. Display the Display Planes tool as described above.

2. While holding down the Alt/Option key, click the region of the Display Planes tool that corresponds to the plane you wish to make the active plane.

Figure 22. Display Planes tool.

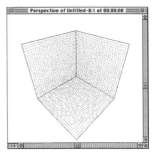

Figure 23. All of the working box's three planes are displayed.

Figure 24. Only the bottom plane of the working box is displayed.

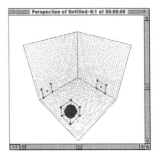

Figure 25. The ground plane is the active plane here.

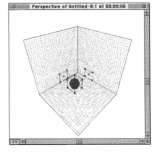

Figure 26. Dragging an object moves it along the active plane (the ground plane here).

Figure 27. Choose
Preferences from the
File menu.

Figure 28. Click
Perspective in the
dropdown list.

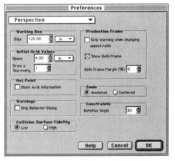

Figure 29. Enter a value and unit of
measurement for the working box.

Figure 30. Choose **Grid**
from the **View** menu.

Figure 31. Set the grid
options in the **Grid**
dialog box.

Setting preferences for the working box

You can set the working box's size, unit of measurements, and initial grid settings with the Preferences dialog box.

To set preferences for the working box:

1. Choose Preferences from the File menu **(Figure 27)**.

2. In the dropdown list of Preferences, click Perspective **(Figure 28)**.

3. In the working box area of the dialog box **(Figure 29)**, enter a value and unit of measurement for the working box.

4. Set the spacing, line drawing, and unit of measurement fields for the working box's grid.

5. Toggle the visibility of axis information for objects' hot points by placing or removing a check in the Show Axis Information checkbox in the hot point area of the dialog box.

Fine-tuning the grid settings

You can also set the working box's grid settings with menu commands. Once again, these operations are very similar to the grid adjustment procedures you learned earlier with respect to the Mesh Form Modeler.

To set the working box's grid settings:

1. Choose Grid from the View menu **(Figure 30)**.

2. In the Grid dialog box, set the Spacing, unit of measurement, "Draw a line every", Show, and "Snap to" options **(Figure 31)**.

3. Press OK to save the changes or Cancel to discard them.

Customizing the working box

One interesting difference between the working box and the Mesh Form modeling box is that the working box is an object. Because it is an object, it possesses properties that can be accessed and edited with the Properties palette.

To set the working box's properties:

1. Click any empty area of the working box while holding the Ctrl/Command key down to select the working box **(Figure 32)**.

2. Choose Properties from the Windows menu **(Figure 33)** to display the Properties palette **(Figure 34)**.

3. If they are collapsed, expand the Color and Grid areas of the dialog box by clicking the plus sign next to each (arrows on the Mac).

4. Set the color of each of the Inactive Plane, the Active Plane, or the Border by double-clicking its corresponding color swatch and selecting a new color from your system's color picker.

5. Configure the grid by setting the Space, "Draw a line every", and "Snap to" options.

6. If the Auto button is not checked, click the Apply button and close the Properties palette.

✔ Tip

■ When selected, the working box is framed by a bounding box. You can resize the working box by dragging the handles on its bounding box.

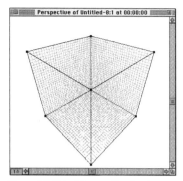

Figure 32. Select the working box by clicking any empty area while holding the Ctrl/Command keys.

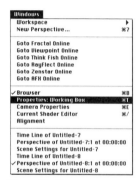

Figure 33. Choose **Properties:Working Box** from the **Windows** menu.

Figure 34. The Properties palette for the working box.

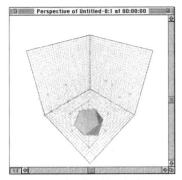

Figure 35. Select the object in the Perspective window.

Figure 36. Choose **Object Invisible** from the **View** menu.

Figure 37. The object disappears.

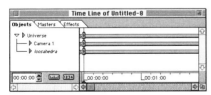

Figure 38. When an object is invisible in the Perspective window, it is italicized in the Time Line window.

Setting other Perspective window preferences

You can further configure the Perspective window by adjusting other available settings in the Perspective Preferences dialog box. For example, you can use the Hot Point Show Axis Information checkbox to toggle the visibility of the local origin (i.e., the intersection of the X, Y, and Z axes at an object's Hot Point).

DISPLAYING OBJECTS IN THE PERSPECTIVE WINDOW

Before you can work with objects, cameras, and lights in the Perspective window, you frequently need to make them visible (or make other objects invisible), position them conveniently in the window, and zoom in or out on them or on the scene itself.

Object visibility

An object's visibility setting determines whether it is visible in the scene. It is sometimes useful to make objects temporarily invisible, either as an aid to visualizing the scene, as an animation effect, or to speed up the time it takes to draw the scene.

To make an object invisible:

1. Click the Selection tool.

2. Select the object in the Perspective window **(Figure 35)**.

3. Choose Object Invisible from the View menu **(Figures 36–37)**.

When an object is set to invisible, it cannot be seen or selected in the Perspective window. In the Objects tab of the Time Line window, the object's name becomes italicized **(Figure 38)** to indicate that it is invisible in the Perspective window.

Make an Object Invisible

To restore the visibility of an object:

1. Display the Objects tab of the Time Line window.

2. Select the invisible object by clicking its italicized name in the Time Line window **(Figure 39)**.

3. Choose Object Visible from the View menu **(Figure 40)**.

Figure 39. Select the invisible object by clicking its italicized name in the Timeline window.

The Hand tool

The Hand tool **(Figure 42)** lets you scroll the contents of the Perspective window both vertically and horizontally at the same time. It also lets you position the contents of the window with reference to its contents rather than with reference to scroll buttons and scroll bars.

To use the Hand tool:

1. Click the Hand tool.

2. Click and drag the window to push or pull its contents into view as desired.

Figure 40. Choose **Object Visible** from the **View** menu.

The Zoom tools

The Zoom tools provide powerful flexibility in object visualization. A total of eight different Zoom tools are located in three different places in the Perspective window:

- One tool is located on the Perspective toolbar between the Virtual Trackball tool and the Hand tool **(Figure 41)**.

- Six tools are located on the Zoom toolbar **(Figure 43)**.

- One final tool is a pop-up menu of zoom settings that is located at the bottom-left corner of the Perspective window itself, directly to the left of the leftmost horizontal scroll-bar button **(Figure 44)**.

These tools work differently. For example, the Zoom tool on the Perspective

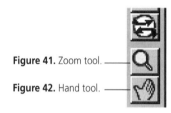

Figure 41. Zoom tool.

Figure 42. Hand tool.

Figure 43. Six zoom-related tools are located in the Zoom toolbar.

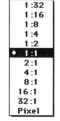

Figure 44. The Perspective window contains a **Zoom** pop-up menu at its bottom-left corner.

Restore Visibility; Hand Tool, Zoom Tools

Figure 45. Zoom tool.

Figure 46. With the Zoom tool, click the location you wish to zoom into.

Figure 47. The window has zoomed into the area of the tabletop.

Figure 48. The Zoom In and Zoom Out tools.

toolbar is actually a zooming cursor that zooms in to or out from a position that you point to with the mouse.

To use the Zoom tool on the Perspective toolbar:

1. If it is not already displayed, display the Perspective toolbar by choosing Toolbars from the View menu and placing a check next to Tools in the list of toolbars.

2. Scroll the Perspective window with the scroll bars or the Hand tool to locate the position into which you wish to zoom.

3. Click the Zoom tool **(Figure 45)**.

4. Click on the location into which you wish to zoom **(Figures 46–47)**.

or

Hold down the Alt/Option key to toggle the Zoom tool to a Zoom out tool (indicated by the substitution of a minus sign for a plus sign in the center of the zoom cursor) and click on the location out of which you wish to zoom.

The Zoom toolbar's tools have their own specialized functions.

To use the Zoom tools on the Zoom toolbar:

1. If it is not already displayed, display the Zoom toolbar by choosing Toolbars from the View menu and placing a check next to Zoom in the list of toolbars.

2. Scroll the Perspective window with the scroll bars or the Hand tool to locate the position into which you wish to zoom.

3. Click on one of the following Zoom tools:

• Use the Zoom In and Zoom Out tools to zoom into or out of the center of the Perspective window **(Figure 48)**.

Zoom Tool, Zoom Toolbar

- Use the Zoom to Actual Size tool **(Figure 49)** to restore objects to the size that they appear in the Reference view.

- Use the Zoom to Selected tool to zoom into the object or objects that are currently selected in the Perspective window.

- Use the Zoom to all Objects tool to zoom to a level at which all of the objects in the scene can be included in the Perspective window.

- Use the Zoom to Working Box tool to zoom to the current view of the working box.

To use the zoom pop-up menu on the Perspective window:

1. Click and hold the current zoom level indicator until the pop-up menu appears **(Figure 50)**.

2. Click the desired zoom level.

✔ Tip

■ The Zoom tools do not affect the orientation of the current view.

MANAGING 3D OBJECTS IN THE PERSPECTIVE WINDOW

The Perspective window supports a wide range of techniques for managing 3D objects:

- Single and multiple object selection.

- Manual object sizing, scaling, and positioning with the mouse.

- Numerical object sizing, scaling, and positioning with the Transformer tab of an object's Properties palette **(Figure 51)**.

- Manual sizing, scaling, and positioning with mouse drags of bounding box handles.

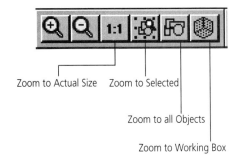

Zoom to Actual Size   Zoom to Selected
Zoom to all Objects
Zoom to Working Box

Figure 49. The Zoom toolbar

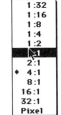

Figure 50. Click and hold the zoom level indicator at the bottom left of the Perspective window to display the pop-up menu.

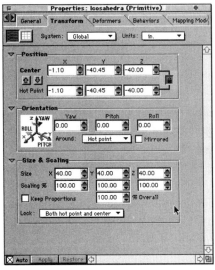

Figure 51. You can use the Transformer tab of an object's Properties palette to perform numerical object sizing, scaling, and positioning.

Figure 52. The **Group** commands under the **Arrange** menu allow you to group objects together.

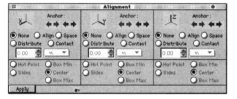

Figure 53. The Alignment window is used to align objects precisely together in the Perspective window, such as stacking one object on top of another.

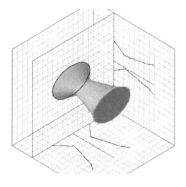

Figure 54. The Free Form Modeler.

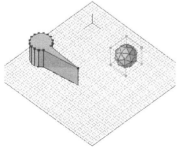

Figure 55. The Mesh Form Modeler.

- Grouping and ungrouping with the Arrange menu commands of the same name **(Figure 52)**.

- Distancing and aligning with the Alignment window **(Figure 53)** that is accessible through the Windows menu.

- Object duplication, selection, replication, and mirroring.

Many of these operations and the tools and techniques that are available for carrying them out are covered elsewhere in this book.

Special instances of the working box

As detailed in the chapters dealing with the Free Form and Mesh Form Modelers, the windows that are opened by those tools are special instances of the Perspective window **(Figures 54–55)**. These windows, and the modeling boxes they contain, manage 3D objects in a way that is similar, though not identical, to the Perspective window and its working box.

HOW PERSPECTIVE AND TIME LINE WINDOWS WORK TOGETHER

Let's conclude this chapter by learning how the Perspective window works with the Time Line window.

Object relationships: spatial vs logical

Two different types of relationships can exist between the objects, lights, and cameras in a scene: spatial and logical.

A spatial relationship is the position of one item relative to the position of another item or some other reference position. For example, two 3D objects may or may not be concentric, co-linear, co-planar, parallel, perpendicular, skewed, oblique, intersecting, non-intersecting, and so on.

A logical relationship is an item's possession of, by, or with another item. For example, two objects might be contained in a group, and that group might itself belong to another group.

As you have already seen in this chapter, the Perspective window is well suited to displaying the spatial relationships between objects. But there are limitations.

For example, if the scene contains objects that are spread far and wide across the universe, it is possible to use the Zoom to all Objects tool to position the camera to bring all of the objects into view, but they may be so small that it is impossible to see them, let alone select or work with them. Zooming in on one or more objects does not necessarily solve the problem, since to do so may cause the camera to be pointed away from other objects.

The Perspective window also has a limited capacity to display the logical relationships between items. For example, a group of objects is indicated by a common bounding box **(Figure 56)**. But the subobjects that comprise the larger object (for example, the parts that make up a lamp) cannot be so indicated.

The Perspective window also may make it difficult to locate and select a specific item with a high level of confidence. Multiple layers of objects and the display of bounding boxes of selected objects may make it very difficult to select or manipulate a specific item.

The Time Line window **(Figure 57)** is optimized for displaying the logical relationships between objects. Its hierarchical interface and functionality make it easy to create, edit, and "drill down" into hierarchical relationships. Its hierarchical relationship also eliminates the spatial

Figure 56. The Perspective window has a limited capacity to communicate the logical relationships between objects. For example, the lamp here is composed of many sub-objects, yet only one bounding box is displayed when the lamp is selected.

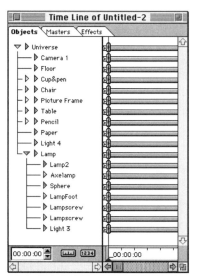

Figure 57. The Time Line window displays the hierarchical relationship between objects in the Perspective window. For example, the lamp in the previous figure is composed of many component objects which are all readily identifiable in the Time Line window.

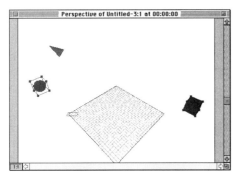

Figure 58. You will often find it more convenient to select and group objects from the Time Line window, since objects in the Perspective window can often be inconveniently spread out, such as the sphere and cube shown here.

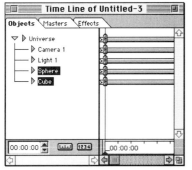

Figure 59. The Time Line window makes it easy to select objects simultaneously.

limitations of the Perspective window. No matter how far apart two objects may be, they are always very close to each other in the hierarchy area of the Time Line window **(Figures 58–59)** and can always be found, selected, grouped, and otherwise manipulated.

Thus, the Perspective window and the Time Line window complement each other perfectly. When objects cannot be readily visualized in the Perspective window, they can be accessed instantly and definitively in the Time Line window. Once selected, objects, object groups, and other items can be visually manipulated in the Perspective window.

In summary, the Perspective window can be thought of as a WYSIWYG word processor, and the Time Line window can be thought of as a hierarchical tree interface to a database of all of the objects, groups, cameras, and lights that are contained in a scene.

Time Line Window

Part II:

Modeling
3D Objects

Figure 1. This tower was built using primitive geometric shapes.

Figure 2. Click and hold the Geometric Primitive tool in the Tools toolbar until the pop-up toolbar appears.

Figure 3. You can also place the primitive you wish into your scene by choosing it from the **Insert** menu.

Primitives are predefined objects built in to Ray Dream that you can quickly incorporate into your scene.

Geometric primitives

Geometric primitives are basic shapes such as cubes, spheres, and cones. Most complex 3D objects can be broken down into a combination of such simple geometric shapes. For example, most buildings can be broken down into a series of stacked cubes and cylinders **(Figure 1)**.

Environmental primitives

Environmental primitives are common environmental objects such as fog, fire, fountains, and clouds.

To place a geometric primitive into your scene:

1. Click and hold the Geometric Primitive tool in the toolbar until the pop-up toolbar appears displaying the primitives **(Figure 2)**.

2. Select the primitive shape in the pop-up toolbar.

3. Drag the primitive object into the Perspective or Hierarchy window to place the object into your scene. When you drag to the Hierarchy window, the object appears by default at the center of your scene. Dragging directly to the Perspective window allows you to immediately position the object wherever you wish.

4. Size the object by dragging the corners of its bounding box.

✔ Tip

■ You can also place a primitive into your scene by choosing it from the Insert menu **(Figure 3)**.

USING ENVIRONMENTAL PRIMITIVES

Environmental primitives allow you to easily add environmental elements to your scene, such as clouds or fog, which are readily accessible by clicking the Environmental Primitives tool **(Figure 4)**. These primitives can be used to create animations such as fire crackling or a fountain spraying, or can be used as a still background object. Each environmental primitive also has its own properties dialog box to control attributes of its animation **(Figure 5)**. The cloud, fire, and fog primitives are visible only after rendering, and you must use the Adaptive or the Ray Tracer renderer.

Unique to environmental primitives is the way in which they are scaled. Normally when you scale any object, the object itself increases in size proportionately. But when scaling an environmental primitive, only the volume enclosing the primitive changes. For example, when scaling the fire primitive, the size of the flame tips does not change, only the volume enclosing them does **(Figures 6–7)**.

To place an environmental primitive into your scene:

1. Click and hold the Environmental Primitives tool, and select the primitive you wish to use **(Figure 4)**.

2. Drag the Environmental Primitives tool into the Perspective window or Hierarchy window.

3. Set the attributes to your specifications in the dialog box that opens for the selected primitive **(Figure 5)**. These attribute settings are described on the following pages.

✔ Tip

■ You can also place an environmental primitive into your scene by choosing it from the Insert menu **(Figure 8)**.

Figure 4. Click and hold the Environmental Primitives tool and choose the environmental primitive you wish to use from the pop-up toolbar.

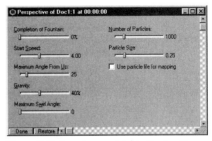

Figure 5. Each environmental primitive has its own **Properties** dialog box.

Figures 6–7. When scaling the size of an environmental primitive, such as fire in this case, only the volume enclosing the primitive changes (fire tips remain the same size).

Figure 8. You can place an environmental primitive by choosing it from the **Insert** menu.

Place an Environmental Primitive

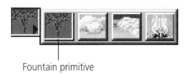

Fountain primitive

Figure 9. Choose the Fountain primitive from the Environmental Primitive pop-up toolbar.

Figure 10. The Fountain primitive is visible without rendering.

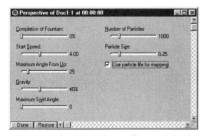

Figure 11. The **Fountain Attributes** dialog box.

Fountain primitive

The Fountain primitive is selected from the Environmental Primitives pop-up toolbar **(Figure 9)**. The fountain is the only primitive visible without rendering **(Figure 10)**. The elements of the fountain attributes **(Figure 11)** are described below:

Fountain Attributes dialog box

Completion of Fountain slider

Use this slider to set the point at which your fountain animation should begin (0%), and the point at which it should end (100%). You can start or end the animation at any percentage point in the animation cycle.

Start Speed Slider

Use this slider to control the speed at which the fountain spouts. A low setting makes the fountain spout fast, while a high setting makes it spout slow.

Maximum Angle From Up slider

Use this slider to control the angle of your fountain. At a 0 setting the fountain sprays straight up; a 180 degree setting makes the fountain spray outward in a radius around the fountain.

Gravity slider

Use this slider to control how quickly the fountain particles fall down. A low setting causes particles to fall slowly; a high setting makes them fall down quickly.

Maximum Swirl Angle slider

Use this slider to control the rotation of the particles as they fall to the ground. A low setting results in minimal rotation, while a higher setting makes the particles rotate farther around the fountain as they fall.

Fountain Primitive

Number of Particles slider

Use this slider to set the number of particles in your fountain.

Particle Size slider

Use this slider to set the size of the particles in your fountain.

Use particle life for mapping option

Select this setting if you wish a shader to be applied over the entire range of particles in your fountain. This means that the shader will be mapped once over the entire fountain, starting at the bottom. If this option is not set, each particle is shaded individually.

Cloud primitive

The Cloud primitive is selected from the Environmental Primitives pop-up toolbar **(Figure 12)**. The cloud is visible only after rendering **(Figure 13)**; there is no on-screen preview. Clouds can be animated. You can place other objects of your scene partially or completely into a cloud. For instance, an airplane can appear to be moving through a cloud. The Cloud Attributes dialog box **(Figure 14)** is described below.

Cloud Attributes dialog box

Color

Click the color chip to adjust the color of your cloud.

Quantity of Clouds slider

Use this slider to increase or decrease the number of clouds in the cloud bounding box.

Cloud Size slider

Use this slider to adjust the size of your cloud within the cloud bounding box.

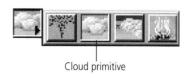

Cloud primitive

Figure 12. Choose the Cloud primitive from the Environmental Primitives pop-up toolbar.

Figure 13. The cloud is visible only after rendering.

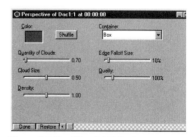

Figure 14. The **Cloud Attributes** dialog box.

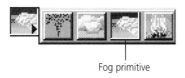

Fog primitive

Figure 15. Choose the Fog primitive from the Environmental Primitives pop-up toolbar.

Figure 16. The fog is visible only after rendering.

Figure 17. The **Fog Attributes** dialog box.

Density slider

Use this slider to control the opaqueness of your cloud. A high setting makes the cloud more opaque, while a low setting makes it more transparent.

Quality slider

Use this slider to control the quality of your cloud, which relates to its level of detail. The higher the setting, the longer the render time.

Container pop-up menu

Choose from this pop-up menu to set the general shape for your cloud.

Edge Falloff Size slider

Use this slider to control the appearance of the edges of your clouds. A low setting causes a sudden change, and a high setting causes gradual change.

Shuffle button

Click the Shuffle button to select a different pattern for your cloud. Each time you click this button, a new pattern appears, while the other attributes stay the same.

Fog primitive

The Fog primitive is chosen from the Environmental Primitives pop-up toolbar **(Figure 15)**. There is no on-screen preview; the fog is visible only after rendering **(Figure 16)**. Fog can be animated, and objects can be placed within the fog. The Fog Attributes dialog box **(Figure 17)** is described below:

Fog Attributes dialog box
Color

Click this chip to select a color for your fog from the color palette.

Patchiness slider

Use this slider to control the patchiness of your fog. A low setting creates a continuous volume of fog, while a higher setting creates more patchiness.

Density slider

Use this slider to control how much light can penetrate your fog.

Quality slider

This slider controls the quality of your fog, which relates to its level of detail. A high setting causes a longer render time.

Container pop-up menu

Use this pop-up menu to select the general shape for your fog.

Completion of Upward Effect slider

Use this slider to set the point at which your fog animation should begin (0%) and the point at which it should end (100%). You can start or end the animation at any percentage point in the animation cycle.

Upward Speed slider

Use this slider to control how quickly the fog rises during your animation.

Swirls slider

Use this slider to control the swirling motion of the fog as it rises.

Swirl Size slider

Use this slider to control the swirl size.

Chaos slider

Use this slider to set the degree of uniformity of the fog. The higher the setting, the more random the fog's appearance.

Figure 18. Choose **Current Scene Settings** from the **Render** menu.

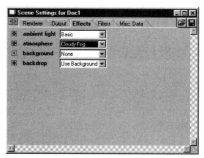

Figure 19. Click the **Effects** tab to access the **Atmosphere** pop-up menu.

Fog Primitive

Fire primitive

Figure 20. Choose the Fire primitive from the Environmental Primitives pop-up toolbar.

Figure 21. The fire is visible only after rendering.

Figure 22. The **Fire Attributes** dialog box.

Edge Falloff slider

Use this slider to control the appearance of the edges of your fog. A low setting causes a sudden change, and a higher setting causes a gradual change.

Shuffle button

Click the shuffle button to select a different pattern for your fog. Each time you click this button, a new pattern appears, while the other attributes stay the same.

✔ Tip

■ When you want fog to pervade your entire scene, rather than a part of it, use the atmosphere pop-up menu in the Scene Settings dialog box. Choose Current Scene Settings from the Render menu **(Figure 18)**, and click the Effects tab to access the atmosphere pop-up menu **(Figure 19)**.

Fire primitive

The Fire primitive is located in the Environmental Primitives pop-up toolbar **(Figure 20)**. There is no on-screen preview; the fire is visible only after rendering **(Figure 21)**. Fire can be animated, and objects can be placed within the fire. The Fire attributes dialog box **(Figure 22)** is described below.

Fire Attributes dialog box
Tip Color

Click the Tip Color chip to select the color for the tips of the flame.

Base Color

Click the Base Color chip to select a color for the base of the flame.

Quantity of Flames slider

Use this slider to adjust the quantity of flames.

Pointiness slider

Use this slider to control what percentage of your fire is made up of flame tips.

Detail slider

Use this slider to control how much detail you want in your fire object.

Density slider

Use this slider to control the opaqueness of your fire. A high setting makes the fire more opaque, while a low setting makes it more transparent.

Quality slider

Use this slider to control the rendering detail of your fire.

Container pop-up menu

Use this pop-up menu to select the general shape of your fire **(Figure 23)**. Three shapes are available **(Figures 24–26)**.

Edge Falloff Size slider

Use this slider to control the appearance of the edges of your fire. A low setting causes a sudden change, and a high setting causes gradual change.

Completion of Burning Fire slider

Use this slider to set the point at which your fire animation should begin (0%) and the point at which it should end (100%). You can start or end the animation at any percentage point in the animation cycle.

Upward Speed slider

Use this slider to set the rate at which the flames shoot up during your animation.

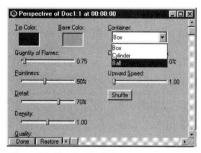

Figure 23. Use the **Container** pop-up menu in the **Fire Attributes** dialog box to select the general shape of your fire.

Figure 24. Container attribute set to **Ball** shape for the Fire primitive.

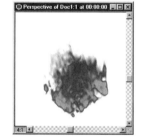

Figure 25. Container attribute set to **Box** shape for the Fire primitive.

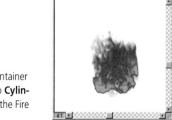

Figure 26. Container attribute set to **Cylinder** shape for the Fire primitive.

Fire Primitive

Figure 27. You can see the edges of an infinite plane in the Perspective window.

Figure 28. Drag the Infinite Plane tool into the Perspective window.

Figure 29. Click the Tiling option in the **Mapping Mode** dialog box to tile a shader across an infinite plane.

Figure 30. In the Browser, click the shader that you wish to apply to the infinite plane.

USING INFINITE PLANES

An infinite plane is used to create a surface in your scene, such as the sky or the ground. Although you can see its edges in the Perspective window **(Figure 27)**, the plane will appear to extend out infinitely when you render it.

To create an infinite plane:

1. Drag the Infinite Plane tool **(Figure 28)** into the Perspective window. The Mapping Mode dialog box appears.

2. Click the Tiling option to tile a shader across an infinite plane **(Figure 29)**. Click the "Mirrored in X axis" option for a shader to be mirrored in the X direction as it's tiled across the plane. Click the "Mirrored in Y axis" option to mirror it in the Y direction across the plane. If you don't select the tiling option, a shader will be applied once over the entire surface of a plane.

To shade an infinite plane:

1. Choose Browser from the Windows menu.

2. Click the Shaders tab in the Browser.

3. Click the shader that you wish to apply to the plane **(Figure 30)**.

4. Drag the selected shader onto the plane in the Perspective window. If you wish to change how the shader is mapped onto the plane, double-click the plane to open the Mapping Mode dialog box. (See "To create an infinite plane" above for a description of the options in this dialog box.)

Create an Infinite Plane

TEXT OBJECTS

You can easily incorporate text into your Ray Dream scene by using the Text tool. The Text Modeling window allows you to specify attributes for your text.

Figure 31. Drag the Text tool into the Perspective window.

To create a text object:

1. Drag the Text tool **(Figure 31)** into the Perspective window. The Text Modeling window appears.

2. In the Text Modeling window, type your text **(Figure 32)**. Text appears at the bottom of the window.

3. Choose the font, style, or size by clicking the appropriate pop-up menu (all TrueType and Type 1 fonts on your system are available).

4. Set the width of the text by using the Depth control.

5. Click the Front or Back Face options to add beveling to your text object.

6. Use the Height and Depth settings to control the contour of the bevel of your text.

7. Select the type of bevel by clicking one of the available bevel options.

8. Click Done. The text appears in the Perspective window **(Figure 33)**.

✔ Tips

■ You can manually change the width and depth of your text object by selecting the object in the Perspective window and dragging the corners of the bounding box.

■ You can determine the approximate size of capital letters in inches by multiplying the font size by 0.333.

To edit text:

1. Double-click a text object in the Perspective window to open the Text Modeling window, where you can edit the contents and attributes of text.

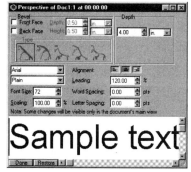

Figure 32. Enter your text in the Text Modeling window.

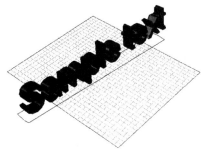

Figure 33. Your text object appears in the Perspective window.

Create a Text Object

Figure 34. Drag the Formula tool into the Perspective window.

Figure 35. Enter your formula in the **Formula Editor** dialog box.

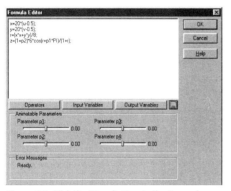

Figure 36. Click the More button in the **Formula Editor** dialog box to display additional parameters.

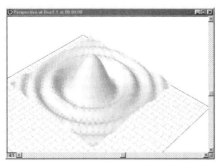

Figure 37. The formula object appears in the Perspective window.

USING FORMULA OBJECTS

Ray Dream allows you to create 3D objects by supplying mathematical formulas. These formulas are entered in the Formula Editor. It should be noted that creating objects in this manner is a complex process, requiring specialized knowledge of mathematics, which is beyond the scope of this guide.

To create a formula object:

1. Drag the Formula tool **(Figure 34)** into the Perspective window. The Formula Editor dialog box appears.

2. Enter your formula in the Formula Editor dialog box **(Figure 35)**.

3. Use the parameter sliders to change the values of parameters in your equations. This changes the shape of your formula object.

4. Click the More button to display additional parameters for your equations **(Figure 36)**.

5. Click Done. The formula object appears in the Perspective window **(Figure 37)**.

✔ Tip

■ Double-click the formula object in the Perspective window to open the Formula Editor.

Create a Formula Object

ALIGNING OBJECTS

You will often find it necessary to align objects in the Perspective window when creating a scene. Ray Dream Studio provides an Alignment window, which allows you to arrange and align objects in a number of different ways. For example, you can align two objects with respect to their hot points (if the hot points are centered, then the objects overlap and are centered), or with respect to any of the sides of the objects' bounding boxes.

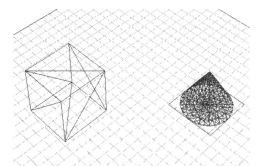

Figure 38. Create a Cone and Cube primitive, with the cone being slightly smaller.

To align a cube with a cone:

The following example places a Cone primitive inside of a slightly larger Cube primitive so that the bottom surfaces of the two objects share the same plane.

1. Choose Wireframe from the View menu (in this example, it's easier to see how the object align in Wireframe view).

2. Create a Cube primitive as outlined earlier in this chapter.

3. Create a Cone primitive that is slightly smaller than the cube **(Figure 38)**.

4. Deselect all objects.

5. Select the cube object. (The first selected object is the anchor object, which means the other selected object will be aligned or moved with respect to this object. The anchor does not move.)

6. While holding the Shift key, select the cone object so that the cube and cone are both selected.

7. Choose Align Objects from the Arrange menu **(Figure 39)**.

8. If the Alignment window is not expanded already, click the key icon to expand the window to display the X, Y, and Z alignment sections **(Figure 40)**.

9. In the X section, click to select the

Figure 39. Choose **Align Objects** from the **Arrange** menu.

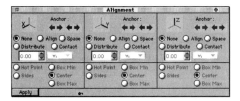

Figure 40. Click the key icon in the Alignment window to expand it.

Aligning Objects

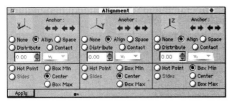

Figure 41. In the X and Y sections of the Alignment window, click the Align and Center buttons. In the Z section, click the Align and Box Min buttons.

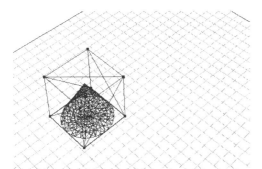

Figure 42. The cone is placed inside the cube and aligned with its bottom surface.

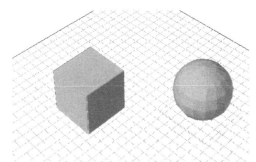

Figure 43. Create a Cube and a Sphere primitive.

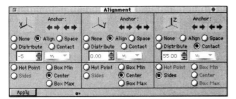

Figure 44. Click the Align and Center buttons in the X and Y axis sections of the Alignment window.

Align and Center buttons **(Figure 41)**. This means that the X coordinate value of the center of the bounding box of the second selected item (the cone) will be changed to be equal to the X coordinate value of the center of the anchor object (the cube). Aligning with respect to the hot point produces the same result if the hot points are centered in each object.

10. In the Y section, click to select the Align and Center buttons.

11. In the Z section, click to select the Align and Box Min buttons. Box Min means that the minimum coordinate values of the bounding boxes along the constraint axis (Z in this case) will be aligned.

12. Click the Apply button in the Alignment window. The cone is placed inside the cube and rests on its bottom surface **(Figure 42)**.

✔ Tip

■ You may wish to zoom the Perspective window into a 4:1 zoom to better see how the objects align.

To stack one object on top of another:

The following example places a Sphere primitive on top of a Cube primitive.

1. Create a Cube and a Sphere primitive as outlined earlier in this chapter **(Figure 43)**.

2. Deselect all objects.

3. Select the cube object first (anchor), then select the sphere.

4. Choose Align Objects from the Arrange menu.

5. In the X axis section, click the Align and Center buttons **(Figure 44)**.

6. In the Y axis section, click the Align and Center buttons.

7. In the Z axis section, click the Contact

and Sides buttons.

8. Click Apply to place the sphere on top of the cube **(Figure 45)**. (If the sphere appears below the cube, read the tip below.)

✔ Tip

■ The Contact Sides option aligns the outer sides of the bounding boxes of the selected objects so that the objects end up either stacked or placed side by side. Ray Dream aligns the two closest outer sides. In the previous example, the sphere is placed on top of the cube if the distance between the bottom of the sphere and the top of the cube is less than the distance between the top of the sphere and the bottom of the cube. Otherwise, the sphere is placed below the cube.

To space apart two objects a specified distance:

1. Select the anchor object.

2. Select the second object you wish to space with respect to the anchor object **(Figure 46)**.

3. Choose Align Objects from the Arrange menu.

4. In the Alignment window, click the Space button for the axis along which you wish to displace the second object **(Figure 47)**.

5. Choose the units of measurement from the Units pop-up menu for the constraint axis **(Figure 48)**.

6. Enter a value or use the arrow keys in the field next to the Units pop-up menu to indicate how far the second object should be displaced (values can be positive or negative).

7. Click Apply to space the objects **(Figure 49)**.

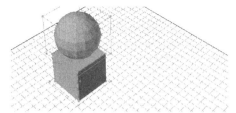

Figure 45. Click the Apply button in the Alignment window to place the sphere on top of the cube.

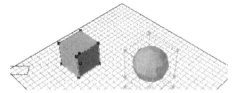

Figure 46. Select the two objects you wish to space, with the first object being the anchor object.

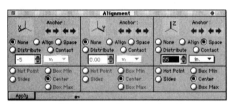

Figure 47. Click the Space button in the Alignment window for the constraint axis (Z in this case).

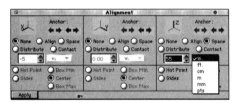

Figure 48. Choose the units of measurement from the pop-up menu and enter a space value beside it.

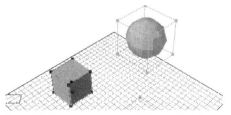

Figure 49. The objects are spaced the specified distance along the axis of constraint (Z in this case).

Space Apart Two Objects a Specific Distance

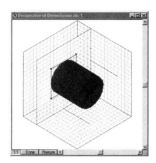

Figure 1. A circle on a cross section has been extruded into a cylinder in the Free Form Modeler.

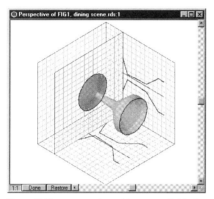

Figure 2. You can create a wide range of objects, such as a wine glass, by manipulating an object's cross sections and sweep path.

Figure 3. The free form objects here (the wine glasses) have been placed into a complete scene.

One of the most important tools in Ray Dream Studio is the Free Form Modeler. The Free Form Modeler is based on the technique known as extrusion.

Extrusion

Extrusion is the process of forming 3D objects by sweeping 2D shapes along a designated path to create a volume. This is much like pushing molten steel through a die to create an elongated 3D form. With the Free Form Modeler, you create single or multiple 2D shapes on a cross-section plane and then give those shapes volume by extruding them along a sweep path such as the circle in **Figure 1**, which has been extruded into a cylinder. The resulting 3D extrusion is known as a **free form object**.

By adding additional cross sections to a free form object's extrusion path, and by manipulating the object's constituent 2D shapes as they "pass through" those cross sections, you can model complex shapes quickly and easily **(Figure 2)**. Similarly, by directly editing the object's sweep path itself, you can quickly shape the object to create complex and fanciful forms .

Free form objects can be further enhanced using other Ray Dream Studio tools. For example, color and texture, such as a tree bark finish, can be added by dragging a shader from the Browser palette directly onto the free form object in the Free Form Modeler.

A free form object can be used by itself, or combined with other objects built with other Ray Dream tools (such as the Mesh Form Modeler) in the scene that is currently being composed in the Perspective window **(Figure 3)**.

Free Form Modeler

Techniques and strategies

The Free Form Modeler provides four different techniques for 3D modeling. The strategy you use depends on the type of object being built.

- Straight extrusion is used to build simple, symmetrical objects that are composed of a single 2D shape of unvarying size, such as a cylinder **(Figure 4)**.

- Scaling is used to build simple, symmetrical objects that are composed of a single 2D shape of varying size **(Figure 5)**.

- Lathing is used to build more complex symmetrical objects that are composed of a single 2D shape of varying size, such as a wine carafe **(Figure 6)**.

- Multiple cross-sectioning is used to build asymmetrical objects that are composed of multiple 2D extruded shapes, such as a fork **(Figure7)**. By adding, connecting, disconnecting, and redirecting multiple cross sections that contain multiple 2D shapes, even complex objects can be modeled efficiently and effectively.

In Chapters 5–7, you will learn how to use the Free Form Modeler in detail. In this chapter, you will learn how to navigate the Free Form Modeler and will extrude a circle into a cylinder. In Chapter 6, you will learn in detail how to work with points and axes and how to build various 2D shapes on planes. In Chapter 7, you will transform a cylinder into a cone using the scaling technique, and you will build a vase and a martini glass.

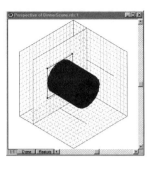

Figure 4. Use straight extrusion to build simple, symmetrical objects such as a cylinder.

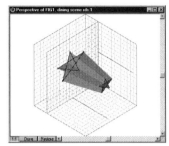

Figure 5. Use scaling to build simple objects composed of a single 2D shape of varying size.

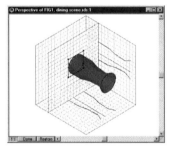

Figure 6. Use lathing to build more complex objects composed of a single 2D shape of varying size, such as a wine carafe.

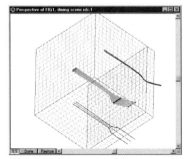

Figure 7. Multiple cross-sectioning is used to build asymmetrical objects composed of multiple 2D cross sectional shapes, such as this fork.

Figure 8.
Free Form tool.

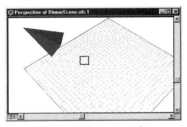

Figure 9. Drag the Free Form tool anywhere into the Perspective window.

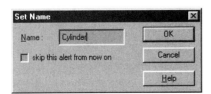

Figure 10. In the **Set Name** dialog box, name the object "Cylinder" and click OK.

CREATING AND EDITING FREE FORM OBJECTS

Free form objects are created and edited within the Free Form Modeler. The Free Form Modeler consists of the Free Form modeling window and the modeling box. The Free Form Modeler is launched by creating a new free form object or by editing an existing free form object.

✔ Tip

■ The Free Form modeling window is actually a special view of the Perspective window that "zooms in" exclusively on the free form object being created or edited.

To create a new free form object called "Cylinder":

1. Start Ray Dream Studio.

2. Choose New from the File menu, and click on the Create Empty Scene button (or open an existing scene).

3. If the Perspective window is not visible and current, choose Perspective of Doc from the Windows menu.

4. Drag the Free Form tool **(Figure 8)** anywhere into the Perspective window **(Figure 9)**.

5. In the Set Name dialog box, name the object "Cylinder" and click OK **(Figure 10)**.

or

1. If the Time Line window is not visible and current, choose Time Line of Doc from the Windows menu.

2. Select the Time Line window's Objects tab to display a hierarchical tree of objects in the current scene.

Create a New Free Form Object

3. Drag the Free Form tool into the tree list of objects in the Time Line window **(Figure 11)**.

4. In the Set Name dialog box, name the object "Cylinder" and click OK.

To edit an existing free form object in the Free Form Modeling window:

1. Select the Time Line Window.

2. Select the Time Line window's Objects tab to display a hierarchical tree of objects.

3. Double-click on any existing free form object to edit it **(Figure 12)**.

or

Select an existing free form object, and then choose Jump In from the Edit menu **(Figure 13)**.

To close the Free Form Modeler:

1. Click the Done button or Restore button at the bottom left corner of the window **(Figure 14)**.

or

Choose Jump Out from the Edit menu **(Figure 15)**.

2. Note that you are returned to the Perspective window.

To delete a free form object:

1. Select it in either the Perspective window or in the Object tab of the Hierarchy window.

2. Press the Delete key.

or

Choose Cut from the Edit menu.

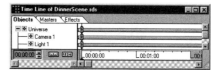

Figure 11. Drag the Free Form tool into the tree list of objects in the Time Line window.

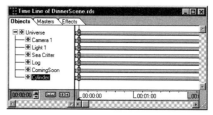

Figure 12. Double-click on any existing free form object to edit it.

Figure 13. Choose **Jump In** from the **Edit** menu.

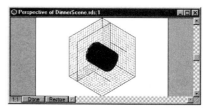

Figure 14. Click Done or Restore at the bottom-left corner of the Free Form Modeling window.

Figure 15. Choose **Jump Out** from the **Edit** menu.

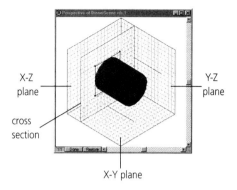

X-Z plane

Y-Z plane

cross section

X-Y plane

Figure 16. The Reference view of the Free Form modeling box.

Figure 17. Click the Planes toolbar item in the Toolbars window to make a check mark appear beside it.

UNDERSTANDING THE MODELING BOX

When the Free Form modeling window is first opened, it displays the Free Form modeling box in its default, or Reference, view. The Reference view looks like the interior of a cube whose sides have been lined with graph paper.

In the Reference view, the X-Y plane of the modeling box is shown as the "bottom" of the cube, the X-Z plane is shown as the "left" side of the cube, and the Y-Z plane is shown as the "right" side of the cube **(Figure 16)**.

The Reference view also displays the default X-Z cross section, which appears immediately to the right of the X-Z plane and makes that cross section the drawing plane.

Navigating the modeling box

Using the Free Form Modeler entails frequent switching among the modeling box's various planes, which display cross sections as well as the sweep paths.

Planes can be displayed, hidden, or selected by clicking on either the modeling box itself or on a specific region of the Display Planes tool.

To show the Display Planes tool:

1. Choose Toolbars from the View menu.

2. If the Planes toolbar item is not checked, click it to make a check mark appear **(Figure 17)**.

3. Click OK.

The Modeling Box

To select a plane for drawing:

1. Click on the Selection tool.

2. Click directly on the desired plane in the modeling box **(Figure 18)**. Notice that a plane's grid lines turn a light aqua color, called "light cyan," to indicate that it is the currently selected plane.

or

Alt/Option click on the region of the Display Planes tool that corresponds to the desired plane.

✔ Tip

■ Clicking on the left plane selects the parallel plane that is directly to its right.

To toggle the visibility of a plane or free form object:

Click on the region of the Display Planes tool corresponding to the plane (left, right, or bottom) or the object (center) whose visibility you wish to toggle.

To isolate the current drawing plane:

1. Press Ctrl+5/Command+5.

or

1. Choose Preset Positions from the View menu, and select Drawing Plane from the submenu **(Figure 20)**.

To return to the Reference view:

1. Press Ctrl+0/Command+0.

or

1. Choose Preset Positions from the View menu, and select Reference from the submenu.

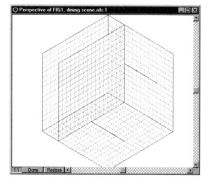

Figure 18. Click on the desired plane in the modeling box to select it.

Figure 19. Click on the region of the Display Planes tool corresponding to the plane or object whose visibility you wish to toggle.

Figure 20. Choose **Preset Position** from the **View** menu, and select **Drawing Plane** from the submenu.

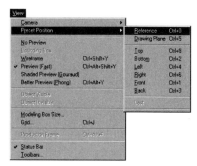

Figure 21. Choose **Preset Position** from the **View** menu and select **Reference** from the submenu.

Figure 22. Click the Primitives tool, and select the Oval tool from the pop-up toolbar.

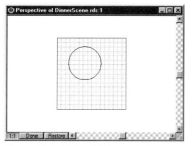

Figure 23. Hold the Shift key and drag to draw a circle on the drawing plane.

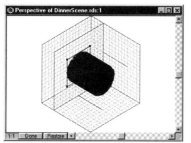

Figure 24. The circle is automatically extruded into a cylinder along the sweep path.

Figure 25. Choose **Center** from the **Sections** menu to center the cylinder on the drawing plane.

BUILDING A FREE FORM OBJECT IN THE MODELING BOX

To build a cylinder:

1. Click on the Selection tool.

2. Make sure the left (X-Z) plane is visible; if not, make it visible by clicking on the corresponding region of the Display Planes tool.

3. Click on the left (X-Z) plane. Note that the default drawing plane appears to the right of the selected X-Z plane.

4. Choose Preset Positions from the View menu, and select Drawing Plane from the submenu. The drawing plane is displayed by itself as a simple 2D grid.

5. Click the Primitives tool (to the left of the Text tool on the toolbar), and select the Oval tool from the pop-up toolbar **(Figure 22)**.

6. While holding down the Shift key (to constrain the oval to a circle), click and hold the mouse near the top-left corner of the drawing plane and drag it toward the bottom-right corner of the drawing plane.

7. When the elastic oval looks like that shown in **Figure 23**, release the mouse button.

8. Choose Reference from the View menu. The circle is automatically extruded into a cylinder along the sweep path **(Figure 24)**. Notice also that the length of the cylinder is equal to the length of the sweep path, as indicated by the light purple ("light magenta") lines shown on the bottom (X-Y) and right (Y-Z) planes. This extrusion occurred automatically because the modeling box uses default values (lengths and shapes) for the sweep path.

9. Choose Center from the Sections menu **(Figure 25)** to center the cylinder on the drawing plane.

Build the Cylinder

ADJUSTING THE SWEEP PATH

Figure 26. Right-click/Ctrl-click to display a pop-up menu, and select **Grid**.

The sweep path, also known as the extrusion path, can be thought of as a flexible spine that dictates the length and shape of an object.

In order to increase or decrease the length of your cylinder without inadvertently changing its shape, follow these steps.

To enable the grid's Snap to option:

1. Click on the Selection tool.

2. Click anywhere on the bottom plane.

3. Right-click/Ctrl-click to display a pop-up menu.

4. Choose Grid from the pop-up menu **(Figure 26)**.

5. Click the "Snap to" checkbox so that it is checked, and click OK **(Figure 27)**.

To select the sweep path:

Click on the bottom plane's sweep path. Note that the sweep path displays all of its points as hollow circles. By default, the extrusion line has only two points: its beginning point and endpoint **(Figure 28)**.

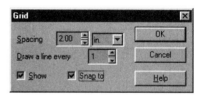

Figure 27. Click the "Snap to" checkbox in the **Grid** dialog box.

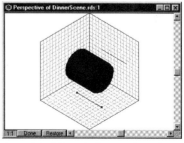

Figure 28. Click on the bottom plane's (X-Y plane) sweep path.

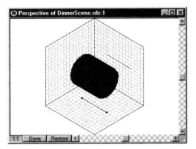

Figure 29. Click the endpoint (lower-right point) of the sweep path on the bottom plane to select it.

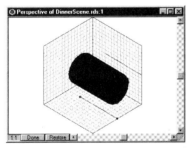

Figure 30. Drag the endpoint to the edge of the bottom plane.

Figure 31. Select the desired zoom ratio from the pop-up menu.

To lengthen or shorten the sweep path:

1. Click on the endpoint of the sweep path (lower-right point) and notice that it becomes a filled point to indicate that it has been selected **(Figure 29)**.

2. Click again and drag the endpoint along the grid so as to lengthen the extrusion path to the full length of the bottom plane and release.

3. Notice that the sweep path (as defined by the two light purple lines shown on the bottom and right planes) and the cylinder were lengthened **(Figure 30)**.

ENHANCING OBJECT VISUALIZATION

Because free form objects are 3D objects, it is useful to view them with differing levels of magnification and from different angles of view.

Zooming

Zooming in or out on the modeling box will give you a larger or smaller view of the box and its contents.

To zoom in or out on the modeling box:

1. Click the Zoom button on the bottom left of the Free Form Modeling window.

2. Select the desired zoom ratio from the pop-up menu **(Figure 31)**.

Scaling

By default, the modeling box is a 32-inch cube. You can increase or decrease the size of the cube as follows.

To scale the modeling box and the free form object:

1. Choose Modeling Box Size from the View menu.

2. Enter the desired size and units of measurement in the Modeling Box Size dialog box **(Figure 32)**.

3. Check the "Scale object with Modeling Box" option if you want the free form object to be scaled in size along with the modeling box.

✔ Tip

■ A useful way to conceptualize scaling is to think of the modeling box as a cardboard box, and the free form object contained in it as an object in that cardboard box. Scaling the modeling box "up" to a larger size without also scaling the object with it is simply like placing the same object in a larger cardboard box.

Virtual Trackball

The Virtual Trackball tool lets you rotate the modeling box—and the free form object it contains—in a 3D manner. Such rotation helps you to visualize the object's appearance from every possible angle.

To use the Virtual Trackball:

1. Click the Virtual Trackball tool, which is located next to the Selector tool **(Figure 33)**. If the One Axis Rotation tool is displayed, click it to toggle it to the Virtual Trackball tool. Note that a circle surrounds the free form object **(Figure 34)**.

2. Place the mouse pointer within the sphere, click and hold the mouse down, and "rotate" the trackball in the desired direction.

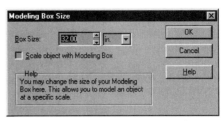

Figure 32. Enter the desired size and units of measurement in the **Modeling Box Size** dialog box.

Figure 33. The Virtual Trackball tool. ———

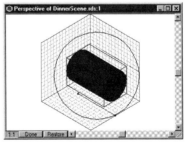

Figure 34. When you select the Virtual Trackball tool, a circle appears surrounding the free form object.

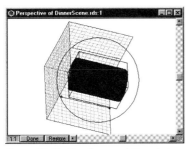

Figure 35. The Free Form modeling window updates to display the object and modeling box in the new position.

Figure 36. Choose **Surface Fidelity** from the **Geometry** menu.

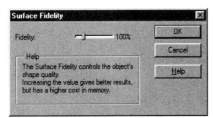

Figure 37. Set the slider to the desired fidelity setting in the **Surface Fidelity** dialog box.

Figure 38. The Hand tool.

3. Note that the Free Form modeling window updates to display the modeling box and the free form object in the new position **(Figure 35)**.

✔ **Tip**

■ The key to controlling the trackball is to imagine that it is a sphere suspended in space, which can slowly and gently be pushed or pulled with your finger in order to rotate it into the desired position.

Surface fidelity

Surface fidelity refers to the accuracy of the shape of a free form object. For example, in the modeling of a sphere, a higher level of fidelity would provide a more perfectly rounded sphere.

To view and set the fidelity level:

1. Choose Surface Fidelity from the Geometry menu **(Figure 36)**.

2. Set the slider to the desired fidelity setting **(Figure 37)**.

✔ **Tip**

■ Higher fidelity causes an object to consume more memory.

Using the Hand tool

The Hand tool **(Figure 38)** lets you move the modeling box within the Free Form modeling window itself. It is especially helpful if you wish to work without expanding the Ray Dream Studio parent window to the full size of your display. It also lets you perform adjustments—such as diagonally moving a target area from the bottom left of the window to the top right of the window—in a single movement that would otherwise have to be made with multiple scroll-bar operations.

To move the contents of the Free Form Modeling window:

1. Click on the Hand tool.

2. Click within the Free Form Modeling window and drag the window contents in the direction opposite from the area you wish to bring into view.

PREVIEW QUALITY OPTIONS

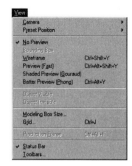

Figure 39. Preview quality commands are located under the **View** menu.

As you model objects, you will sometimes want to show, hide, or alter the quality of the preview of the object being built. You can choose between the following commands, which are chosen from the View menu **(Figure 39)**:

The **No Preview** command hides the free form object so that it does not have to be redrawn **(Figure 40)**. This setting yields the fastest response time and is useful when working on sweep paths and cross sections.

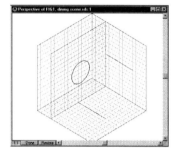

Figure 40. The **No Preview** setting.

The **Wireframe** command hides the surfaces of the free form object and resembles an x-ray that shows skeletal structure but not covering tissue like skin **(Figure 41)**. By temporarily hiding an object's surfaces, you can have an unobstructed view of its structure.

The **Preview (Fast)** command is the default setting. It provides opaque surfaces and helps you understand the overall shape of the object **(Figure 42)**.

The **Shaded Preview (Gouraud)** provides a bit more information about how the object will look under the lights that are currently configured in your scene **(Figure 43)**.

The **Better Preview (Phong)** is actually the best preview; it gives the most detail about the appearance of the object when it is finally rendered. Because it provides the most detail, it takes the longest to generate **(Figure 44)**.

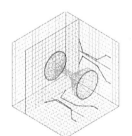

Figure 41. The **Wireframe** setting.

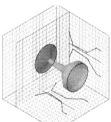

Figure 42. The **Preview (Fast)** setting.

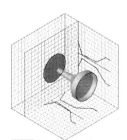

Figure 43. The **Shaded Preview (Gouraud)** setting.

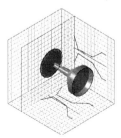

Figure 44. The **Better Preview (Phong)** setting.

Preview Quality Options

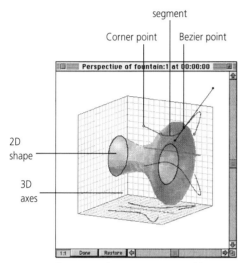

Figure 1. Various components used in building a 3D object are shown in the Free Form modeling box.

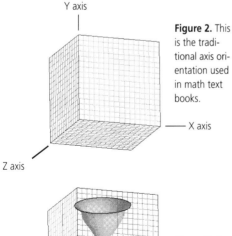

Figure 2. This is the traditional axis orientation used in math text books.

Figure 3. A wine glass is shown in a traditional axis orientation.

As you may recall from grade school, a coordinate system lets you chart points, lines, segments, shapes, and volumes in space. Ray Dream's 3D modeling tools—such as the Free Form Modeler and the Mesh Form Modeler—are a combination of a computer-assisted coordinate system and some specialized drawing tools that, together, help you create and manage points, lines, segments, shapes, and volumes and the relationships they enjoy.

In this chapter you will gain an in-depth understanding of working with the following 3D modeling components **(Figure 1)** that are common to Ray Dream Studio's different modules:

- 3D axes
- Points
- Point types
- Lines
- Segments
- 2D shapes

UNDERSTANDING 3D AXES

When you first learned about graphs in grade school, you were probably taught to represent the X axis with a horizontal line and the Y axis with a vertical line. You may have also learned to represent the Z axis as a diagonal line through the intersection of the X and Y axes **(Figure 2)**. Thus, if you were drawing a wine glass on a traditional representation of 3D space, the glass would be shown standing normally, with its height dimension parallel to the Y axis **(Figure 3)**.

The Free Form Modeler's modeling box, however, represents things in a way that can be just a bit disorienting. In the modeling box, the axis that is displayed in the vertical orientation is the Z axis, not the Y axis **(Figure 4)**. The axis visible on the left side of the Z axis is the X axis, and the axis to the right of Z is the Y axis. So a wine glass built in the Free Form Modeler would appear as shown in **Figure 5**, where longitudinal axis of the glass remains parallel to the Y axes so that the glass appears flipped on its side.

✔ Tip

■ You can always rotate your view of the modeling box with the Virtual Trackball tool (as described in the previous chapter) so that the axes appear in the traditional positions.

UNDERSTANDING POINTS, LINES, SEGMENTS, AND SHAPES

Points, lines, segments, and shapes play a crucial role in several of Ray Dream Studio's tools, such as the Free Form Modeler.

Point, line, segment and 2D shape defined

Ray Dream Studio defines points, lines, and segments as follows **(Figure 6)**:

• A **point** is a nondimensional position in 3D space, such as the position represented by the intersection of the X, Y, and Z axes.

• A **line** is a straight or curved path between two known points in 3D space: the starting point and the ending point.

• A **segment** is the portion of a line that is located between two consecutive points on that line.

• A **2D shape** is an area that is fully enclosed by a line.

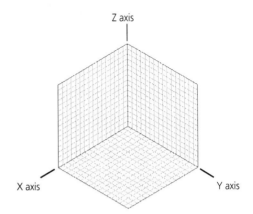

Figure 4. This is the orientation of the X, Y, and Z axes in Ray Dream Studio.

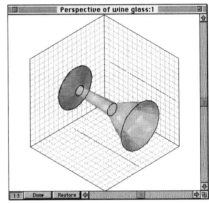

Figure 5. The orientation of the wine glass illustrates the typical orientation of objects built in Ray Dream's Free Form Modeler.

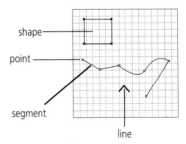

Figure 6. A point, line, segment, and shape are shown in the Drawing Plane view of the Free Form modeling box.

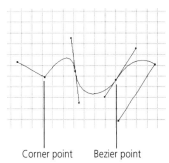

Figure 7. Ray Dream uses two types of points: Corner points and Bezier points.

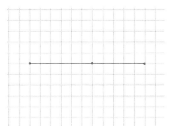

Figure 8. A line that passes through a Corner point is like a piece of cord that is wrapped around a nail.

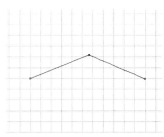

Figure 9. If the point is moved out of line with the other points, the line becomes angled.

Types of points

Ray Dream uses two types of points **(Figure 7)**:

- Corner points
- Bezier curve points

A line that passes through a Corner point is like a piece of cord that is wrapped around a nail. If the nail is moved out of line with the other points in the line, the line becomes angled **(Figures 8–9)**. A Bezier curve point differs from a Corner point in two important respects:

- A Bezier curve point is used to produce curves and not corners **(Figure 10)**; and
- A Bezier curve point's position relative to the other points in the line need not change for it to produce a change in the line's shape **(Figure 11)**. As you will soon see, a point's type can be converted between a Corner point and a Bezier curve point using the Convert Point tool.

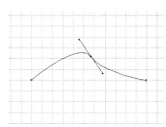

Figure 10. A Bezier point is used to produce curves, and not corners.

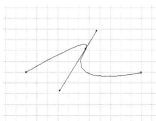

Figure 11. A Bezier point's position need not change for it to produce a change in the line's shape.

Factors affecting points, lines, segments, and shapes

Generally speaking, because points, lines, segments, and shapes play similar roles, you manipulate them with similar techniques throughout Ray Dream Studio. However, as you will see later in this chapter, their precise uses and capabilities depend on the following factors:

- The Ray Dream Studio module you are using.

- The tool, object, or view you are using.

- The operation you are performing.

- The type of point (Corner vs Bezier curve) you are manipulating.

- The functional relationship between the lines and segments (e.g., whether they are part of the same, or separate, 3D shapes).

- The status of a 2D shape (whether it is open or closed).

- The method you use to create a shape, line, or point.

An example illustrates these variations:

- Bezier curve points and, by extension, the Convert Point tool are available in the Free Form Modeler but not in the Mesh Form Modeler **(Figures 12–13)**.

Figure 12. The Convert Point tool is available from the Free Form Modeler toolbar.

Figure 13. The Convert Point tool is not available from the Mesh Form Modeler toolbar.

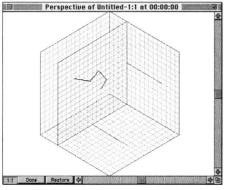

Figure 14. Create or select the cross section that does or will contain the 2D shape or line that does or will hold the target point.

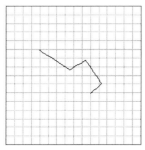

Figure 15. Select an appropriate view such as the Drawing Plane view shown here.

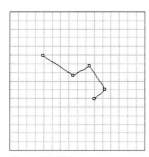

Figure 16. Click on, or create, the line or shape that does or will contain the target point.

Displaying and selecting points, lines, sections, and shapes

The reasons and procedures for adding, moving, deleting, and converting points, lines, sections, and shapes are generally consistent throughout Ray Dream Studio, although, again, there are some variations between modules, tools, objects, and views.

These procedures frequently involve the creation and management of points. Point management can be summarized with the generic steps and illustrated with the specific Free Form Modeler example set forth below:

To manipulate points on a Ray Dream object:

1. Create the new object, or select the existing object, that will host the targeted points.

2. If working in the Free Form Modeler, create or select the cross section that does or will contain the 2D shape or line that does or will hold the target point **(Figure 14)**.

3. Select an appropriate view for performing the function (usually an isolated view of the current drawing plane) **(Figure 15)**.

4. Click on the Selection tool to avoid inadvertent drawing or other actions.

5. Click on the grid to deselect any already selected points or other objects.

6. Click on, or create, the line or shape that does or will contain the target point **(Figure 16)**.

7. Identify the target point among the available points, which are displayed as hollow circles, or the target position for a new point.

Manipulate Points on a Ray Dream Object

8. Select the correct tool: the Pen tool (which is adjacent to the Hand tool), or the Add Point tool, the Remove Point tool, or the Convert Point tool (which are represented as a single tool that is adjacent to the Pen tool which opens up to a pop-up toolbar) **(Figure 17)**.

9. Click on the target point **(Figure 18)**.

10. If necessary, convert the target point between a Corner or Bezier curve point, move it, and (in the case of a Bezier curve point) manipulate its handles to achieve the desired line or curve.

✔ Tip

■ To choose among the Add Point tool, the Remove Point tool, and the Delete Point tool, click repeatedly on the Point tool until the desired tool is displayed.

To build a new 2D shape using the Pen tool:

1. Create a new free form object, name it "Test FFO" **(Figure 19)**, and display it in the Reference view, all as instructed in the last chapter.

2. Display the default cross section by pressing Ctrl+Left/Command+Left

3. Isolate the cross section as the current drawing plane by pressing Ctrl+5/Command 5 **(Figure 20)**.

4. Click on the Pen tool, which is adjacent to the Hand tool.

5. Position the cursor near the top-left corner of the drawing plane and click once to create a new point **(Figure 21)**.

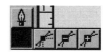

Figure 17. From the pop-up toolbar, select either the Pen, Add Point, Remove Point, or Convert Point tool.

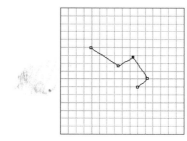

Figure 18. Click on the target point to select it.

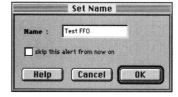

Figure 19. Create a new Free Form object and name it "Test FFO".

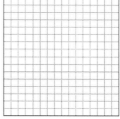

Figure 20. Display the default cross section in the Drawing Plane view.

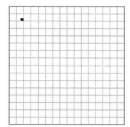

Figure 21. Create a point near the top-left corner of the drawing plane.

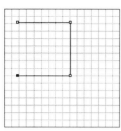

Figure 22. Add three more points to form a rectangle.

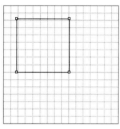

Figure 23. Create the fourth point directly over the first point to close the shape.

Figure 24. A closed shape appears filled-in in **Preview (Fast)** mode.

6. Hold down the Shift key to constrain alignment by 90 degrees, while clicking to add three more points to form a rectangle **(Figure 22)**.

7. Make sure you create the fourth point directly over the first point; this causes the 2D shape to "close" **(Figure 23)**.

8. Choose Preview (Fast) from the View menu to shade the free form object. If closure was achieved, the shape will appear as a filled-in area **(Figure 24)**.

9. Press Ctrl+0/Command+0 to return to the Reference view. Note that the shape was extruded along the entire sweep path **(Figure 25)**.

10. Choose Wireframe or No Preview from the View menu to view the free form object without shading.

Removing points

Points can be removed with the Remove Point tool. Removing a point can have a range of impacts on a Ray Dream object, depending on its structural significance—that is, its relationship to the other elements that comprise the object. Fortunately, you can choose Undo from the Edit menu to reverse any untoward point deletions!

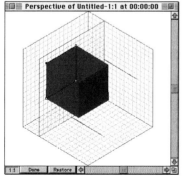

Figure 25. The rectangle is extruded along the sweep path.

To remove a point from an existing line or 2D shape using the Remove Point tool:

1. Click on the Selection tool.

2. Click on the bottom plane to deselect any selected object or cross section.

3. Click on the object that contains the point to be deleted (in this case, the last point that you added at the top-left to close the rectangle), and note that its points are displayed as hollow circles **(Figure 26)**.

4. Click and hold the Point tool and select the Remove Point tool from the pop-up toolbar **(Figure 27)**.

5. Click on the target point to remove it **(Figure 28)**.

6. Note that the target point was removed and that the 2D shape automatically maintained its closure by revising itself into a triangle **(Figure 29)**.

7. Press Ctrl+Z/Command+Z to undo the deletion of the point and to restore the original shape.

Adding points with the Add Point tool

Complex 3D objects are constructed by adding points to lines and shapes and then moving them to architecturally strategic positions.

To add a point to an existing line or 2D shape with the Add Point tool:

1. Click on the Selection tool.

2. Click on the bottom plane to deselect any selected object or cross section.

3. Click on the object to which you wish to add a point (in this case, the rectangle), and note that its points are displayed as hollow circles.

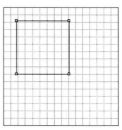

Figure 26. Click on the object that contains the point to be deleted.

Remove Point tool

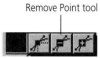

Figure 27. Click and hold the Point tool, and select the Remove Point tool from the pop-up toolbar.

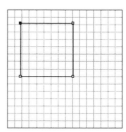

Figure 28. Click on the target point to remove it.

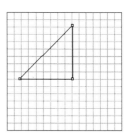

Figure 29. The target point is removed, and the 2D shape maintains its closure by revising itself into a triangle.

Remove and Add Points to Lines and Shapes

Add Point tool

Figure 30. Click and hold the Point tool, and select the Add Point tool from the pop-up toolbar.

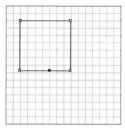

Figure 31. Click on the center area of the rectangle's bottom line. A Corner point has been added above.

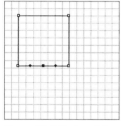

Figure 32. A Bezier point has been added to the rectangle's bottom line.

4. Click and hold the Point tool, and select the Add Point tool from the pop-up toolbar **(Figure 30)**.

5. Click on the center area of the bottom line of the rectangle. Note that the new point is displayed as a filled-in circle, indicating that it is currently selected **(Figure 31)**.

6. Note also that merely adding a point does not affect the contours of the host shape.

7. Determine the type of point that was added. If only a single, filled point appears, then the point is a Corner point; but if three new points appear, then a Bezier curve point was added in the center, and its manipulation handles were added on either side **(Figure 32)**.

✔ Tip

■ Any point added with either the Pen tool or the Add Point tool can be converted from a Corner point to a Bezier curve point, or vice versa, with the Convert Point tool.

Moving Points

Moving a point, like removing a point, can impact the shape of a line, segment, or 2D shape; and that impact can be either negligible or great.

For example, laterally moving a point on a straight, horizontal line segment will have no impact on the segment's shape. On the other hand, moving that point up or down will disrupt the segment in an angular or curved fashion, depending on whether the point is a Corner point or a Bezier curve point.

Points are moved simply by selecting them and dragging them.

Moving Points

To move a point on a 2D shape:

1. Click on the Selection tool.

2. Click on the desired point and drag it to the desired position (in this case, click the point you just added to the middle of the rectangle's bottom line and drag it downward several spaces) **(Figures 33–34)**.

3. Note the effect on the 2D shape's overall appearance.

✔ Tip

■ Make sure that only the target point is selected.

Converting points

To fix an error or carry out an inspiration, you may want to convert a Corner point to a Bezier curve point, or vice versa. Without the Convert Point tool, it would be necessary to remove the target point and then add a replacement of the correct type.

To convert a Corner point to a Bezier curve point (or vice versa):

1. Click on the Selection tool.

2. Click anywhere on the grid to deselect any selected lines or points.

3. Click on the line that contains the target point in order to display all points on that line as hollow circles.

4. Click and hold the Point tool, and select the Convert Point tool from the pop-up toolbar **(Figure 35)**.

5. Click on the target point (in this case, the point that you just dragged down from the center of the bottom of the rectangle) to convert its type **(Figure 36)**.

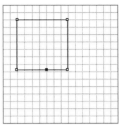

Figure 33. Click the desired point you wish to move.

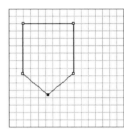

Figure 34. Drag the selected point to the new position.

Convert Point tool

Figure 35. Click and hold the Point tool, and select the Convert Point tool from the pop-up toolbar.

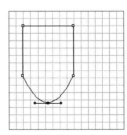

Figure 36. Click on the target point to convert its type.

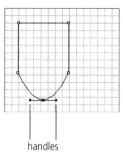

handles

Figure 37. Click on the target point to convert its type.

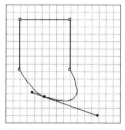

Figure 38. Contour a Bezier curve point by dragging and rotating one of its handles.

Contouring Bezier curve points

Once placed into a drawing, a Bezier curve point appears in the middle of a short line. Two additional points, called handles **(Figure 37)**, are placed on either side of the Bezier point. At first it may be difficult to see this line, especially if you added the Bezier point to a straight line. But if you click and drag either of the handles at the end of the line, you will see that the host line will curve in real time. Once the desired curve is achieved, the handle is released and the curve is fixed.

To contour Bezier curve points:

1. Click on the handle and drag it away from, and rotate it around, the Bezier curve point **(Figure 38)**.

2. When you have the desired curve, release the mouse.

✔ Tip

■ As you manipulate a Bezier curve point's handle and line, note the relationship between the curve that is produced and the position of the handle and the length of the line. The more the control line is extended away from the center point, the more the curve is stretched; and the more the control handle is rotated around the center point, the more the curve is sloped.

MASTERING THE FREE FORM MODELER

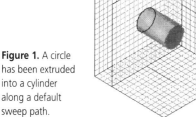

Figure 1. A circle has been extruded into a cylinder along a default sweep path.

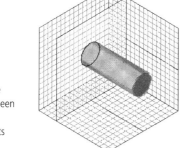

Figure 2. The cylinder has been extended by lengthening its sweep path.

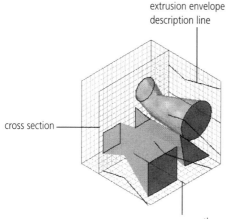

cross section

extrusion envelope description line

sweep path description line

Figure 3. You can sculpt complex and fanciful objects by mastering features of the Free Form Modeler.

In Chapter 5 you created a new free form object, drew and centered a circle on the free form object's default cross section, and watched Ray Dream automatically extrude the circle into a cylinder along a default sweep path **(Figure 1)**. Then you extended the length of this cylindrical free form object by selecting and lengthening one of its sweep path description lines **(Figure 2)**.

In Chapter 6, you delve deeply into the concepts of the coordinate system, points, point types, lines, segments, curves, and 2D shapes.

In this chapter you will continue to work with the Free Form Modeler, and in the process, you will learn about the following features:

- Single and multiple cross sections
- The sweep path
- The sweep path description lines
- Extrusion envelope
- The extrusion envelope description lines

By mastering these features, you will be able to sculpt complex and even fanciful objects with great precision and efficiency. **(Figure 3)**.

Mastering the Free Form Modeler

UNDERSTANDING CROSS SECTIONS

A cross section is a plane that is parallel to the modeling box's left (X-Z) plane and that intersects the sweep path of a free form object **(Figure 4)**. A free form object can have one or more cross sections. Only one cross-sectional plane is visible at any one time, but if an object has multiple cross sections, the outlines of the shapes on the various cross-sectional planes can be visible at the same time (this depends upon the setting of the Show command under the Sections menu). You can draw single or multiple 2D shapes on each such cross section, and connect or disconnect the extrusion between those cross sections to sculpt free form objects with complex shapes.

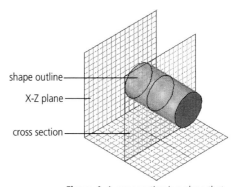

shape outline
X-Z plane
cross section

Figure 4. A cross section is a plane that is parallel to the Free Form modeling box's left (X-Z) plane and that intersects the sweep path of a free form object.

The default cross section

When you drew the 2D circle in chapter 5, you drew it on the default cross section. Whenever you create a new free form object or open an existing one for editing in the modeling box, the default cross section is the one that is displayed parallel to, and immediately to the right of, the left (X-Z) plane **(Figure 5)**.

To select and display the default cross section:

1. Click on the left (X-Z) plane.

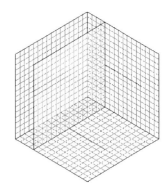

Figure 5. The default cross section.

The implied cross section

When viewing the cylinder you created, it appears as though a second cross section —one at the right end of the cylinder— was also created **(Figure 6)**. In fact, the right "face" of the cylinder is not a cross section, but rather the illusion or suggestion of a cross section that could be drawn at the end of the sweep path. We can refer to this apparent cross section as the **implied cross section**.

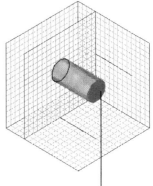

Figure 6. Implied cross section.

Default Cross Section, Implied Cross Section

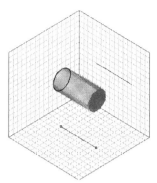

Figure 7. Click on the sweep path description line on the bottom plane.

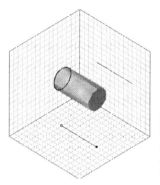

Figure 8. Click on the right endpoint on the bottom sweep path description line to select it.

Figure 9. Choose **Create** from the **Sections** menu.

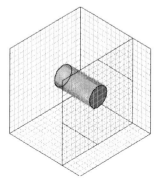

Figure 10. To select and display the new cross section, press Ctrl/Command+ Right Arrow.

Similarly, when you lengthened the sweep path by moving the endpoint of its description line on the bottom (X-Y) plane, you also moved the position of the implied cross section.

✔ Tip

■ Because the implied cross section does not exist and cannot be accessed, you cannot perform functions such as filling or hollowing out its 2D shapes. You can, however, add a cross section at the endpoint of a free form object's sweep path and then select that cross section like any other.

Adding single and multiple cross sections

The Free Form Modeler permits you to add multiple cross sections at a single time. As you will learn later in this chapter, multiple cross sections are useful for adding and scaling 2D shapes, and for interrupting and redirecting the extrusion of those shapes in a free form object.

To add a single cross section at the end of the sweep path:

1. Display the cylinder in the Reference View.

2. Click on the Selection tool.

3. Click on the sweep path description line on the bottom plane. Note that the beginning and ending points of that line are displayed as hollow points **(Figure 7)**.

4. Click on the end (rightmost) point to select it.

5. Note that the endpoint confirms your selection by turning solid **(Figure 8)**.

6. Choose Create from the Sections menu **(Figure 9)**.

7. Note that the newly created cross section is not automatically displayed.

8. To select and display the new cross section, press Ctrl/Command+Right Arrow **(Figure 10)**.

To create multiple cross sections simultaneously:

1. Display the free form object in the Reference view and click on the Selection tool.

2. Navigate to the cross section to the right of where the multiple cross sections will be inserted by pressing Ctrl/Command+Left or Ctrl/Command+Right (in this case, select the default cross section by pressing Ctrl/Command+Left).

3. Choose Create Multiple from the Sections menu **(Figure 11)**.

4. Enter 3 in the "Number to create" field and click OK **(Figure 12)**.

5. Click on the sweep path description line on the bottom plane to see the three new points that were created at the locations of the new cross sections **(Figure 13)**.

✔ Tip

■ The Create Multiple Cross Sections command is available only if you've selected an existing cross section that is not located at the endpoint of the sweep path description line. In other words, if you have replaced the implied cross section with an actual cross section and select that cross section, you cannot invoke the Create Multiple Cross Sections command.

Figure 11. Choose **Create Multiple** from the **Sections** menu.

Figure 12. Enter 3 in the **Create Multiple Cross-Sections** dialog box and click OK.

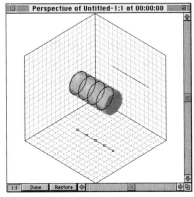

Figure 13. Click on the sweep path description line on the bottom plane to see the three new points where the cross sections were created.

Create Multiple Cross Sections

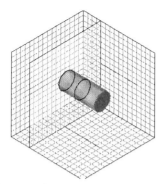

Figure 14. If there is an actual cross section to the right of the current cross section, then the new cross sections are placed between them.

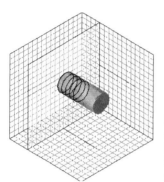

Figure 15. New cross sections have been added between two previous cross sections.

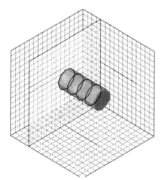

Figure 16. If you create multiple cross sections starting from the default cross section, and there are no other cross sections on the object, then Ray Dream adds the new sections between the default section and the implied cross section.

Placement and spacing of cross sections

Here's how Ray Dream Studio places and spaces one or more cross sections that were created using the Create Multiple Sections command:

- If there is an actual cross section to the right of the current cross section, then the new cross sections are placed between those two explicit cross sections **(Figures 14–15)**; otherwise, the new cross sections are placed evenly between the current cross section and the implied end cross section **(Figure 16)**.

- If the number of cross sections specified in the dialog box is less than the number of points, then Ray Dream adds a cross section for each such point, even though you specified fewer new cross sections.

✔ Tip

■ Before adding multiple cross sections, consider how many you need and how far apart you want them in your object. If you need equal spacing throughout the entire sweep path, then replace the implied cross section with an actual cross section and select the number you need. Similarly, to achieve equal spacing for a segment of the free form object, place cross sections at the beginning and end of that segment, and then invoke the Create Multiple cross sections command from the beginning cross section.

Placement and Spacing of Cross Sections

Removing cross sections

When you remove a cross section, Ray Dream also removes the shapes that it contains. If a shape on a target cross section has a contour, scale, or position that differs from a corresponding shape on any adjoining cross section, and if such shapes are connected, then deletion of the target plane will have an impact on the overall shape of the free form object **(Figures 17–18)**.

Cross sections may be removed directly, by selecting and removing them, or indirectly, by deleting the point that corresponds to the cross section from either sweep path description line.

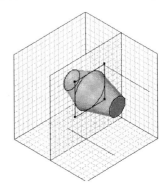

Figure 17. A cross section has been selected to be removed.

To remove a cross section:

1. Navigate to the cross section.

2. Choose Remove from the Sections menu **(Figure 19)**.

or

1. Click on the Selection tool.

2. Click on the bottom (X-Y) plane.

3. Click on the sweep path description line on the bottom plane.

4. Click on the point that corresponds to the plane to be deleted **(Figure 20)**.

5. Press the Delete key.

or

Choose Cut from the Edit menu.

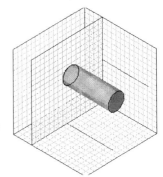

Figure 18. Removing the cross section in this case changes the shape of the object.

Figure 19. Choose **Remove** from the **Sections** menu.

If you are dissatisfied with the resulting change in the free form object's shape, press Ctrl/Command+Z or choose Undo from the Edit menu.

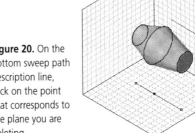

Figure 20. On the bottom sweep path description line, click on the point that corresponds to the plane you are deleting.

Figure 21. Choose **Go To** from the **Sections** menu.

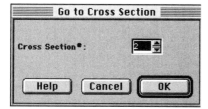

Figure 22. Use the arrow buttons in the **Go to Cross Section** dialog box to enter a cross section to jump to and click OK.

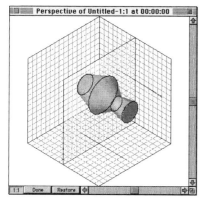

Figure 23. The entered cross section becomes the current cross section.

Rules to remember

The following rules govern the interplay between the deletion of a point on a sweep path description line and the deletion of a cross section:

- There must always be at least one cross section. Thus, the default cross section cannot be removed unless another cross section has already been created.

- Deleting a point on a sweep path description line also deletes the cross section, if any, that exists at that point.

- Deletion of a cross section does not necessarily delete its corresponding point on the sweep path description line. (The point continues to be available for use in adjusting the shape of the sweep path itself, as described later in this chapter).

- If there are only two points on the sweep path description line, you cannot delete the endpoint (i.e., the rightmost point), although you can delete a cross section if you added one there.

Navigating cross sections

A quick way to locate (and count) the cross sections that currently exist is to navigate them.

To navigate a free form object's cross sections from the menu:

1. Choose Go To from the Sections menu **(Figure 21)** to display the Go to Cross Section dialog box **(Figure 22)**.

2. Click on the up and down arrow buttons to increase or decrease the number of the current cross section and click OK. The entered cross section becomes the current one **(Figure 23)**.

✔ Tip

■ The Arrow up and down buttons will not let you enter a number higher than the highest numbered (rightmost) cross section.

Navigating Cross Sections

To navigate a free form object's cross sections from the keyboard:

1. Press and hold Ctrl/Command+Left Arrow for a few seconds, in order to make the leftmost cross section the currently selected one.

2. Press Ctrl/Command+Right Arrow once and wait a second. If another cross section exists, then the first one will be hidden and the next one will be displayed and made current. If the first cross section is the only cross section, it will remain displayed.

3. Repeat Step 2 until the last cross section is reached and made current.

Moving cross sections

You can reposition one or more cross sections by moving their corresponding point on either sweep path description line.

To move one or more cross sections:

1. Click on an empty section on the bottom plane to deselect any selected items.

2. Click on the sweep path description line on the bottom plane to display its points as hollow circles **(Figure 24)**.

3. Click on the point that corresponds to the cross section to be moved **(Figure 25)**. Hold the Shift key to select several points.

4. Release the mouse button and the Shift key.

5. Hold the Shift key to constrain the movement along the Y axis.

6. Drag the leftmost point in the selection to its new position, and release the Shift key **(Figure 26)**.

7. Navigate the cross sections to verify their new locations **(Figure 27)**.

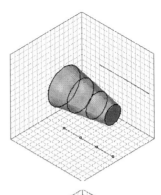

Figure 24. Click on the sweep path description line on the bottom plane to display its points.

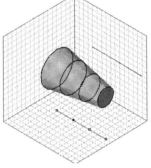

Figure 25. Click on the point that corresponds to the cross section to be moved.

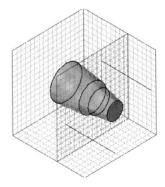

Figure 26. Drag the point to its new position.

Figure 27. Navigate the cross sections to verify the new locations.

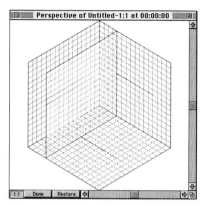

Figure 28. Go to the first, leftmost cross section.

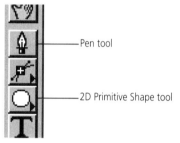

Pen tool

2D Primitive Shape tool

Figure 29. Select either the Pen tool or one of the 2D Primitive shape tools.

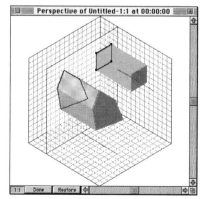

Figure 30. Two shapes have been drawn on the first cross section.

The current cross section and the current drawing plane

The mere display of a cross section indicates that it is currently selected. Note that its grid becomes light cyan (which is the graphics designation for light aqua), and the 2D shapes that were drawn on or extruded through it become displayed and selected, too.

The current cross section is also the current drawing plane. As you learned in Chapter 6, you can isolate the current cross section to get an uncluttered view for precision drawing. To do this, choose Preset Positions from the View menu and select Drawing Plane from the submenu.

It is not necessary to isolate the drawing plane; instead, you can draw on the current cross section whenever it is displayed in the modeling box. But depending on what other planes are visible, and the orientation of the modeling box, you may find the view too cluttered for precision drawing.

To draw shapes directly on a cross section:

1. Go to the first, leftmost cross section (or any other existing cross section) as described above **(Figure 28)**.

2. Click on either the Pen tool or one of the 2D Primitive Shape tools **(Figure 29)**.

3. Hold down the Shift key when you want the Pen tool to draw straight lines, or the Primitive Shapes tool to draw equilateral polygons or regular (circular) ovals **(Figure 30)**.

Draw Shapes Directly on a Cross Section

Understanding how shapes, cross sections, and extrusions interact

Three rules govern the interaction between preexisting and newly added 2D shapes and cross sections and the free form object's sweep path:

- When a free form object has only one cross section, any shape that you draw on that cross section will automatically be extruded along the sweep path **(Figure 31)**.

- If you add a second cross section and then draw a new shape on the first cross section, that shape will not be automatically extruded along the sweep path **(Figure 32)**. If you want that shape extruded, you must manually "connect" the new shape to a shape on another cross section, as described later in this chapter **(Figure 33)**.

- If one or more shapes have been extruded along the sweep path and you add a new cross section so that it intersects the extrusion, each such extruded shape will automatically be drawn—and can be scaled and otherwise edited—on the new cross section **(Figure 34)**.

Scaling 2D shapes on cross sections

In Chapter 5 you learned how to adjust the scale of the modeling box and, optionally, of the free form object it contains.

The modeling box offers other kinds of scaling. For example, you can scale any 2D shape that is contained on any of the free form object's cross sections. Such scaling is an efficient way to taper an object along its entire length or, if the free form object contains more than one cross section, along either its entire length or one or more segments of its length.

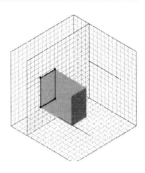

Figure 31. When a free form object has only one cross section, any shape drawn on it is automatically extruded along the sweep path.

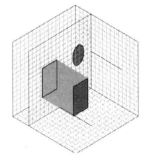

Figure 32. If you add a second cross section, new shapes drawn on the first are not automatically extruded along the sweep path.

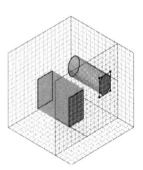

Figure 33. To extrude the new shape, you must connect it to another shape on the second cross section.

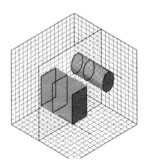

Figure 34. When you add a new cross section that intersects an object's extrusion, the 2D shapes that appear on the new cross section can be edited by scaling, for instance.

Scaling 2D Shapes on Cross Sections

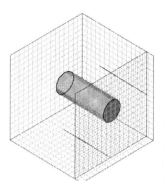

Figure 35. Navigate to the cross section that contains the target 2D shape to be scaled.

Figure 36. Choose **Preset Positions** from the **View** menu, and select **Drawing Plane** from the submenu.

Figure 37. Choose **Scale** from the **Geometry** menu.

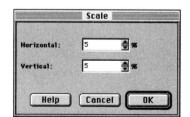

Figure 38. Reduce the horizontal and vertical scale to 5% each.

To illustrate one possible use of scaling, let's hone the cylinder into a tapered cone by scaling down the shape of the circle as it passes through the last cross section.

To scale a 2D shape on a cross section:

1. Display the free form object in the modeling box's Reference view.

2. Click on the Selection tool.

3. Navigate to the cross section that contains the target 2D shape (in this case, select the rightmost cross section by pressing Ctrl/Command+Right) **(Figure 35)**.

4. Choose Preset Positions from the View menu, and select Drawing Plane from the submenu **(Figure 36)**.

5. Click the shape on the cross section, and note that it is surrounded by a bounding box to indicate that the shape is selected.

6. Choose Scale from the Geometry menu **(Figure 37)**.

7. Reduce the horizontal and vertical scale to 5% each and click OK **(Figure 38)**.

8. Return to the Reference view.

9. Note that the free form object is displayed as scaled **(Figure 39)**.

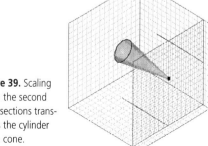

Figure 39. Scaling down the second cross sections transforms the cylinder into a cone.

How scaling a 2D shape on a cross section affects a free form object:

- Scaling a 2D shape will affect the free form object across its entire length, only if:

  Only one cross section exists.

  or

  Only two cross sections exist, and the rightmost cross section with the scaled shape is placed at the end of the sweep path—i.e., at the location of the implied cross section **(Figure 40)**.

- In any other case, scaling a 2D shape will affect only those segments of the extrusion that fall between: the cross section holding the scaled shape and the cross section to its immediate right **(Figures 41–42)**, and the cross section holding the scaled shape and the cross section to its immediate left.

Connecting, disconnecting, and redirecting 2D shapes on a cross section

The Free Form Modeler permits you to draw single or multiple 2D shapes on single or multiple cross sections, and lets you connect, disconnect, and redirect those shapes between cross sections however you like. By "mixing and matching" shapes across cross sections, you can create complex free form objects very easily.

To create a multishaped free form object:

1. Create a new free form object and name it Wild Thing **(Figure 43)**.

2. On the default cross section, use the Primitive Shapes tool to draw a square on the left-center area of the cross section, and draw a circle on the right-center area **(Figure 44)**.

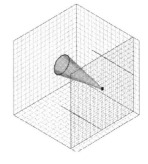

Figure 40. When only two cross sections exist on a free form object, scaling a shape on the right-most cross section affects the entire object.

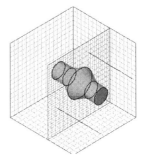

Figure 41. When more than two cross sections exist on a free form object, scaling a shape affects the object between the section with the scaled shape and the two adjacent sections, shown here in the Reference view.

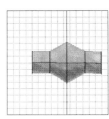

Figure 42. When more than two cross sections exist on a free form object, scaling a shape affects the object between the section with the scaled shape and the two adjacent sections, shown here in the Left view.

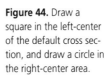

Figure 43. Create a new free form object and name it Wild Thing.

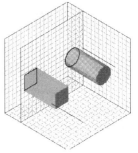

Figure 44. Draw a square in the left-center of the default cross section, and draw a circle in the right-center area.

Figure 45. Enter 2 in the **Create Multiple Cross-Sections** dialog box.

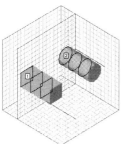

Figure 46. The square is assigned shape number 1, and the circle shape number 2.

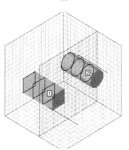

Figure 47. The shape number assignments carry through each cross section.

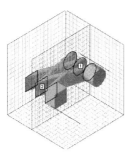

Figure 48. The shapes are cross-connected between the first and second cross sections.

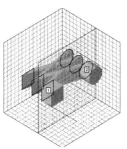

Figure 49. The shapes are also cross-connected between the third and second cross sections.

3. Center the shapes in the plane by choosing Center from the Cross Sections menu.

4. Return to the Reference view if not already there, and click on the Selection tool.

5. Create two new cross sections by choosing Multiple from the Sections menu, entering two in the dialog box, and clicking OK **(Figure 45)**.

6. Choose Show Shape Numbers from the Sections menu.

7. Note that the square is assigned shape number 1 and the circle is assigned shape number 2 **(Figure 46)**.

8. Navigate to the second and third cross sections by pressing Ctrl/Command+Right Arrow and Ctrl/Command+Left Arrow.

9. Note that the shape numbering assignments carry through each cross section **(Figure 47)**.

To redirect shape connections:

1. Navigate to the second cross section.

2. Click the shape number on the square on the second cross section to open the Shape Number dialog box, and change the square number to 2. The circle number automatically changes to 1.

3. Note that the shapes are cross-connected between the first and second cross section **(Figure 48)**.

4. Note also that the shapes are cross-connected between the third and second cross sections, because the third cross section retains the original number assignments **(Figure 49)**.

5. Click on the bottom plane to temporarily hide the cross section and examine the object.

Next, let's remove the connection between the shapes on the second and third cross sections.

Redirect Shape Connections

To disconnect 2D shapes between cross sections:

1. Navigate to the second cross section **(Figure 50)**.

2. From the Sections menu choose Cross Section Options.

3. Click "Disconnect from next Cross Section" in the Cross Section Options dialog box and click OK **(Figure 51)**.

4. Note that the extrusion has been interrupted between the second and third cross sections **(Figure 52)**.

5. Turn off shape numbering by choosing Show Shape Numbers from the Sections menu to uncheck it **(Figure 53)**.

Cross section options

By default, each new cross section that you add to a free form object is "filled in." Thus, you cannot see through the cylinder unless you deselect the "Fill Cross Section" property for each cross section through which the circle shape is extruded.

As noted earlier, the implied ending cross section is not a true cross section, and thus it has no options to set. However, it has the appearance of being filled in. So, in order to be able to see through the cylinder, you must create a new section at the ending (rightmost) point of the sweep path description line and then uncheck its default Fill Cross Section option.

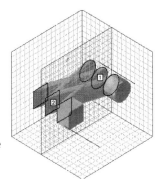

Figure 50. Navigate to the second cross section.

Figure 51. Click "Disconnect from next Cross Section" in the **Cross Section Options** dialog box.

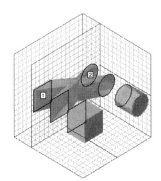

Figure 52. The extrusion has been disconnected between the second and third cross sections.

Figure 53. Choose **Show Shape Numbers** from the **Sections** menu.

Disconnect 2D Shapes Between Sections

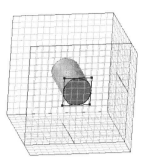

Figure 54. Navigate to the second cross section.

Figure 55. Choose **Cross Section Options** from the Sections menu.

Figure 56. Check or uncheck the Fill Cross Section option in the **Cross Section Options** dialog box.

To set the cross section's fill option:

1. Navigate to the target cross section **(Figure 54)**.

2. Choose Cross Section Options from the Sections menu **(Figure 55)**.

3. Check or uncheck the Fill Cross Section option in the Cross Section Options dialog box and click OK **(Figures 56–57)**.

Another cross section option involves the "skinning" of a free form object. Point-to-point skinning is used to connect shapes on adjacent cross sections that are similar; it connects the vertices of one shape to the corresponding vertices of the other shape.

To set the cross section's skinning option:

1. Navigate to the target cross section.

2. Choose Cross Section Options from the Sections menu.

3. Check "Skin shape-to-shape" or "Skin point-to-point" in the Skinning area of the Cross Section Options dialog box, and click OK.

Cross Section Fill and Skinning Options

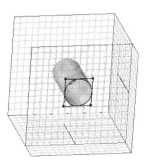

Figure 57. The second cross section has been unfilled.

UNDERSTANDING THE SWEEP PATH AND ITS DESCRIPTION LINES

The overall shape of a free from object is defined in large part by its sweep path (also known as its extrusion path).

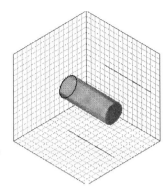

Figure 58. The overall shape of a free form object is largely defined by its sweep path.

The sweep path can be thought of as an imaginary, flexible, thread-like spine that runs through the geometric center of a free form object **(Figure 58)**. While you cannot directly lengthen, twist, or otherwise manipulate this imaginary spine, you can indirectly manipulate it by selecting and editing either or both of the free form object's sweep path description lines. The sweep path description lines can be thought of as the shadows that would be cast by that spine.

Thus, the sweep path description line that is displayed on the bottom (X-Y) plane can be thought of as the shadow that would be cast if a light were placed directly over the spine **(Figure 59)**; and the sweep path description line that is displayed on the right (Y-Z) plane can be thought of as the shadow that would be cast if a light were placed directly to the left of the spine **(Figure 60)**.

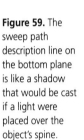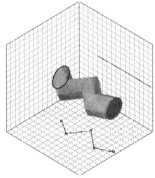

Figure 59. The sweep path description line on the bottom plane is like a shadow that would be cast if a light were placed over the object's spine.

✔ Tip

■ Ray Dream's manual describes these lines as being red. In fact, they are light magenta, which is the graphics designation for light purple.

Like other modeling box features, sweep path description lines are subject to certain rules:

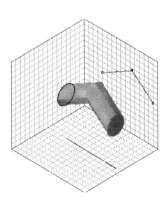

Figure 60. The sweep path description line on the right plane is like a shadow that would be cast if a light were placed to the left of the object's spine.

• A free form object always has two—and only two—sweep path description lines. The "horizontal" sweep path description line is displayed on the lower, or X-Y plane; and the "vertical" sweep path description line is displayed on the right, or Y-Z plane.

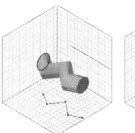 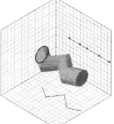

Figures 61–62. The number and position of points on both sweep path description lines are identical.

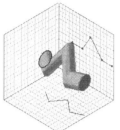

Figure 63. Editing the sweep path description line on the right plane allows you to sculpt the vertical shape of the free form object.

Figure 64. Add three points to either sweep path description line.

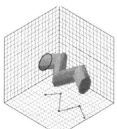
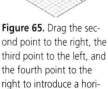

Figure 65. Drag the second point to the right, the third point to the left, and the fourth point to the right to introduce a horizontal zig zag.

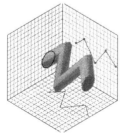

Figure 66. Drag the second point upward, the third point downward, and the fourth point upward to introduce a vertical zig zag.

- Sweep path description lines must always have at least two points: a beginning and an ending. Attempting to delete one of these necessary points will result in a warning indicating that the operation failed.

- The number and position of points on the sweep path's description line displayed lower (X-Y) plane are identical to the number and position of points on the sweep path's description line that is displayed on the right (Y-Z) plane **(Figures 61–62)**.

By selecting and editing the sweep path description line displayed on the bottom plane, you can sculpt the "horizontal" shape of the free form object's sweep path; and by selecting and editing the sweep path description line displayed on the right plane, you can sculpt the "vertical" shape of the free form object's sweep path **(Figure 63)**.

To add a horizontal (or vertical) zig zag to a free form object's sweep path:

1. Using the Add Point tool, add three points to either sweep path description line **(Figure 64)**.

2. Click on the Selection tool.

3. Click on the ground plane to deselect any selected elements.

4. Click on the sweep path description line on the ground plane to display its points.

5. Drag the second point to the right, the third point to the left, and the fourth point to the right to introduce a horizontal zig zag to the sweep path **(Figure 65)**.

6. Click the sweep path description line on the right plane to display its points.

7. Drag the 2nd point upward, the 3rd point downward, and the 4th point upward to introduce a vertical zig zag to the sweep path **(Figure 66)**.

Add a Zig Zag to the Sweep Path

Ray Dream also provides some interesting preset sweep paths that can be applied to a free form object.

To return the sweep path to a straight line:

1. Choose Extrusion Preset from the Geometry menu, and select Straight in the submenu **(Figure 67)**.

Figure 67. Choose **Extrusion Preset** from the **Geometry** menu and select **Straight** from the submenu.

To apply a spiral sweep path to a free form object:

1. Choose Extrusion Preset from the Geometry menu, and select Spiral in the submenu **(Figure 68)**.

2. In the dialog box, configure the spiral's parameters. For example, to create a spiral whose core takes three full turns, whose diameter is reduced by 90% over those three turns, and whose turns are separated by increasingly large spaces, set the "Number of turns" to 3, the Cross Section Scaling to 10%, and the Spiral Scaling to 300% **(Figures 69–70)**.

Figure 68. Choose **Extrusion Preset** from the **Geometry** menu and select **Spiral** from the submenu.

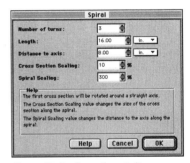

Figure 69. Configure the spiral's parameters in the **Spiral** dialog box.

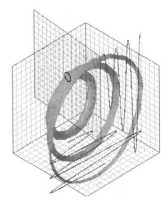

Figure 70. This spiral was created with "Number of turns" set to 3, Cross Section Scaling at 10%, and Spiral Scaling at 300%.

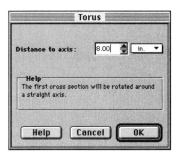

Figure 71. Enter the Distance to axis in the **Torus** dialog box.

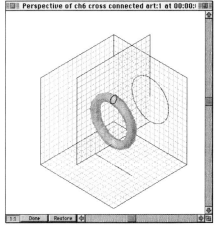

Figure 72. A torus sweep path.

To apply a torus (circular) sweep path to a free form object:

1. Choose Extrusion Preset from the Geometry menu and select Torus in the submenu.

2. Enter the Distance to axis **(Figure 71)**.

3. Click OK to draw the torus sweep path **(Figure 72)**.

✔ Tips

■ Individual settings are not "remembered" by the spiral and torus dialog boxes. Thus, to refine a spiral or torus sweep path extrusion, you must reenter the desired value for each parameter in place of its default setting.

■ Applying a preset sweep path can add many new points to the sweep path. For example, for the spiral settings above, 11 new points were added. But, with the exception noted below, new cross sections are not added at these points.

■ If, however, only a single cross section existed when the sweep path was spiraled, a new cross section would be added at the location of the implied cross section at the rightmost point of the sweep path description lines.

■ You can verify the addition of new points and, if applicable, the substitution of an explicit cross section for the implied cross section by selecting the sweep path to display its new points and by navigating cross sections.

Apply a Torus Sweep Path

POSITIONING CROSS SECTIONS IN RELATION TO THE SWEEP PATH

You can choose one of two methods for positioning cross sections in relation to the sweep path. In the first method, known as the **Translation Extrusion method**, cross sections always remain perpendicular to both the ground plane and the right plane **(Figures 73–74)**. This method is the default, and all of the figures we have shown you so far have this placement. In this view, the cross sections hold one position regardless of whether there are any vertical or horizontal jogs in the sweep path.

But there is another possibility: a second method, known as the **Pipeline Extrusion method**. This placement "frees up" the cross sections and causes them to be rotated so that they are always perpendicular to the sweep path **(Figures 75–76)**. Thus, if a sweep path takes a vertical or horizontal jog, the cross sections that occur along that jog are perpendicular to it. The resulting extrusion frequently looks something like a pipe, which explains how this method got its name.

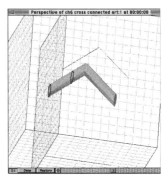
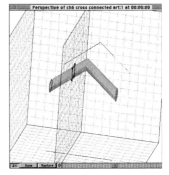

Figures 73–74.
With the Translation Extrusion method (default), cross sections always remain perpendicular to both the ground plane and the right plane.

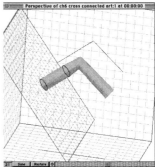
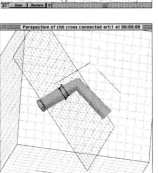

Figures 75–76.
With the Pipeline Extrusion method, cross sections always remain perpendicular to the sweep path.

Translation and Pipeline Extrusion

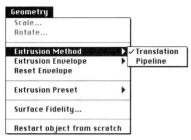

Figure 77. Choose **Extrusion Method** from the **Geometry** menu and select either **Translation** or **Pipeline** from the submenu.

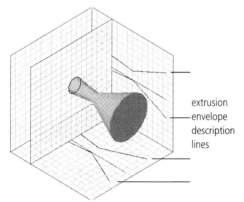

extrusion envelope description lines

Figure 78. Extrusion envelope description lines are used to depict the vertical and horizontal shadows of the free form object itself.

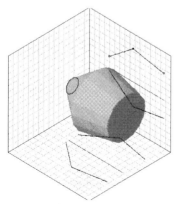

Figure 79. The extrusion envelope is edited by manipulating the extrusion envelope description lines.

To set the extrusion method:

1. Choose Extrusion Method from the Geometry menu, and select Translation or Pipeline to specify the desired method **(Figure 77)**.

PERFORMING SCALING ALONG A SWEEP PATH

The extrusion envelope is a tool that allows you to perform scaling along a free form object's sweep path. The extrusion envelope lets you build complex objects in seconds that would otherwise take hours adding numerous cross sections, and drawing and scaling numerous shapes.

The relationship between a free form object and its extrusion envelope—like the relationship between the free form object and its sweep path—can best be visualized in terms of the shadows they would cast if illuminated from above and from the side.

Just as sweep path description lines are used to depict the vertical and horizontal shadows of the free form object's spine, the modeling box uses extrusion envelope description lines to depict the vertical and horizontal shadows of the free form object itself **(Figure 78)**.

And, just as the free form object's imaginary spine cannot be manipulated directly, but must rather be manipulated indirectly through its "shadows"—i.e., the sweep path description lines—the extrusion envelope cannot be manipulated directly, but must rather be manipulated indirectly through *its* "shadows"—i.e., the extrusion envelope description lines **(Figure 79)**.

To toggle the visibility of the extrusion envelope:

1. Display the cylindrical free form object in the Reference view.

2. Make sure that the circle from which the cylinder was extruded is centered in its drawing plane, by choosing Center from the Sections menu.

3. Select and display a symmetrical extrusion envelope by choosing Extrusion Envelope from the Geometry Menu and Symmetrical from the submenu **(Figure 80)**.

4. Note that the symmetrical extrusion envelope is represented as two pairs of blue lines placed parallel to, and around, the two sweep path description lines **(Figure 81)**.

Rules to remember

Like its modeling box's sweep path description lines, a free form object's extrusion envelope description lines are subject to certain rules:

- Extrusion envelope description lines must always have at least two points: a beginning point and an ending point. Attempting to delete one of these necessary points will result in a warning dialog box indicating that the attempted operation failed.

- The extrusion envelope description line displayed on the bottom (X-Y) plane has the same number and position of points as are displayed on the extrusion envelope description line for the right (Y-Z) plane.

At first glance, it may appear that the two extrusion envelope description lines on the bottom plane (or those on the right plane) do not depict the shadow of a true 3D object, because they do not appear to form a completely enclosed area.

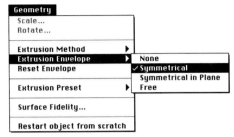

Figure 80. Choose **Extrusion Envelope** from the **Geometry** menu and select **Symmetrical** from the submenu.

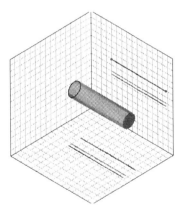

Figure 81. The extrusion envelope is represented as two pairs of blue lines placed parallel to, and around, the two sweep path description lines.

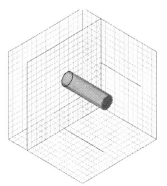

Figure 82. Create a new cylindrical free form object.

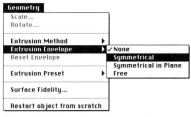

Figure 83. Choose **Extrusion Envelope** from the **Geometry** menu, and select **Symmetrical** from the submenu.

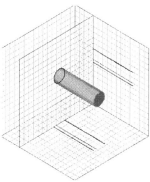

Figure 84. Two blue lines appear on either side of each sweep path description lines.

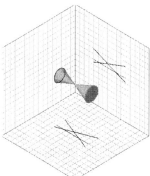

Figure 85. Drag the endpoint down and to the left, so that the extrusion envelope description lines cross each other like swords.

This is because the modeling box uses a slightly stylized representation of these shadows. In effect, the modeling box depicts a segment of the area that is covered by each shadow, by omitting the following details from its representation:

- The two segments of the boundary line that run parallel to any edge of the first (leftmost) and last (rightmost) cross sections.

- The shading that is traditionally used to denote an area of shadow.

Sculpting a free form object with the extrusion envelope description lines

By placing and manipulating points on the extrusion envelope description lines, you can instantly generate complex and creative free form objects.

To sculpt an hour glass using the extrusion envelope:

1. Create a new free form object, and draw and center a circle on the default cross section **(Figure 82)**.

2. Choose Extrusion Envelope from the Geometry menu, and select Symmetrical from the submenu **(Figure 83)**.

3. Note that two blue lines appear on either side of each of the sweep path description lines **(Figure 84)**.

4. Click on the bottom plane to deselect any selected items.

5. Click on the upper extrusion envelope description line on the bottom plane to display its points.

6. Click on the endpoint of that line, and drag that point down and to the left, so that it crosses over the sweep path description line and so that the extrusion envelope description lines cross each other like swords **(Figure 85)**.

To create a vase:

1. Repeat steps 1–4 in the hour glass example.

2. Add two points to the lower extrusion envelope description line on the bottom plane **(Figure 86)**.

3. Convert the leftmost of the two newly added points to a Bezier curve point with the Convert Point tool by dragging it briefly.

4. Drag the converted point to the left (i.e., parallel to the X axis) for a few grid lines and then down toward the bottom of the screen **(Figure 87)**.

5. Click on the Selection tool, click on the bottom plane, and click on the lower extrusion envelope description line on the bottom plane to display its points.

6. Click on the second point you added (which is still a Corner point) and drag it to the right, toward the purple sweep path description line **(Figure 88)**.

7. Use the Virtual Trackball tool to rotate the vase and inspect its shape **(Figure 89)**.

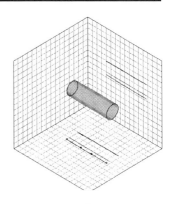

Figure 86. Add two points to the lower extrusion envelope description line on the bottom plane.

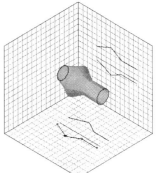

Figure 87. Drag the point to the left and down toward the bottom of the screen.

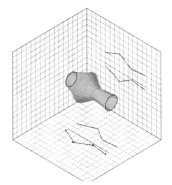

Figure 88. Drag the second point to the right, toward the sweep path description line.

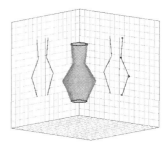

Figure 89. Use the Virtual Trackball tool to rotate the vase and inspect its shape.

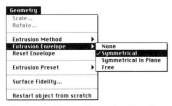

Figure 90. Choose **Extrusion Envelope** from the **Geometry** menu, and select **Symmetrical** from the submenu.

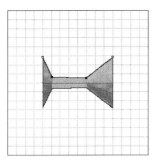

Figure 91. Add two new points to the extrusion envelope description line, and reposition them as shown.

Figure 92. Choose **Preview (Fast)** from the **View** menu.

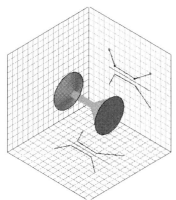

Figure 93. A martini glass.

LATHING

The last sculpting technique to use the extrusion envelope and the extrusion envelope description lines is called **lathing**.

Lathing is the rotation of a 2D shape around a central axis. The 2D shape can be thought of as the profile of the object being sculpted.

To lathe a martini glass:

1. Create a new free form object.

2. Draw and center a circle on the default cross section.

3. Choose No Preview from the View menu.

4. Click on the Selection tool.

5. Click on an empty space on the right plane.

6. Choose Extrusion Envelope from the Geometry menu and click on Symmetrical in the submenu **(Figure 90)**.

7. Isolate the drawing plane by pressing Ctrl/Command+5.

8. Click on the Pen tool.

9. Add two new points to the extrusion envelope description line, and reposition them as shown to describe the shape of the martini glass's profile, being careful not to draw below the sweep path description line **(Figure 91)**.

10. Return to the Reference view by pressing Ctrl/Command+0.

11. Restore the preview by choosing Preview (Fast) from the View menu **(Figure 92)** to see the martini glass **(Figure 93)**.

12. Select the rightmost point on either sweep path description line.

13. Choose Create from the Sections menu.

Lathe a Martini Glass

14. Navigate to the new cross section at the rightmost point.

15. Choose Cross Section Options from the Sections menu.

16. Uncheck the Fill Cross Section check box in the Cross Section Options dialog box **(Figure 94)** to open the top end of the glass **(Figure 95)**.

Figure 94. Uncheck the Fill Cross Section option in the **Cross Section Options** dialog box.

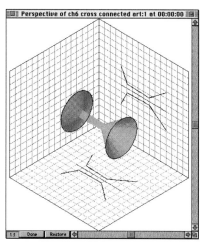

Figure 95. The cross section at the right end of the glass has been unfilled so that the martini glass appears open.

Lathe a Martini Glass

INTRODUCING THE MESH FORM MODELER

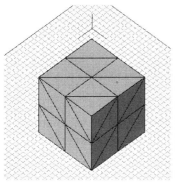

Figure 1. Working with objects in the Mesh Form Modeler can be compared to sculpting with clay.

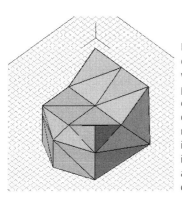

Figure 2. By directly moving vertices and polygons, you can stretch, deform, and reshape existing structures into just about any shape you can imagine.

The Mesh Form Modeler is new to version 5 of Ray Dream Studio. If you are like us, you will probably spend more time working with the Mesh Form Modeler than with any other tool in the suite.

Why? Because the **Mesh Form Modeler** enables you to model complex 3D objects by sculpting chunks of what might be called "cyber-material." In fact, using the Mesh Form Modeler is very similar to working with modeling clay—it is a direct, intuitive, and hands-on experience that provides instant feedback **(Figures 1–2)**.

And, there is more good news. You will be happy to discover that many of the concepts and techniques that you have already mastered in the Free Form Modeler—such as the creation and manipulation of points, shapes, cross sections, and extrusions—are also used in the Mesh Form Modeler. Indeed, as you will learn in a moment, you can even open objects created with the Free Form Modeler in the Mesh Form Modeler for further customization **(Figures 3–4)**.

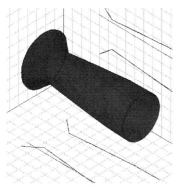

Figure 3. An object created in the Free Form Modeler (body of a glass).

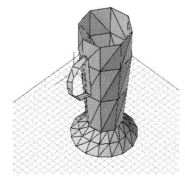

Figure 4. The object has been opened in the Mesh Form Modeler, and a handle has been added to complete the glass.

GETTING STARTED WITH THE MESH FORM MODELER

Before working with the Mesh Form Modeler, it is helpful to define a few terms and to illustrate them with a few examples.

Key concepts and definitions

In the Mesh Form Modeler:

- A **vertex** is a point in 3D space **(Figure 5)**.

- An **edge** is a line that connects two vertices.

- An **open polyline** is a set of two or more connected edges that do not form a loop.

- A **polygon** is a closed and filled polyline that doesn't encompass other edges or vertices.

- A **closed polyline** is a polyline that is closed and forms a loop. A closed polyline can be filled or empty, and can include other vertices, edges, or polygons.

- A **polymesh** is a set of connected polylines that form an enclosed volume **(Figure 6)**, an unenclosed 3D form, or both.

A mesh form object can contain any combination of vertices, edges, polygons, open or closed polylines, and polymeshes **(Figure 7)**.

Creating and editing mesh form objects

Mesh form objects are created and opened for editing much the same as free form objects: by dragging the Mesh Form Modeling tool directly into either the Perspective window or into the Time Line window.

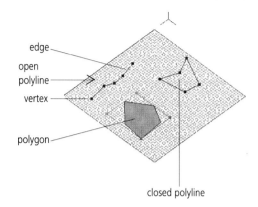

Figure 5. Key concepts and definitions

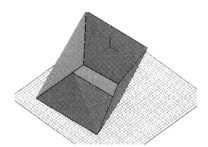

Figure 6. A polymesh is a set of connected polylines that form an enclosed volume, an unenclosed 3D form, or both.

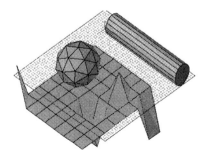

Figure 7. A mesh form object can contain any combination of vertices, edges, polygons, open or closed polylines, and polymeshes.

Figure 8. Mesh Form Modeling tool.

Figure 9. Enter a name for the mesh form object.

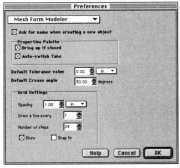

Figure 10. Enter the desired values in the **Mesh Form Modeler Preferences** dialog box.

Figure 11. "Draw a line every" controls the number of drawn lines. It is set to 1 here.

Figure 12. "Draw a line every" controls the number of drawn lines. It is set to 2 here.

To create a new mesh form object:

1. Create a new scene, or open an existing one.

2. Display and select the Perspective window (or the Time Line window).

3. Click on the Mesh Form Modeling tool **(Figure 8)**, and drag it into the Perspective window (or the Time Line window).

or

Choose Jump In from the Edit menu.

4. Give the mesh form object a name (or accept the proposed default name) and click OK **(Figure 9)**.

✔ Tips

■ The Perspective window zooms in exclusively on the mesh form object you are about to create. Note also that a new toolbar and menu items become available.

■ Various attributes of the Mesh Form Modeler—such as those affecting the appearance and behavior of the grid—can be set in the Mesh Form Modeler Preferences dialog box.

To adjust the Mesh Form Modeler preferences:

1. Choose Preferences from the File menu.

2. Choose Mesh Form Modeler from the dropdown list in the dialog box.

3. Enter the desired values for the following fields **(Figure 10)**:

• Spacing controls the distance between actual grid lines.

• "Draw a line every" controls the number of drawn lines—i.e., the visible lines that are displayed for every actual grid line. For example, entering a value of 1 will cause one drawn line to be displayed for every actual grid line **(Figure 11)**; and entering a value of 2 will cause one drawn line to be displayed for every two grid lines **(Figure 12)**.

- "Number of steps" controls the number of grid lines that are displayed on either side of the center of each of the Mesh Form modeling box's displayed planes. For example, a value of 6 will size each plane to 12 actual grid lines by 12 actual grid lines **(Figure 13)**.

- "Show" displays the drawn lines if it is checked, or hides them if it is unchecked.

- "Snap to" causes dragging actions to jump to the nearest grid line or intersection of grid lines if it is checked, or permits "free" dragging if it is unchecked.

- Click OK to apply the settings and to close the dialog box.

To illustrate the tools and concepts that are unique to the Mesh Form Modeler, let's create and explore a simple primitive mesh form object—a cube.

To create a Cube primitive with the Mesh Form Modeler:

1. Click repeatedly on the Primitives tool until the Create Cube tool appears, and then release the mouse.

or

Click and hold the mouse in the currently displayed Primitives tool until all of the Primitives tools are displayed, drag the mouse to the Create Cube tool, and then release the mouse **(Figure 14)**.

2. Click and drag the mouse on the drawing plane, and drag toward the bottom and right of the screen.

3. Release the mouse, and observe the resulting cube **(Figure 15)**.

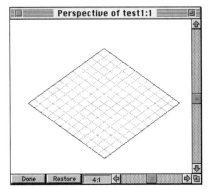

Figure 13. Number of steps controls the number of grid lines that are displayed on either side of the center of each of the modeling box's displayed planes. The value is set to 6 here which produces 12 grid lines by 12 grid lines.

Figure 14. Drag the mouse to the Create Cube tool.

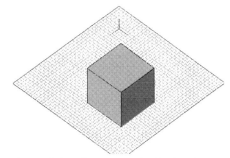

Figure 15. Drag the mouse on the drawing plane toward the bottom and right of the screen to draw the cube.

Create a Cube Primitive

Figure 16. Click on the object's name in the Objects Tab of the Time Line window.

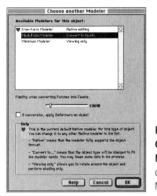

Figure 17. In the **Choose another Modeler** dialog box, click Mesh Form Modeler.

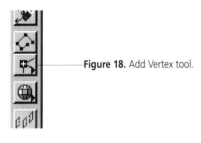

Figure 18. Add Vertex tool.

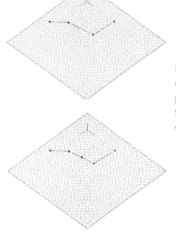

Figures 19–20. Click the desired position on the segment to add a vertex.

To save a mesh form object:

1. Click Done on the Mesh Form modeling window.

or

Choose Jump Out from the File menu.

To open an existing mesh form object for editing:

1. Double-click on the mesh form object's name in the Time Line window.

or

1. Click on the mesh form object's name in the Objects Tab of the Time Line window (in this case, click on the mesh form object you just created) **(Figure 16)**.

2. Choose Jump In or Jump In New Window from the Edit menu.

To open an existing free form object in the Mesh Form Modeler for editing:

1. Click on the free form object's name in the Objects Tab of the Time Line window.

2. Choose Jump In Another Modeler from the Edit menu.

3. In the Choose another Modeler dialog box, click Mesh Form Modeler **(Figure 17)**.

4. Adjust the Fidelity slider.

5. Click OK to perform the conversion and close the dialog box.

To add a vertex to an edge:

1. Click the Selection tool.

2. Click any empty area of the grid to deselect any selected items.

3. Click repeatedly on the Vertex tool until the Add Vertex On Edge tool appears **(Figure 18)**.

4. Click the desired position on the target edge **(Figures 19–20)**.

To select and move a vertex:

1. Click the Selection tool.

2. Click any empty area of the grid to deselect any selected items.

3. Click any empty portion of the host edge that does not contain a vertex to display and select the entire edge and all of its vertices **(Figure 21)**.

4. Make a mental note of the location of the target vertex.

5. Repeat Step 2 to deselect the edge.

6. Click the location of the target vertex to select it **(Figure 22)**.

7. To move the vertex along the current drawing plane (e.g., the bottom, or X-Y plane), click and drag the vertex to the desired location, and then release the mouse **(Figure 23)**.

8. To move the vertex perpendicular to the current drawing plane (e.g., "up" or "down" along the Z axis), press the Alt/Option key before clicking and dragging the vertex **(Figure 24)**.

and

Use the horizontal guidelines that are displayed to measure the movement along the perpendicular axis, and then release the mouse.

To select and move an edge:

1. Click the Selection tool.

2. Click any empty area of the grid to deselect any selected items.

3. Click any empty portion of the edge that does not contain a vertex to select the entire edge.

4. To move the edge along the current drawing plane, or perpendicular to it, follow Steps 7 and 8 in the last section on selecting and moving a vertex.

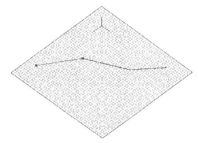

Figure 21. Click an empty part of the host edge to display all of its vertices.

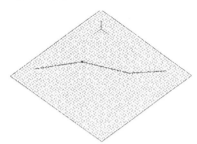

Figure 22. Click the location of the target vertex to select it.

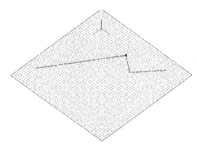

Figure 23. Drag the vertex to the desired new location and release the mouse.

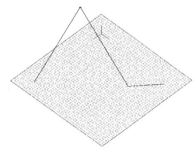

Figure 24. Hold the Alt/Option key to move the vertex perpendicularly to the drawing plane.

Select and Move a Vertex, Edge

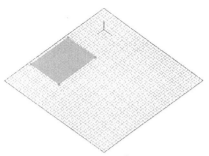

Figure 25. Click the interior of the polygon.

Figure 26. Drag the polygon to the new location.

Figure 27. Choose **Cut** from the **Edit** menu.

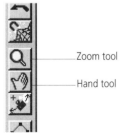

Zoom tool

Hand tool

Figure 28.

To select and move a polygon:

1. Click the Selection tool.

2. Click any empty area of the grid to deselect any selected items.

3. Click the interior of the polygon **(Figure 25)**.

4. To move the polygon along the current drawing plane, or perpendicular to it, follow Steps 7 and 8 in the section on selecting and moving a vertex **(Figure 26)**.

To delete a selected vertex, edge, or polygon:

1. Select the target object.

2. Press the Delete key.

or

Choose Cut from the Edit menu **(Figure 27)**.

✔ Tip

■ To select multiple objects for simultaneous movement or deletion, simply hold the Shift key while making each selection.

VISUALIZING OBJECTS WITH THE MESH FORM MODELER

The Mesh Form Modeler's tools for visualizing objects under construction are similar, though not necessarily identical, to those in the Free Form Modeler.

The following tools and menu options, which were described in the chapters dealing with the Free Form Modeler, are available in the Mesh Form Modeler and work in the same manner as in the Free Form Modeler:

- The Hand tool lets you perform simultaneous horizontal and vertical scrolling of the contents of the Mesh Form Modeling window **(Figure 28)**.

Move a Polygon

- The Zoom tools let you zoom in on a specific area of the Mesh Form modeling window.

- The Preset View menu options let you view the mesh form object from the Reference view, from the Top, Bottom, Left, Right, Front, Back, or from the current drawing plane **(Figure 29)**.

- The Display Planes tool lets you display or hide the left, right, or bottom plane or the mesh form object itself **(Figure 30)**.

- The Preview quality menu options let you display the mesh form object with a wireframe, or a Fast Preview quality **(Figure 31)**.

By default, the Mesh Form Modeler displays the mesh form object as a wireframe. Also by default, the Mesh Form Modeler displays only the bottom, or X-Y plane, of the Mesh Form modeling box.

✔ Tip

■ In the Mesh Form modeling box, you cannot select a plane to make it the current drawing plane by clicking on it, as you can with the Free Form Modeler. Instead you must choose Send Drawing Plane from the View menu and then choose a location (Selection, Screen, Position, Top, Bottom, Left, Right, Front, or Back) from the submenu.

The Mesh Form Modeler also features a Virtual Trackball tool, but it performs a different function from that of the Free Form Modeler's trackball. The Free Form Modeler Virtual Trackball tool lets you rotate your view of the free form object, whereas the Mesh Form Modeler's trackball lets you actually rotate the mesh form object itself. **(Figures 32–33)**. In other words, the Free Form Modeler's trackball is a visualization tool, while the Mesh Form Modeler's trackball is a positioning tool.

Figure 29. The **View** menu options let you view your mesh form object from many different viewpoints.

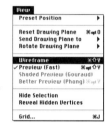

Figure30. Display Planes tool.

Figure 31. The Preview quality menu options let you display your mesh form object with a **Wireframe**, or a **Fast Preview** quality.

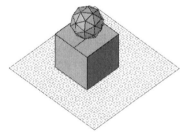

Figure 32. A mesh form object before rotation with the Virtual Trackball tool.

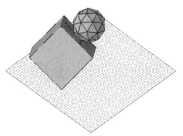

Figure 33. A mesh form object after rotation with the Virtual Trackball tool.

Figure 34. Camera Dolly tool.

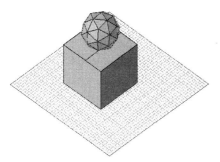

Figure 35. The Mesh Form Modeling window before using the Camera Dolly tool.

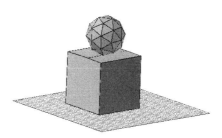

Figure 36. The Mesh form modeling window after using the Camera Dolly tool.

Figure 37. Polyline Drawing tool.

To make up for this specialized use of the Virtual Trackball tool, the Mesh Form Modeler provides a Camera Dolly tool. This tool lets you change your frame of reference with respect to the entire mesh form object.

To use the Camera Dolly tool:

1. Click the Camera Dolly **(Figure 34)**.

2. Click in a location in the Mesh Form Modeling window, and drag the mouse to alter the frame of reference **(Figures 35–36)**.

or

1. Press the numeric keypad key that corresponds to the desired dolly movement:

- 8 to dolly up.
- 2 to dolly down.
- 4 to dolly left.
- 6 to dolly right.
- 1 to dolly downward along the drawing plane's axis.
- 3 to dolly upward along the drawing plane's axis.

TOOLS AND TECHNIQUES: A FUNCTIONAL OVERVIEW

The Mesh Form Modeler offers many drawing, sculpting, positioning techniques that can be used either to customize primitives or to construct custom objects from scratch. What follows is a functional classification of the Mesh Form Modeling tools and techniques that are covered in the next chapter:

Basic sculpting tools and techniques

- Polyline Drawing tool—for creating 1D, 2D, and 3D open and closed polylines **(Figure 37)**.

- Rectangle and Oval—for creating 2D shapes **(Figure 38)**.
- Sphere, Cylinder, and Cube Primitive tools—for creating 3D volumes.
- Mesh Primitive tool—for automatically creating a sparsely or richly populated "fabric" of vertices that can be sculpted as desired.

Selection and drawing plane tools and techniques

- Basic selection techniques—for selecting single and multiple vertices, edges, polygons, polylines, adjacent polyline segments, and polymeshes.
- Marquee tool—for selecting multiple embedded structures.
- Select All command—for selecting all structures in the Mesh Form Modeler.
- Hide Selection and Reveal Hidden Vertices commands—for improving access to hard-to-reach portions of an object's surface **(Figure 39)**.
- Save/Restore commands and features—for the manual and automatic saving and recalling of complex selections **(Figure 40)**.
- Invert command—for deselecting the current selection, and selecting all other vertices and edges that were not included in that selection.
- Drawing Plane commands—to send the current drawing plane to the plane of an edge, polyline segment, or polygon, or to some other preset or arbitrary position **(Figure 41)**.

Sizing and positioning tools and techniques

- Numerical Properties tab—for directly sizing, scaling, and positioning a selection in 3D space **(Figure 42)**.
- Manual sizing and positioning techniques—for directly scaling a selection in a symmetrical or asymmetrical way.

Selection & Drawing Plane Tools

Figure 38. The Sphere, Cube, Cylinder, Mesh, Rectangle, and Oval Primitive tools can be used to create basic shapes that you can quickly customize into more complex 3D forms.

Figure 39. Use the **Hide Selection** command under the **View** menu to hide vertices and edges.

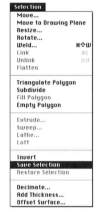

Figure 40. Use **Save Selection** to save the current pattern of selected objects.

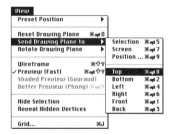

Figure 41. Use the **Drawing Plane** commands under the **View** menu to reposition the current plane.

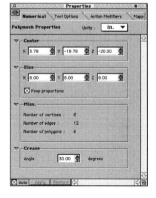

Figure 42. Use the Numerical Properties tab to size, scale, and position a selection directly.

Figure 43. Use the **Resize** command under the **Selection** menu to increase or decrease the size of a selection.

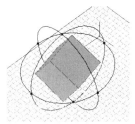

Figure 44. Virtual Trackball tool.

Figure 45. Sphere of Attraction tool.

Figure 46. Use the Virtual Trackball tool to freely rotate a 3D selection.

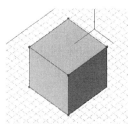

Figure 47. Use the **Empty Polygon** command under the **Selection** menu to make selected polygons transparent.

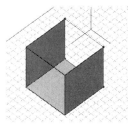

Figure 48. The front, top, and back polygons of this cube have been emptied.

- Resize command—for increasing or decreasing the size of a selection **(Figure 43)**.

- Adjust (Align) command—for arranging two selections.

- Rotate command—for rotating a selection in a specific direction around a specific axis by a specific number of degrees.

- Move command—for precisely moving a selection by specific amounts in specific directions along one or more axes.

- The Nudge technique—for moving a selection to a desired position with the arrow keys, in increments of one actual grid line per keystroke.

- Virtual Trackball tool—for rotating a selection in 3D space **(Figures 44 and 46)**.

- 2D Rotation tool—for rotating a selection in 2D space around the axis that is perpendicular to the current drawing plane.

- Sphere of Attraction tool—for stretching a selection toward a spherical source of attraction **(Figure 45)**.

Surface manipulation commands

- Fill/Empty Polygon commands—for toggling the transparency of a selection of polygons **(Figures 47–48)**.

- Triangulation command—for replacing irregular polygons in a selection with regular polygons, for improved rendering.

- Subdivision/Decimation commands—for adding or removing polygons to a selection in order to increase or decrease its "granularity."

Surface Manipulation Commands

- Smooth/Sharpen Edges commands—for decreasing or increasing the angles of intersection between a selection of edges in order to smoothen or sharpen its surfaces.
- Offset Surface command—for moving selected polygons in the direction of the surface normal.

Object linking and fusing tools and techniques

- Link/Unlink commands—for creating or destroying an edge between two selected vertices.
- Weld command—for fusing a selection of two or more vertices into a single vertex.

Volumetric tools and techniques

- Loft command—for stretching a "skin" between two selected polylines that are both open or closed and are located on different planes.
- Add Thickness command—for extruding a selection along a straight path.
- Send to Drawing Plane command and Flatten command—for "flattening" a 3D selection into a 2D shape on the current drawing plane or to some other arbitrary plane.
- Boolean Operation command—for performing union, subtraction, and intersection operations on a selection of two objects to form a single resultant object **(Figures 49–51)**.
- Extrude command—for extruding a selected "cross section," such as a polygon or polyline, along either a default extrusion path, or along a custom extrusion path that consists of another selected polygon or polyline **(Figures 52–53)**.

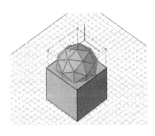

Figure 49. Use the **Boolean Operation** command under the **Polymesh** menu to perform union, subtraction, and intersection operations on two selected objects to form one object.

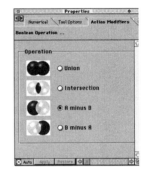

Figure 50. The Action Modifiers tab of the **Properties** dialog box lists the different Boolean operations you can perform.

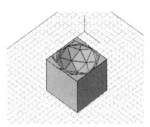

Figure 51. The sphere has been subtracted from the cube, forming a crater at the top.

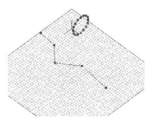

Figure 52. Use the **Extrude** command under the **Selection** menu to extrude a cross section along an extrusion path.

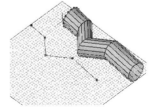

Figure 53. The circle cross section has been extruded along the polyline extrusion path.

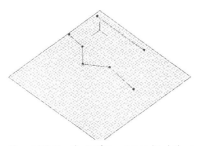

Figure 54. Use the **Lathe** command to lathe a selected cross section around a default or custom axis.

Figure 55. The **Lathe** command is found under the **Selection** menu.

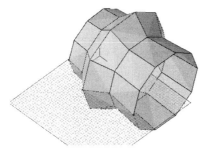

Figure 56. The bent polyline in the figure above has been lathed around the straight polyline.

Figure 57. Action Modifier tools.

- Sweep command—for sweeping a selected "cross section," such as a polygon or polyline, along a custom sweep path that consists of another selected polygon or polyline.

- Lathe command—for lathing a selected "cross section," such as a polygon or polyline, along either a default lathing axis or along a custom lathing axis that consists of another selected polygon or polyline **(Figures 54–56)**.

- Action Modifier Tools—for increasing or decreasing some aspect of the last-performed action, such as increasing or decreasing the number of polygons used to make up a sphere primitive **(Figure 57)**.

Some of these tools and techniques have counterparts in the Free Form Modeler, but most do not. Throughout the next chapter, the similarities and differences between the tools in these modelers will be analyzed, so that you can start and end with the right tools and techniques for your particular modeling needs.

Volumetric Tools and Techniques

MASTERING THE MESH FORM MODELER

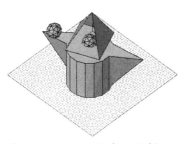

Figure 1. You can manipulate 3D objects directly within the Mesh Form Modeler without having to create cross sections as in the Free Form Modeler.

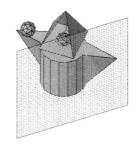

Figure 2. You can send the current drawing plane to any edge, polygon, or polyline.

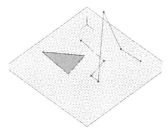

Figure 3. The Polyline tool can draw both on and perpendicularly to the current drawing plane.

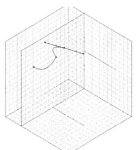

Figure 4. The Mesh Form Modeler does not use Bezier curve points as shown here in the Free Form Modeler.

Mastery of the Mesh Form Modeler begins with a clear understanding of the five key differences between it and the Free Form Modeler, and of the central role that vertices play in every mesh form object.

Comparing the Mesh Form and Free Form Modelers

- Both modelers support extrusions and sweeps of 2D shapes drawn on a cross section; but only the Mesh Form Modeler permits you to add and manipulate vertices, polygons, 2D and 3D polylines and polymeshes anywhere in the 3D space of an object, all without first having to create an explicit cross section **(Figure 1)**.

- The Mesh Form Modeler also lets you "send" the current drawing plane to any edge, polygon, or polyline **(Figure 2)**—and not just to a handful of preset positions that are parallel to the four sides of the modeling box, as does the Free Form Modeler.

- The Mesh Form Modeler's Polyline tool can draw both on and perpendicular to the current drawing plane **(Figure 3)**—i.e., in 3D—while the Free Form Modeler's Pen tool can draw only 2D shapes on the current cross section.

- The Mesh Form Modeler does not use Bezier curve points **(Figure 4)** and therefore has no equivalent to the Free Form Modeler's Convert Point tool.

The ubiquitous vertex

Vertices can be thought of as the very atoms that comprise a polymesh built in the Mesh Form Modeler. Every edge, surface, polyline, and polymesh is either:

- A relationship between two or more vertices **(Figure 5)**.

  or

- A relationship between two or more such relationships between vertices **(Figure 6)**.

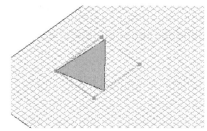

Figure 5. Every edge, surface, polyline, and polymesh is either a relationship between two or more vertices as shown, or...

The Mesh Form Modeler is a flexible and efficient tool that lets you move between working with vertices and their relationships, both at the "macro" level with tools like the Primitives tools, and at the "micro" level with the Polyline tool.

BASIC SCULPTING TOOLS

In this section you will learn some basic Mesh Form Modeler drawing techniques using the Polyline tool, the Primitives tools, and the Action Modifier tools.

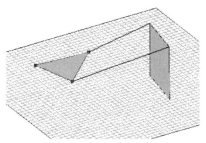

Figure 6. A relationship between two or more such relationships between vertices.

To create a polyline with the Polyline tool:

1. Create or open a mesh form object using one of the commands you learned in the previous chapter.

2. Click the Vertex tool repeatedly until the Add Vertex tool is displayed **(Figure 7)**.

3. Click the bottom plane to create a vertex.

4. Click again to create additional vertices as shown **(Figure 8)**.

Figure 7. Click the Add Vertex tool.

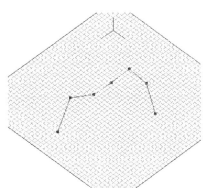

Figure 8. Click repeatedly on the bottom plane to create additional vertices.

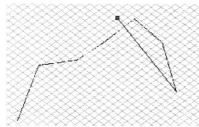

Figure 9. Drag the mouse up or down to the desired position on the axis that is perpendicular to the current drawing plane.

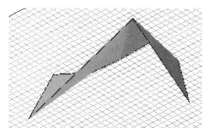

Figure 10. Close the polyline by clicking on the first vertex.

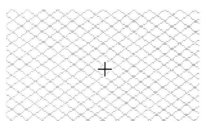

Figure 11. Before creating the first vertex, the cursor is a single crosshair.

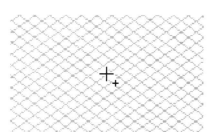

Figure 12. After creating the first vertex, the cursor is a double crosshair.

5. To add a vertex that is above or below the bottom plane, click on the current drawing plane (e.g., the bottom plane) to designate the vertex's position (e.g., its X-Y coordinates) on that plane.

and

Without releasing the mouse, press and hold the Alt/Option key.

and

Drag the mouse up or down to the desired position on the axis that is perpendicular to the current drawing plane (e.g., up or down the Z axis, which is perpendicular to the bottom plane) and release the mouse **(Figure 9)**.

6. Close the polyline by clicking on the first vertex you created **(Figure 10)**.

or

End the polyline without closing it by clicking the last vertex you created.

or

Click on any other tool, e.g., the Selection tool.

✔ Tips

■ Note the subtle change in the cursor before creating the first vertex (it is a single crosshair) **(Figure 11)**, after creating the first vertex (it becomes and remains a double crosshair) **(Figure 12)**, and after ending or closing the polyline (it reverts to a single crosshair).

■ Remember that a double crosshair cursor means that the next vertex to be added will be connected by an edge to the last vertex that was added.

The Primitives tools

In the previous chapter, you learned about creating, cutting, copying, and pasting Mesh Form Modeler primitives.

The Mesh Form Modeler's Primitives toolset differs from the Free Form Modeler's toolset in two important respects:

- It lets you specify and manipulate the number of polygonal surfaces that are used to define a 3D primitive.

- It lets you add vertices to resulting 2D or 3D shapes.

✔ Tip

■ Changes to the Primitive tools' properties affect only those objects that are created after the changes are made. Thus, it is useful to inspect and, if desired, edit the properties of a tool before using it.

To set the tool options for the Mesh Form Modeler's Sphere, Cylinder, Mesh, or Oval primitive tool:

1. Click repeatedly on the tool to display and select the desired primitive tool.

2. Choose Properties from the Windows menu **(Figure 13)**.

3. Click the Tool Options tab.

4. For the Sphere tool, enter the number of polygons that will be drawn to create a sphere **(Figure 14)**.

or

For the Cylinder tool enter the number of edges that will be drawn to create the sides of a cylinder **(Figure 15)**.

or

For the Mesh tool, enter the number of

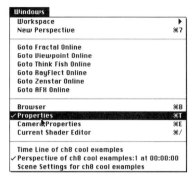

Figure 13. Choose **Properties** from the **Windows** menu.

Figure 14. Enter the number of polygons that will be drawn to create a sphere.

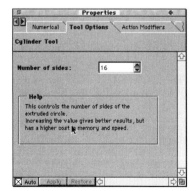

Figure 15. Enter the number of edges to be drawn to create the sides of a cylinder.

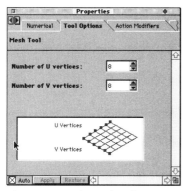

Figure 16. Enter the number of "U" vertices and "V" vertices for the Mesh tool.

Figure 17. Select the desired primitive from the pop-up toolbar.

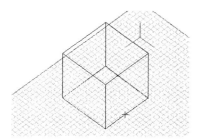

Figure 18. Drag to size the given primitive.

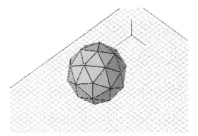

Figure 19. Release the mouse to create the given primitive.

"U" vertices (i.e., vertices that run along the X axis) and the number of "V" vertices (i.e., vertices that run along the Y axis) **(Figure 16)**.

or

For the Ellipse tool, enter the number of edges that will be drawn to create the sides of an ellipse.

To use the Mesh Form Modeler Primitives tool:

1. Click and hold the Primitive tool and select the desired primitive from the pop-up toolbar (Sphere, Cube, Cylinder, Mesh, Rectangle, or Oval) **(Figure 17)**.

2. Move the selected tool directly to the desired position in the Mesh Form Modeler Box, and then drag to size and create the given primitive **(Figures 18–19)**.

You can, of course, select, cut, copy, paste, and move the vertices, edges, polygons, and polylines that are contained in any primitive, as well as the entire primitive itself. Detailed steps for these processes are provided below.

Mesh Form Modeler Primitives

SELECTION AND DRAWING PLANE TOOLS

In the Mesh Form Modeler, the great majority of modeling and sculpting actions—from scaling to sweeping—begin with the creation of a selection of one or more target structures.

In the previous chapter, you learned how to select single and multiple vertices, polygons, and edges.

In the next few pages, you'll learn how to make single and multiple, and partial and complete selections of adjacent and non-adjacent polylines, primitives, and poly-meshes, in any combination you may need.

Basic selection techniques

Before making a new selection, it is often necessary to deselect any currently-selected items.

To deselect all currently selected items:

1. Click the Selection tool.

2. Click on any empty portion of the current drawing plane.

✔ Tip

■ The deselection process should be performed immediately before you perform most of the procedures and techniques described throughout the rest of this chapter.

The Angle of Selection Propagation

In the last chapter you learned to select a single edge and its vertices by clicking on a portion of it that does not contain a vertex **(Figure 20)**. You also learned to select multiple edges by holding the Shift key while clicking on each edge **(Figure 21)**.

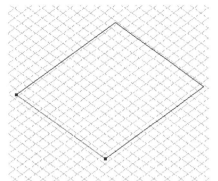

Figure 20. Select an edge by clicking on a portion of it that does not contain a vertex.

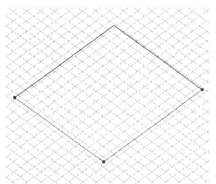

Figure 21. Select multiple edges by holding the Shift key while clicking on each edge.

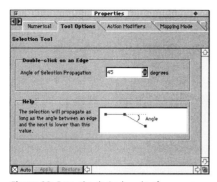

Figure 22. Enter the desired angle of propagation in the Tool Options tab of the **Properties** dialog box.

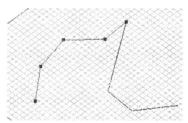

Figure 23. Double-click any portion of the edge that does not contain a vertex to select all adjacent edges that form angles less than or equal to the Angle of Selection Propagation, which is set to 90 here.

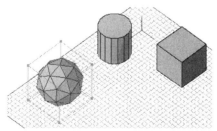

Figure 24. Triple-click anywhere within the sphere to select it.

You can also select all adjacent edges that are joined with angles that are less than or equal to the Angle of Selection Propagation. The default angle value is 45 degrees, but you can set the value to anywhere from 0 to 360 degrees in the Tool Options tab of the Properties palette for the Selection tool.

To set the Angle of Selection Propagation value:

1. Click the Selection tool.

2. If it is not already displayed, display the Selection tool's Properties palette by choosing Properties from the Windows menu.

3. Click the Tool Options tab.

4. Enter the desired Angle of Propagation and click OK **(Figure 22)**.

To select adjacent edges of a polyline or polymesh that form angles less than or equal to the Angle of Selection Propagation:

1. Click the Selection tool.

2. Double-click any portion of the edge that does not contain a vertex and that does fall within the desired selection area **(Figure 23)**.

3. To add additional edges, repeat Step 2 while holding down the Shift key.

To select an entire polyline, primitive, or polymesh:

• For rectangle and oval primitives, click once anywhere within the bounds of the primitive.

• For sphere, cylinder, cube, and mesh primitives, and for any polymesh, triple-click anywhere within the target object **(Figure 24)**.

- For any type of primitive or poly-mesh, click and drag the Selection tool to create a selection box around the entire primitive until its bounding box is displayed.

Figure 25. Marquee tool.

✔ Tip

■ Certain objects display a bounding box when they are completely selected. For more about bounding boxes, see the discussion on scaling and sizing selections later in this chapter.

The Marquee tool

The Selection tool can be used to draw a marquee around an entire structure in a mesh form object, such as an entire primitive. But, if you have ever tried to select a subset of structures within a larger structure—such as a group of polygons within a polymesh—with the Selection tool, you may have noticed that it doesn't work very well. This is because the Selection tool makes and completes a selection as soon as you click it on a selectable object. Thus, instead of dragging a marquee around the subset, you end up dragging the first polygon, edge, or vertex you clicked on.

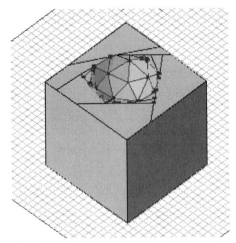

Figure 26. Click and drag to draw a marquee around the target to select its vertices.

Fortunately the Mesh Form Modeler features a Marquee tool which solves this problem.

To make a selection with the Marquee tool:

1. Click the Marquee tool (**Figure 25**).

2. Click and drag the mouse to draw a marquee around the target selection (**Figure 26**).

3. Release the mouse.

4. To add additional items to the current selection, repeat Steps 2 and 3 while holding down the Shift key (**Figure 27**).

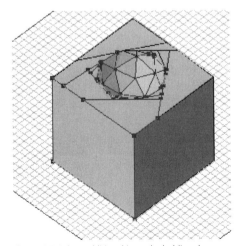

Figure 27. Select additional items by holding down the Shift key while dragging the marquee around additional items.

Marquee Tool

Figure 28. Choose **Select All** from the **Edit** menu.

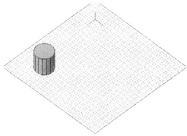

Figure 29. Initial position of an object shown.

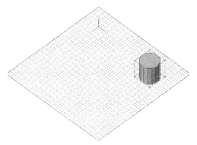

Figure 30. Drag to the desired location and release the mouse.

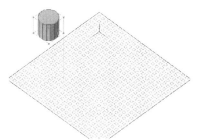

Figure 31. Hold the Alt/Option key while dragging to move the object perpendicularly to the current drawing plane.

The Select All Command

Sometimes it is desirable to select the entire contents of the Mesh Form Modeler window.

To select all items in the Mesh Form Modeler window:

1. Choose Select All from the Edit menu. **(Figure 28)**.

Dragging, cutting, copying and pasting selections

Selections are frequently made for the purpose of dragging, cutting, copying, and pasting them in order to sculpt the overall shape of a mesh form object.

To drag, cut, copy, or paste a selection:

- To move a selection along the current drawing plane (e.g., along the bottom, or X-Y plane), drag it to the desired location and then release the mouse **(Figures 29–30)**.

- To move a selection along the axis that is perpendicular to the current drawing plane (e.g., up or down the Z axis when the current drawing plane is the bottom plane), hold the Alt/Option key and drag the selection to the desired location, as indicated by the guidelines that are displayed, and then release the mouse **(Figure 31).**

- To delete a selection, press the Delete key.

  or

  Choose Cut from the Edit menu.

- To copy a selection to the clipboard, choose Copy from the Edit menu.

  or

  Press Ctrl/Command+C.

133

- To paste a selection from the clipboard, choose Paste from the Edit menu.

  or

  Press Ctrl/Command+V.

  The new copy appears directly over the original primitive and is the currently selected object.

✔ Tip

■ When copying and pasting a polyline or mesh primitive, immediately after the copy step, click anywhere on the drawing plane to deselect the copy, then reselect the copy by triple-clicking directly on it, and then move it. If you don't deselect and reselect before moving the copy, you will only end up moving the edge, vertex, or polygon that you click on when you attempt the drag.

The Hide Selection and Reveal Hidden Vertices commands

Complex mesh form objects can be difficult to visualize. Fortunately, selections can be hidden and revealed as needed.

To hide or reveal a selection:

1. Using the Selection or Marquee tool, select the group of vertices, edges, polygons, and/or polymeshes within the mesh form object that you wish to hide or reveal **(Figure 32)**.

2. Choose Hide Selection or Reveal Hidden Vertices from the View menu **(Figure 33)**. When a selection is hidden, its vertices and any links between them disappear **(Figure 34)**.

The Save and Restore Selection commands

Complex selections can involve dozens or hundreds of edges and vertices. Repeatedly defining such a selection can waste a great deal of time.

Hide or Reveal a Selection

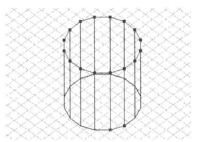

Figure 32. Select the group of vertices, edges, polygons, and/or polymeshes that you wish to hide or reveal.

Figure 33. Choose **Hide Selection** or **Reveal Hidden Vertices** from the **View** menu.

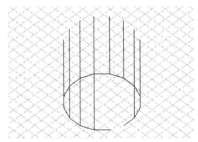

Figure 34. When a selection is hidden, its vertices and any links between them disappear.

Figure 35. Choose **Save Selection** from the **Selection** menu.

Figure 36. Choose **Restore Selection** from the **Selection** menu.

Figure 37. Choose **Invert** from the **Selection** menu.

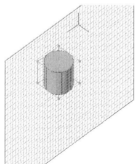

Figure 38. You can send the drawing plane to many different preset or custom locations to make it more convenient to edit your objects.

Fortunately, the Mesh Form Modeler provides two very efficient ways of saving and recalling selections.

The first method is automatic and persistent across editing sessions. Any selection that is present when you press the Done button will automatically reappear whenever you reopen the object for editing—even if you have exited Ray Dream Studio in the interim.

The second method is manual and temporary. That is, a selection can be saved and recalled, but is lost once the Done button is pressed.

To save and restore a selection:

1. To save a selection, choose Save Selection from the Selection menu **(Figure 35)**.

2. To restore a selection, choose Restore Selection from the Selection menu **(Figure 36)**.

The Invert Selection command

The Mesh Form Modeler also permits you to invert the currently displayed selection—that is, it permits you to deselect all selected items and to select all items that were not included in the original selection.

To invert a selection:

1. Choose Invert from the Selection menu **(Figure 37)**.

The Send Drawing Plane commands

Most Mesh Form Modeler operations, such as drawing and scaling, can be performed either in the Mesh Form modeling box's Reference view, or in another preset or custom view that sends the current drawing plane to a more convenient location **(Figure 38)**.

Typically, the drawing plane is sent to the plane of a selected polygon or selected edge in a polyline or polymesh. Or the drawing plane may be sent to another, more arbitrary position, in which new structures are added and fused to existing structures **(Figure 39)**.

To send the drawing plane to a specific location:

1. Choose "Send Drawing Plane to" from the View menu, and select one of the options listed below in the Send Drawing Plane submenu **(Figure 40)**.

- Selection for the current selection.

- Screen for the Screen **(Figure 41)**.

- Position for a coordinate in 3D space that you specify in the resulting dialog box **(Figure 42)**.

- Top for the top of the Mesh Form modeling box.

- Bottom for the bottom of the Mesh Form modeling box. **(Figure 43)**.

- Left for the left side of the Mesh Form modeling box **(Figure 44)**.

- Right for the right side of the Mesh Form modeling box.

- Front for the front side of the Mesh Form modeling box.

- Back for the back side of the Mesh Form modeling box.

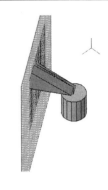

Figure 39. You can send the drawing plane to an arbitrary position where new structures can be added and fused to existing objects.

Figure 40. Choose **Send Drawing Plane to** from the **View** menu.

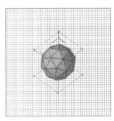

Figure 41. The Screen view.

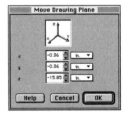

Figure 42. You can specify the center of the drawing plane by entering coordinates in the **Move Drawing Plane** dialog box.

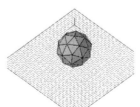

Figure 43. Bottom view.

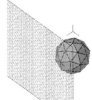

Figure 44. Left view.

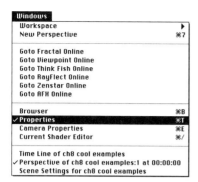

Figure 45. Choose **Properties** from the **Windows** menu.

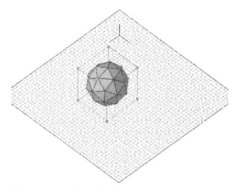

Figure 46. A polymesh object has been selected.

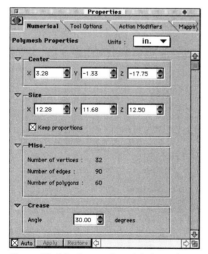

Figure 47. Selecting a polymesh in its entirety allows you to set both its size and position attributes.

✔ **Tip**

■ Don't try to use the Position option to reorient the current drawing plane. Instead, use a preset position (e.g., left) to reorient the current drawing plane, and then use the Position option to position it as desired.

Having learned how to make selections and how to access them with optimal orientations of the current drawing plane, you are now ready to learn what can be done with those selections. To start, we'll learn how to size and position selections.

SIZING AND POSITIONING TOOLS

The Mesh Form Modeler offers several ways of sizing, scaling, rotating, and positioning selected objects within the Mesh Form Modeler Box.

The Numerical tab of the Properties palette

Certain types of selections can be sized and/or positioned precisely in the Mesh Form Modeler by entering values in the Numerical tab of the Properties palette.

To display the Numerical tab of the Properties palette:

1. Choose Properties from the Windows menu **(Figure 45)**.

2. Click the Numerical tab of the Properties palette.

The nature of the selection dictates what fields, if any, are displayed and editable in the Numerical tab. For example:

• Selecting an edge, polyline, primitive, or other polymesh in its entirety enables you to set both its size and its position **(Figures 46–47)**.

- Selecting a polygon enables you to specify the coordinates for its center point but not its overall size **(Figure 48)**.

- Selecting multiple polygons or polymeshes prevents you from setting either their sizes or positions **(Figure 49)**.

To size a selection with the Numerical tab of the Properties palette:

1. Enter the desired units in the Edge, Polygon, or Polymesh Properties area of the tab **(Figure 50)**.

2. Toggle proportional scaling on or off by checking or unchecking the Keep Proportions box in the Sizes area of the tab.

3. Enter the desired values and units in the X, Y, and Z fields of the Size section of the dialog.

4. To redraw the selection immediately after each change is made, check the Auto checkbox.

or

To redraw the selection only on your command, uncheck the Apply checkbox.

and

Click Apply to redraw the selection.

To position a selection with the Numerical tab of the Properties palette:

1. Enter the desired units in the Edge, Polygon, or Polymesh Properties area of the tab.

2. Enter the desired values and units in the X, Y, and Z fields of the Center section of the tab.

3. Manually or automatically redraw the selection as described in Step 4 of the instructions on sizing a selection with the Numerical tab of the Properties palette.

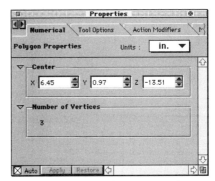

Figure 48. You can specify the position of a polygon, but not its overall size, in the Properties palette.

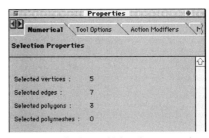

Figure 49. Selecting multiple polygons or polymeshes prevents you from setting either their sizes or positions.

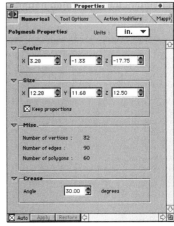

Figure 50. Enter the desired units in the Edge, Polygon, or Polymesh Properties area of the tab.

Size and Position a Selection

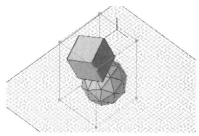

Figure 51. You can scale an object by directly manipulating the handles on its bounding box.

Figure 52. You can also scale an object by choosing **Resize** from the **Selection** menu.

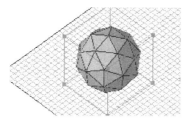

Figure 53. For spheres and cylinders, the bounding box appears as a 3D frame that surrounds but is separate from the primitive.

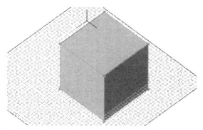

Figure 54. For cubes, rectangles, ovals, and meshes, the bounding box is displayed around, and is co-linear with the primitive's perimeter.

Scaling and sizing tools and techniques

Scaling can be performed either by

- Directly manipulating the handles on a selection's bounding box, if available **(Figure 51)**.

  or

- Invoking the Mesh Form Modeler's Resize command, which is the equivalent of the Free Form Modeler's Scale command **(Figure 52)**.

The presence and appearance of a bounding box depends on the nature of the object that is selected. Obviously, selections that do not produce a bounding box—such as an open polyline, or a subset of a closed polyline—cannot be directly scaled with bounding box handles. In any event, the Resize command permits more accurate scaling because it requires numerical inputs.

✔ Tips

- ◼ Bounding box availability and appearance can be summarized as follows:
- For spheres and cylinders, the bounding box appears as a 3D frame that surrounds the primitive but is separated from it by a visible border **(Figure 53)**.
- For cubes, rectangles, ovals, and meshes, the bounding box is displayed around, and is co-linear with, the primitive's perimeter **(Figure 54)**.

The direct scaling technique

When closed 2D and 3D polylines are selected, they are surrounded by a bounding box. You can scale such objects by manipulating the bounding box's handles, or by using the Resize command from the Selection menu.

To scale a selection directly with its bounding box handles:

1. To scale the selection symmetrically (i.e., proportionally in all three dimensions), click and drag a bounding box handle in the desired direction while holding the Shift key.

2. To scale the selection asymmetrically along either axis of the current drawing plane, click and drag a bounding box handle in the desired direction **(Figure 55)**.

3. To scale the selection asymmetrically along the axis that is perpendicular to the current drawing plane (e.g., above or below the bottom plane), click and drag a bounding box handle in the desired direction while holding the Alt/Option key **(Figure 56)**.

To scale a polyline or selection with the Resize command:

1. Choose Resize from the Selection menu.

2. Enter the percentage by which to scale the target item up or down in the X, Y, and/or Z axes **(Figure 57)**.

The Adjust (align) Command

Ray Dream makes it very easy to align a vertex, edge, or polygon surface of one polymesh with the vertex, edge, or polygon of another polymesh.

To adjust (align) a vertex, edge, or surface of one polymesh with the vertex, edge, or surface of another polymesh:

1. Make the first selection.

2. While holding down the Shift key, make the second selection **(Figure 58)**.

3. Choose Adjust from the Polymesh menu **(Figure 59)**.

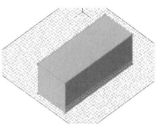

Figure 55. Scale asymmetrically by dragging a handle in the desired direction.

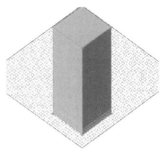

Figure 56. Scale in the perpendicular direction by dragging a handle while holding the Alt/Option key.

Figure 57. Enter the percentage by which to scale the target item along the X, Y, and Z axes.

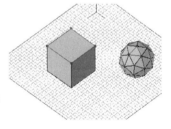

Figure 58. Make the second selection while holding the Shift key.

Figure 59. Choose **Adjust** from the **Polymesh** menu.

Scale a Selection, Adjust (Align) Command

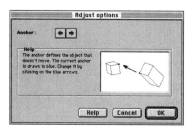

Figure 60. Click OK in the **Adjust options** dialog box.

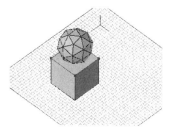

Figure 61. The second selection is aligned with the first.

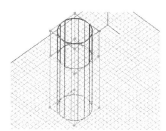

Figure 62. First, align the surfaces of the cylinders.

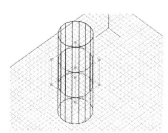

Figure 63. Set the Z values for each of the cylinders to the same value.

4. To move the second selection so that it aligns within or around the first selection, click OK in the Adjust options dialog box **(Figures 60–61)**.

or

To move the first selection so that it becomes aligned within or around the second selection, press the right-pointing blue arrow key and then press OK in the Adjust options dialog box.

✔ Tips

■ Only like items can be aligned with the Adjust command—e.g., only a polygon can be aligned with another polygon.

■ Only two objects can be aligned at one time.

■ To select an object that is not directly accessible (e.g., the base surface of a cylinder), choose an appropriate Preset Position (e.g., the Bottom view) from the View menu.

■ When aligning vertices, the anchor vertex is displayed in blue, and the vertex to be moved is displayed in red. However, when aligning edges and polygon surfaces, the anchor object is not displayed in blue.

■ The first object you select is, by default, the anchor object.

■ To align objects within each other, such as a thinner cylinder within a thicker cylinder, a two-step process is required:

• First, align their corresponding surfaces **(Figure 62)**.

• Then, individually select each polymesh, and set the Z value for its center in the Numerical tab of the Properties dialog to the same value **(Figure 63)**.

Adjust (Align) Command

The Rotate command

The Mesh Form Modeler lets you rotate selections in 3D space to any desired orientation.

To rotate a selection:

1. Make the selection **(Figure 64)**, and choose Rotate from the Selection menu **(Figure 65)**.

2. In the Rotate Selection dialog, click the axis around which the selection is to be rotated **(Figure 66)**.

and

Enter a value between 360 and –360 in the degrees field for a specific axis.

and

Click OK **(Figure 67)**.

✔ Tip

■ Edges that are adjacent to the rotated selection are moved and/or resized to permit their continued attachment to the selection. The Rotate command, therefore, can have a substantial impact on the overall shape of the mesh form object.

The Virtual Trackball tool

The Mesh Form Modeler's Virtual Trackball is another way of rotating a selection in the 3D space of the Mesh Form modeling box. It differs from the Rotate command in the three ways:

• The Virtual Trackball tool can operate only on a fully selected polyline, primitive, or other polymesh, while the Rotate command can operate on a partial selection of such an object—e.g., three non-adjacent polygons on a sphere.

• The Virtual Trackball tool can be characterized as being positionally heuristic (i.e., approximate), while the Rotate command is positionally specific (i.e., it requires a specific number of degrees).

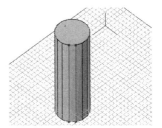

Figure 64. Make your selection. In this figure, a single rectangle on the cylinder has been selected.

Figure 65. Choose **Rotate** from the **Selection** menu.

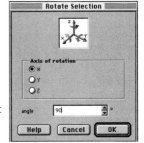

Figure 66. Enter an angle value for a specific axis in the **Rotate Selection** dialog box.

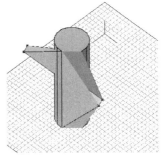

Figure 67. The cylinder has been rotated 90 degrees around the X axis.

Figure 68. Virtual Trackball tool.

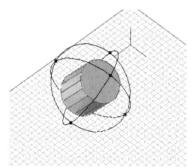

Figure 69. Click and drag to rotate the selection as desired. A spherical bounding box appears around the selection.

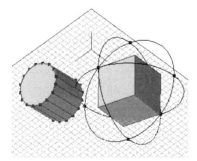

Figure 70. When multiple unconnected objects are selected, the Virtual Trackball tool will rotate all of them simultaneously.

- The Virtual Trackball tool lets you rotate around one, two, or three axes simultaneously, while the Rotate command lets you rotate around only one axis at a time.

To reorient a selected polymesh in 3D with the Virtual Trackball tool:

1. Click the Virtual Trackball tool **(Figure 68)**.

2. Click and drag the mouse to rotate the selection as desired, and release the mouse **(Figure 69)**.

✔ Tip

■ This tool affects or creates selections differently depending on what selections, if any, were defined with the Selection tool before the Virtual Trackball tool was clicked. For example:

- If an object is partially selected with the Selection tool and then is clicked on with the trackball tool, the tool will select and operate on the entire object.

- If multiple unconnected objects —such as an entire cylinder primitive and an entire cube primitive—are fully selected with the Selection tool, then the Virtual Trackball will rotate all such fully selected objects simultaneously **(Figure 70)**.

- If some objects are fully selected and others are only partially selected when the tool is used, then only the fully selected object will be rotated.

Virtual Trackball Tool

The 2D Rotation tool

The 2D Rotation tool enables you to rotate a selection around the axis that is perpendicular to the current drawing plane.

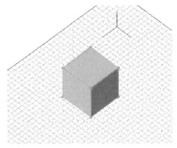

Figure 71. Select the object you wish to rotate.

To rotate a selection with the 2D Rotation tool:

1. Make the selection in advance **(Figure 71)**.

2. Click the 2D Rotation tool **(Figure 72)**.

3. Click and drag the mouse to rotate the selection as desired around the current drawing plane, and release the mouse **(Figure 73)**.

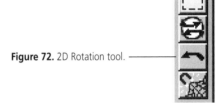

Figure 72. 2D Rotation tool.

The 2D Rotation tool differs from the Virtual Trackball tool and the Rotate command in the following ways:

- The 2D Rotation tool and the Rotate command can operate on multiple partial selections from single or multiple polylines, primitives, or other polymeshes, while the Virtual Trackball tool can operate only on one, fully selected edge, polyline, primitive, or polymesh.

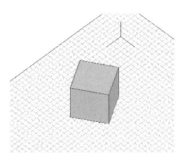

Figure 73. Drag to rotate the selection around the current drawing plane.

- Unlike the Mesh Form Modeler's Virtual Trackball tool, you cannot use the 2D Rotation tool as a pointer or selection tool to select the target item to be rotated if no selection has been defined. Instead, you must first make the selection with the Selection tool before clicking the 2D Rotation tool.

- Unlike the Mesh Form Modeler's Virtual Trackball, the 2D Rotation tool and the Rotate command will rotate only those elements of a polymesh that have been selected or are directly connected to selected elements. For example, if only one polygon in the side of a cylinder is selected, then only that side and its directly adjoining elements are rotated **(Figure 74)**.

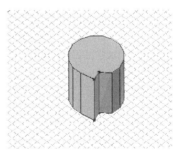

Figure 74. The selected rectangle in the cylinder is rotated.

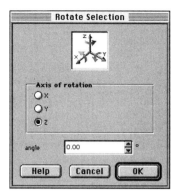

Figure 75. The Rotate command lets you specify the axis and degrees.

- The 2D Rotation tool lets you rotate only on one axis at a time—i.e., the axis that is perpendicular to the current drawing plane, while the Rotate command lets you specify an axis, a direction, and a specific number of degrees **(Figure 75)**.

The Nudge technique

You can easily "nudge" selections using the numeric keyboard.

To nudge a selection along a specific axis, toward or away from the Mesh Form modeling box's point of origin:

1. Press the Left Arrow or Right Arrow to move the selection along the "horizontal" axis of the current drawing plane (i.e., the X axis in the Reference view) **(Figures 76–77)**.

or

Press the Up Arrow or the Down Arrow to move the selection along the "vertical" axis of the current drawing plane (i.e., the Y axis).

or

Hold the Alt/Option key and press the Up Arrow or the Down Arrow to move the selection up or down the axis that is perpendicular to the current drawing plane (i.e., the Z axis).

✔ Tips

- Nudging moves an item one actual grid line (as opposed to one displayed grid line). Thus, if a selected vertex is located on a drawn line, and if the Grid preferences are set so that only one drawn grid line is displayed for every two actual grid lines, you will have to nudge twice to move a selection to the next drawn line.

- To change the fineness or coarseness of nudging, change the increment between actual grid lines in the Grid Preferences dialog box, as explained in the previous chapter.

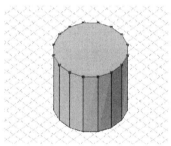

Figure 76. Selection before nudging.

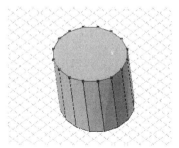

Figure 77. Selection after nudging.

Nudge Technique

The Move command

The Move command lets you move a selection using a distance and unit of measurement that you provide.

To move a selection from its current location by a specific distance along a specific axis:

1. Choose Move from the Selection menu **(Figure 78)**.

2. Enter the desired values and unit of measurement in the Move Selection dialog box and click OK **(Figure 79)**.

✔ Tips

■ Entering a positive value with respect to a particular axis will move the selected items in the positive direction along that axis and away from the Mesh Form modeling box's point of origin (X = 0, Y = 0, Z = 0) **(Figures 80–81)**.

■ Entering a negative value moves the selection along that axis and toward the point of origin.

The Sphere of Attraction tool

A selection can be attracted toward an imaginary gravitational source with the Sphere of Attraction tool.

The Sphere of Attraction tool can identify the vertices that fall within the constraints that you define. Moreover, this tool will affect different vertices in different ways, depending upon the following factors:

• The curve type, effective radius, and mode settings you specify in the tool's Properties palette.

• The vertices' distance and angle from the attracting sphere.

Figure 78. Choose **Move** from the **Selection** menu.

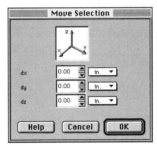

Figure 79. Enter the desired values and unit of measurement in the **Move Selection** dialog box.

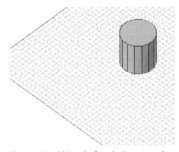

Figure 80. Object before being moved.

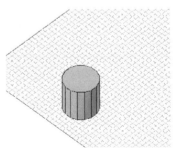

Figure 81. Object after being moved in the positive X direction.

Move Command, Sphere of Attraction Tool

Figure 82. Sphere of Attraction tool.

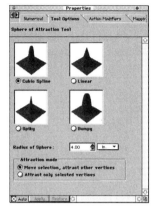

Figure 83. Click on the desired curve type in the **Sphere of Attraction tool Properties** dialog box.

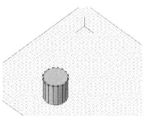

Figure 84. Select the vertices that you wish to attract.

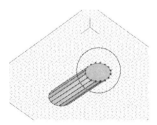

Figure 85. Drag the Sphere of Attraction tool along the direction in which you wish to attract the vertices.

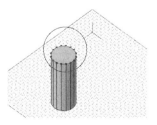

Figure 86. Attract the vertices perpendicularly to the drawing plane by holding the Alt/Option key while dragging.

To move vertices with the Sphere of Attraction tool:

1. Click the Sphere of Attraction tool **(Figure 82)**.

2. Display the tools' Properties palette if it is closed by selecting Properties from the Windows menu.

3. Click on the Tool Options tab of the Properties palette.

4. Click on the desired curve type (Cubic spline, Linear, Spiky, or Bumpy) **(Figure 83)**.

5. Enter the desired radius, and select the desired of unit of measurement.

6. Select the desired attraction mode:

(a) Select the "Move selection, attract other vertices" mode to move the vertices you select in the next step, and to attract other vertices that are within the specified radius.

or

(b) Select the "Attract only selected vertices" mode to attract only the vertices you select in the next step.

7. Press and hold the Shift key, and click on each vertex you want to select **(Figure 84)**.

8. To attract the vertices along the drawing plane, drag the tool in the direction of the attraction **(Figure 85)**.

9. To attract the vertices perpendicular to the drawing plane (e.g., above or below the bottom plane), hold the Alt/Option key and drag the tool in the direction of the attraction **(Figure 86)**.

10. Release the mouse.

Sphere of Attraction Tool

Offset Surface command

The Offset Surface command is used to move single or multiple polygon selections by a specific amount in the "direction of the surface normal."

To offset a selection of one or more surfaces (polygons):

1. Choose Offset Surface from the Selection menu.

2. In the Offset Surface dialog, enter the desired distance and unit of measurement and click OK **(Figure 87)**.

For a discussion of the concept of "the direction of the surface normal," see the section on the Add Thickness command later in this chapter.

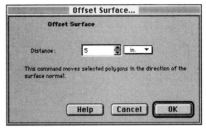

Figure 87. In the **Offset Surface** dialog box, enter the desired distance and unit of measurement and click OK.

MANIPULATING A POLYMESH SURFACE

The surfaces of 3D objects can be refined by manipulating the attributes and interactions of their constituent polygons.

Deleting, emptying, and filling polygons

Selected polygons can be deleted, emptied, or filled.

Deleting a specific polygon usually has a more extensive impact on the overall shape of a polymesh than does emptying it. This is because the deletion of a polygon also results in the deletion of its edges; thus, any other polygon that shares one of the deleted edges is also deleted.

By contrast, emptying a polygon simply toggles it between being transparent and opaque. Adjacent, unselected polygons are not deleted, emptied, or otherwise affected by the emptying operation.

The difference is easily illustrated with any polygon that comprises the side of a cylindrical primitive **(Figures 88–90)**.

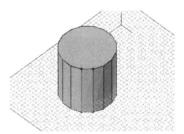

Figure 88. A rectangular polygon has been selected in this cylinder object.

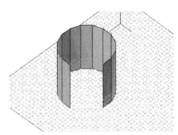

Figure 89. The rectangular polygon has been deleted in this cylinder object.

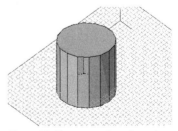

Figure 90. The rectangular polygon has been emptied in this cylinder object.

Figure 91. Choose **Empty Polygon** from the **Selection** menu.

Figure 92. Choose **Fill Polygon** from the **Selection** menu.

Figure 93. Choose **Triangulate Polygon** from the **Selection** menu.

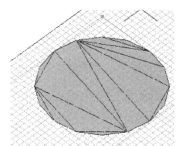

Figure 94. The circle primitive shown has been triangulated.

To delete a selection of one or more polygons:

1. Press the Delete key.

or

Choose cut from the Edit menu.

To empty a selection of one or more polygons:

1. Choose Empty Polygon from the Selection menu **(Figure 91)**.

To fill a selection of one or more polygons:

1. Choose Fill Polygon from the Selection menu **(Figure 92)**.

Triangulate Polygon command

The Triangulate Polygon command lets you subdivide a polygon into a series of smaller, triangular polygons. The resulting triangles are normal polygons that can be manipulated individually. Triangulation also enables smoother rendering.

To triangulate a selection of one or more polygons:

1. Choose Triangulate Polygon from the Selection menu **(Figures 93–94)**.

The Subdivision and Decimation commands

Subdividing is similar to triangulating in that it subdivides an existing polygon into a set of new, smaller polygons. But it differs from Triangulating in two respects:

- Subdividing a polygon creates more polygons than triangulating since it adds vertices and edges, whereas triangulating only adds edges.

- After the first subdivision, the original polygon can remain selected, and the operation can be repeated to generate additional subdivisions.

Delete, Empty, Fill, Triangulate Polygons

To subdivide a polygon:

1. Choose Subdivide from the Selection menu **(Figures 95–96)**.

2. Repeat Step 1 as desired to generate additional polygons **(Figure 97)**.

The Decimation command

Decimation is the opposite of subdivision: it reduces the number of polygons in a selection. Thus, the Decimation command is applied to a selection of contiguous polygons, and not to a single polygon.

Removing polygons can be used to reduce the excess complexity of a model.

To decimate a set of polygons:

1. Choose Decimate from the Selection menu.

2. In the Decimate dialog box, drag the Threshold slider to indicate what percentage of vertices are to be removed in the selected polygons and click OK **(Figures 98–99)**.

3. Repeat Steps 1–2 as desired to decimate additional polygons.

✔ Tip

■ Alternately triangulating, subdividing, and decimating an object yields a constantly changing set of polygons and can help stimulate the creative impulse when working with abstract or stylized objects.

Smooth Edges, Sharpen Edges, and Set Crease Angle commands

There are two ways to smoothen or sharpen the surfaces of a selection:

● Selected polygons can be adjusted with the Smooth Edges and Sharpen Edges commands.

or

● An entire polymesh can be smoothed or sharpened by decreasing or increasing its crease angle with the Set Crease Angle command.

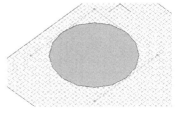

Figure 95. An object before being subdivided.

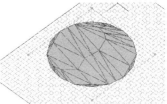

Figure 96. An object after being subdivided.

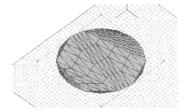

Figure 97. An object after being subdivided twice.

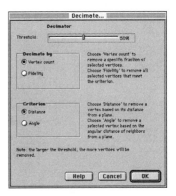

Figure 98. In the **Decimate** dialog box, drag the Threshold slider to indicate the percentage of vertices to be removed.

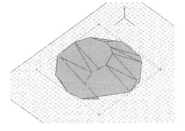

Figure 99. The object in Figure 97 after being decimated.

Figure 100. Choose **Smooth Edges** from the **Polymesh** menu.

Figure 101. Choose **Sharpen Edges** from the **Polymesh** menu.

Figure 102. Choose **Set Crease Angle** from the **Polymesh** menu.

Figure 103. Enter the desired Angle value in the **Crease angle** dialog box.

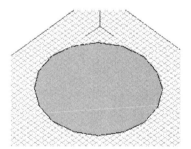

Figure 104. Two vertices before being linked.

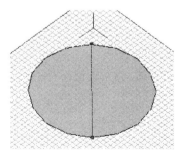

Figure 105. Two vertices after being linked.

To smooth or sharpen a selection of surfaces:

1. Choose Smooth Edges or Sharpen Edges from the Polymesh menu **(Figures 100–101)**.

2. Preview the effect by choosing one of the Preview commands from the View menu.

To smooth or sharpen an entire polymesh by setting its crease angle:

1. Choose Set Crease Angle from the Polymesh menu **(Figure 102)**.

2. Enter the desired Angle value **(Figure 103)**.

3. To override any operations previously performed on one or more of the edges in the selection with the Smooth Edges or Sharpen Edges commands, click the Override option to place a check mark in it.

4. Press OK.

OBJECT LINKING AND FUSING TOOLS

Complex 3D objects can be built by linking, unlinking, and fusing selections.

The Link and Unlink Commands

Any two vertices that exist anywhere in a mesh form object and that are not already linked by an edge can be linked by an edge with the Link command. Conversely, any edge that links two vertices can be removed without disturbing the vertices—i.e., the vertices can be unlinked—with the Unlink command.

To link two selected vertices:

1. Choose Link form the Selection menu, and note the new edge that forms between the two vertices **(Figures 104–105)**.

Smooth, Sharpen Surfaces, Link Vertices

To unlink two selected vertices that are linked by an edge:

1. Choose Unlink from the Selection menu **(Figure 106)**, and note that the linking edge has been removed.

✔ Tip

■ As noted above, the Unlink command deletes only the selected edge and leaves its two vertices undisturbed. By contrast, removing a selected edge with the Delete key or the Cut command removes both the edge itself and its two vertices.

The Weld command

Welding is used to fuse a group of vertices into single vertex at a new position. It also stretches all edges that are connected to the welded vertices out to that new point and therefore can have a substantial impact on the mesh form object's overall shape.

To weld a selection of vertices:

1. Choose Weld from the Selection menu **(Figure 107)**.

2. To weld only the vertices that are currently selected, check the "Weld all selected vertices" option in the Weld dialog box **(Figures 108–110)**.

or

To weld only those vertices that fall within the "Default Tolerance" from the position of the current selection, check Use Default Tolerance option in the Weld dialog box.

or

To weld only those vertices that fall within a specific distance from the position of the current selection, check Use Custom Tolerance option and enter the value and unit of measurement in the Weld dialog box.

3. Click OK and note the changes that result.

Figure 106. Choose **Unlink** from the **Selection** menu.

Figure 107. Choose **Weld** from the **Selection** menu.

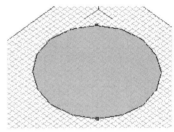

Figure 108. Two vertices before being welded.

Figure 109. Select "Weld all selected vertices" to weld only currently selected vertices.

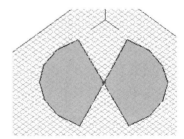

Figure 110. Two vertices after being welded.

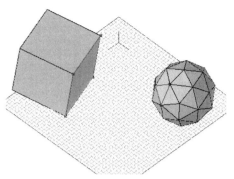

Figure 111. Select two items between which the surface will be stretched. Two polygons are selected here.

Figure 112. Choose **Loft** from the **Selection** menu.

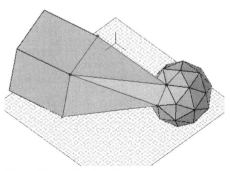

Figure 113. Results after lofting.

✔ Tip

■ The Weld command's Default Tolerance value is specified in the Mesh Form Modeler Preferences dialog box, which is accessed by choosing Preferences from the File menu and specifying the Mesh Form Modeler in the dropdown list.

VOLUMETRIC TOOLS AND TECHNIQUES

The Mesh Form Modeler provides myriad ways to create and manipulate volume in your models. Its volume-related tools and techniques range from the very simple to the very complex. The effects generated by its tools and techniques range from the highly predictable to the occasionally unpredictable.

As always, we shall attempt to start with the simpler tools and techniques, and then gradually build on what you have learned. In just a few minutes, you'll be lathing 3D objects around 3D polylines with the best of them!

The Loft command

One of the Mesh Form Modeler volumetric techniques that should be easiest for Free Form Modeler veterans to learn and use is the Loft command. This command lets you stretch surfaces between a selection of multiple polygons or closed polylines.

To loft a surface between two selections:

1. Select the two items between which the surface will be stretched **(Figure 111)**.

2. Choose Loft from the Selection menu **(Figures 112–113)**.

As noted earlier, the Mesh Form Modeler's Loft command is similar to skinning in the Free Form Modeler; but it does not offer the point-to-point or shape-to-shape options that are available in the Free Form Modeler.

The Add Thickness command

Another very easy way to extrude a 2D shape—or to add additional thickness to a 3D object—is to use the Add Thickness command. This command extrudes a selection along a straight path by a distance that you specify.

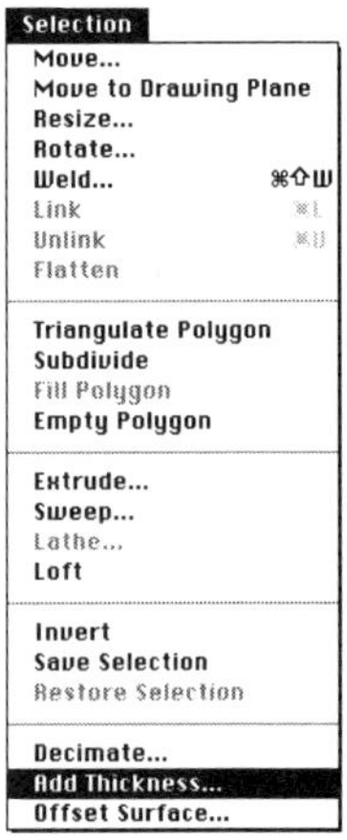

To thicken a selected polygon or polymesh:

1. Choose Add Thickness from the Selection menu **(Figure 114)**.

2. In the Add Thickness dialog box, enter the value and unit of measurement **(Figure 115)** and click OK to see the addition **(Figures 116–117)**.

✔ Tip

■ The Add Thickness command provides the best illustration of the concept of "the direction of the surface normal," which is used by other Mesh Form Modeler tools and commands. To determine which direction this is, simply perform the Add Thickness command. The direction in which thickness is added is the direction of the surface normal.

Figure 114. Choose **Add Thickness** from the **Selection** menu.

Figure 115. Enter the value and unit of measurement in the **Add Thickness** dialog box.

Figure 116. Object before the **Add Thickness** command has been applied.

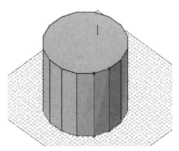

Figure 117. Object after the **Add Thickness** command has been applied.

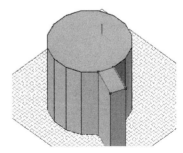

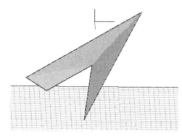

Figure 118. Choose **Flatten** from the **Selection** menu.

The Flattening command and the Move To Drawing Plane command

It may sometimes be desirable to "flatten" points that are not co-planar so that they become co-planar. The Mesh Form Modeler provides two flattening methods:

- The Flatten command lets you flatten a multi-planar selection onto either the current drawing plane or on another, arbitrary plane, depending on the nature of the selection.

- The Move To Drawing Plane command, by contrast, always flattens the selection to the current drawing plane.

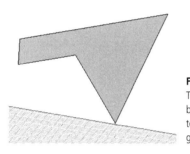

Figure 119. A 3D object before being flattened.

Figure 120. The object has been flattened to a single plane.

To flatten a selection:

The Flatten command sends the selections to the current drawing plane, or to an automatically and arbitrarily selected plane.

1. Choose Flatten from the Selection menu **(Figure 118)** to place your selection onto a single plane **(Figures 119–120)**.

To flatten a selection to the current drawing plane with the Move To Drawing Plane command:

1. Choose Move to Drawing Plane from the Selection menu **(Figure 121)** to place your selection onto the current drawing plane **(Figure 122)**.

Figure 121. Choose **Move to Drawing Plane** from the **Selection** menu.

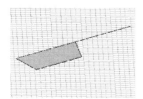

Figure 122. The selection has been placed onto the current drawing plane.

Flatten, Move To Drawing Plane Commands

The Boolean Operation command

Moving gently up the slope of complexity, we come next to the Boolean Operation command. Boolean operations are used to combine two volumes in one of four possible ways:

- Union fuses the two volumes into a single, unified volume **(Figure 123)**.

- Intersection fuses those portions of the volume that overlap and discards those portions that do not **(Figure 124)**.

- Subtraction of A from B removes all of the A volume and that portion of the B volume that intersected the A volume **(Figure 125)**.

- Subtraction of B from A removes all of the B volume and that portion of the A volume that intersected the B volume **(Figure 126)**.

To perform a Boolean operation on a selection of two intersecting, closed volumes:

1. Choose Boolean Operation from the Polymesh menu.

2. Click on the specific operation to be performed in the Tool Options tab of the Properties palette **(Figure 127)**:

- Union

- Intersection

- Subtraction of A from B

  or

- Subtraction of B from A.

3. If the Auto option is not checked, click the Apply button to view the resulting object.

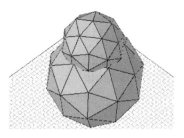

Figure 123.
Union fuses two volumes into a single volume.

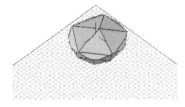

Figure 124.
Intersection fuses those portions of the volume that overlap.

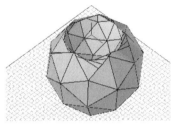

Figure 125.
Subtraction of A from B.

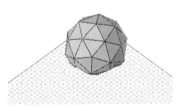

Figure 126.
Subtraction of B from A.

Figure 127.
Click on the operation to be performed in the Tool Options tab of the Properties palette.

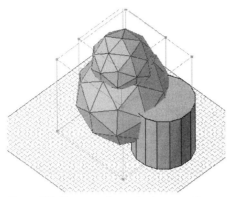

Figure 128. You can perform a Boolean operation even when more than two volumes overlap, provided that only two volumes are selected when the operation is performed.

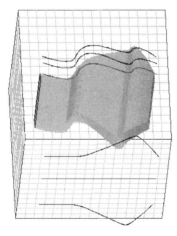

Figure 129. The Free Form Modeler is shown with the sweep path and extrusion envelope description lines visible.

✔ **Tips**

■ The A volume is the larger volume, and the B volume is the smaller one.

■ A Boolean operation can be used when more than two volumes overlap, provided that only two volumes are selected when the operation is performed **(Figure 128)**.

■ To perform Boolean operations on more than two volumes, operate on two volumes to create a single volume and then operate on that volume with another, and so on.

The Extrusion, Sweep, and Lathe commands

The Mesh Form Modeler's most complex volumetric techniques are embodied in the Extrusion, Sweep, Loft, and Lathe commands. But, as noted earlier, these techniques are similar to the basic extrusion, sweep, and lathe concepts and techniques you learned in the Free Form Modeler.

Extruding, sweeping, and lathing with the Mesh Form Modeler versus the Free Form Modeler

While working with the Free Form Modeler in Chapter 7, you created 2D shapes, scaled them as they passed through various cross sections, and contoured the resulting extrusion by modifying the free form object's sweep path description lines and extrusion envelope description lines **(Figure 129)**. The Mesh Form Modeler provides many enhancements and supplements to these techniques.

Comparing the Mesh Form Modeler Extrude, Sweep, and Lathe commands with their Free Form Modeler counterparts

- In the Mesh Form Modeler, the difference between extruding and sweeping is analogous to the difference between the Free Form Modeler's Translation and Pipeline methods of extrusion:

  - A Mesh Form Modeler Extrusion is analogous to the Translation method of extrusion in the Free Form Modeler, because the orientation of the cross section is kept constant throughout the extrusion, regardless of the undulations of the extrusion path **(Figures 130–131)**.

  - A Mesh Form Modeler Sweep in the Mesh Form Modeler is analogous to the Pipeline method of extrusion in the Free Form Modeler, because the orientation of the cross section is automatically and continuously changed throughout the extrusion, so that it is always perpendicular to the sweep path **(Figure 132)**.

- The Free Form Modeler lets you only extrude, sweep, and lathe 2D shapes around a single set of sweep path description lines and within a single set of extrusion envelope description lines.

- By contrast, the Mesh Form Modeler lets you extrude, sweep, and lathe a "cross section" that consists of any polygon or any open or closed, 2D or 3D polyline that exists in a mesh form object, along or around an extrusion or sweep path or lathe axis that is constructed with any other such polygon or polyline that exists in a mesh form object **(Figure 133)**.

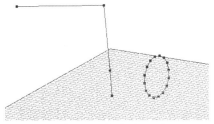

Figure 130. When extruding in the Mesh Form Modeler, the orientation of the cross section remains constant along the extrusion path. Here, the "L" shaped polyline is the extrusion path and the circle is the cross section, shown before extruding.

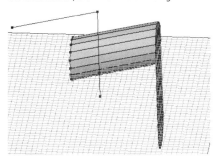

Figure 131. After extrusion.

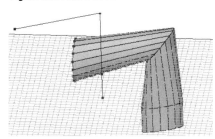

Figure 132. A sweep in the Mesh Form Modeler.

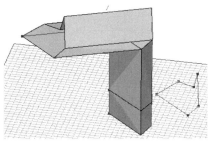

Figure 133. A 3D closed polyline is shown extruded along an open polyline.

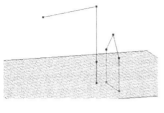

Figure 134. A polygon cross section is shown before extrusion.

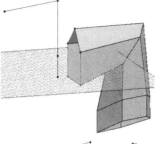

Figure 135. The polygon cross section has been extruded.

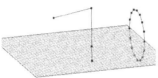

Figure 136. An "L" shaped open polyline is shown before extrusion.

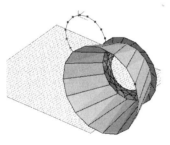

Figure 137. The "L" shaped open polyline has been extruded along a circular path.

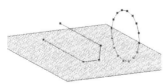

Figure 138. A 3D open polyline is shown before extrusion.

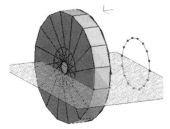

Figure 139. The 3D open polyline has been extruded along a circular path.

Ray Dream's use of the term "cross section" to refer to a selection that is extruded, swept, or lathed in the Mesh Form Modeler is ironic, in view of the fact that cross sections need not, and indeed can not, be explicitly created in the Mesh Form Modeler. Nevertheless, this term communicates the idea that some selected shape is about to be stretched along or around a path in order to create a volume.

Finally, as noted earlier, Bezier curves cannot be created in the Mesh Form Modeler. Thus, if you need to use a curved extrusion path, sweep path, lathe profile, or lathe axis, you can create it in the Free Form Modeler and then open it for editing in the Mesh Form Modeler by following steps provided earlier in this chapter for using the Jump In Another Modeler command.

Factors affecting the results of the Extrude, Sweep, and Lathe commands

The Mesh Form Modeler provides many different ways to extrude, sweep, and lathe objects. The precise result you get with each command will depend on many factors, including:

- Whether the object being extruded, swept, or lathed is a polygon **(Figures 134–135)**, an open polyline **(Figures 136–137)**, a closed polyline, a 2D polyline, or a 3D polyline **(Figures 138–139)**.

- In the case of extrusions and lathes, whether the object is being extruded along or lathed around a default and implied path or axis, or along or around a second, explicitly selected path or axis. And, in the case of a selected extrusion path, whether that path is a polygon, an open polyline, a closed polyline, a 2D polyline, or a 3D polyline.

Because it is impossible to illustrate every possible combination in the space of this book, we encourage you to experiment with various combinations. When all is said and done, there simply is no substitute for experience.

The Extrude command

A selected "cross section" can be extruded either along an implied extrusion path or along an explicitly selected extrusion path, such as a polyline.

To extrude a cross section along an implied extrusion path:

1. Deselect any selected items, and click the Selection tool.

2. Select the cross section (i.e., the polygon or the open or closed, 2D or 3D polyline) to be extruded **(Figure 140)**.

3. Choose Extrude from the Selection menu.

4. Enter the Length value and unit of measurement in the Extrude Options dialog, and click OK **(Figures 141–142)**.

✔ Tip

■ This technique is similar, but not always identical, to the Add Thickness command. For example, the Extrude command can be applied to both polylines and polygons, while the Add Thickness command can be applied to polygons but not polylines.

To extrude a cross section along an explicitly selected extrusion path:

1. Deselect any selected items and click the Selection tool.

2. Select the polyline or group of edges that will serve as the extrusion path **(Figure 143)**.

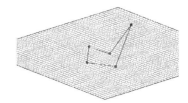

Figure 140. Select the cross section or open polyline to be extruded.

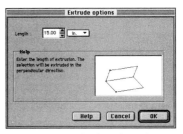

Figure 141. Enter the desired Length value and unit of measurement.

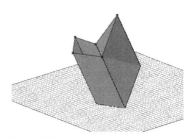

Figure 142. The selection is extruded.

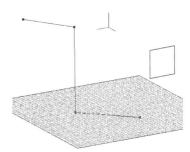

Figure 143. The extrusion path selected here is the "Z" shaped polyline.

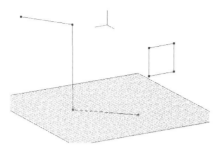

Figure 144. The square has been selected here as the cross section to be extruded.

Figure 145. Choose **Extrude** from the **Selection** menu.

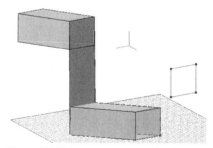

Figure 146. The square cross section has been extruded along the "Z" shaped path.

Figure 147. Use the Action Modifiers tab to select which selection is used as the extrusion path and which as the cross section.

3. While holding the Shift key, select the cross section (i.e., the polygon or the open or closed, 2D or 3D polyline) that will be extruded **(Figure 144)**.

4. Choose Extrude from the Selection menu **(Figure 145)** to view the extrusion **(Figure 146)**.

5. If the Properties palette is not visible, choose Properties from the Windows menu.

6. Click on the Action Modifiers tab of the Properties palette **(Figure 147)**.

7. Press the blue double-arrow buttons labeled Extrusion Path to toggle which selection is designated as the extrusion path and which selection is designated as the cross section.

8. Press the single blue buttons labeled Starting Vertex to toggle the starting position for the extrusion (which is designated with a blue handle).

The Sweep command

As noted above, the primary difference between the Extrude command and Sweep command is in the way that the cross section being extruded or swept is oriented. The Extrude command maintains the original orientation of the cross section throughout the extrusion path, while the Sweep command alters the cross section's orientation so that it is always perpendicular to the sweep path.

Some other differences include the following:

The Extrude command can be applied to a single selection (and will extrude that selection along a default, implied extrusion path by the amount you specify).

By contrast, the Sweep command can only be applied when two appropriate items are selected. By default, the first item that is selected serves as the sweep path, and the second item serves as the cross section to be swept along that path.

Extrude, Sweep Commands

To sweep a cross section around a sweep path:

1. Deselect any selected items, and click the Selection tool.

2. Select the polygon or the open or closed 2D or 3D polyline that will serve as the sweep path.

3. While holding the Shift key, select the cross section (i.e., the polygon or the open or closed 2D or 3D polyline) that will be swept **(Figure 148)**.

4. Choose Sweep from the Selection menu **(Figure 149)** to view the swept cross section **(Figure 150)**.

5. If the Properties palette is not visible, choose Properties from the Windows menu.

6. Click on the Action Modifiers tab of the Properties palette **(Figure 151)**.

7. Press the blue double-arrow buttons labeled Sweep Path to toggle which selection is designated as the sweep path and which is the item being swept.

8. Press the single blue buttons labeled Starting Vertex to toggle the starting position for the sweep (which is designated with a blue handle).

The Lathe command

Like the Extrude command, the Lathe command can be applied to a single selection (so that it is lathed around an implied lathing axis) or to a multiple selection (so that the second selection is lathed around the first selection).

And, like both the Extrude and Sweep commands, the Lathe command will not let you lathe a 3D primitive sphere or cube.

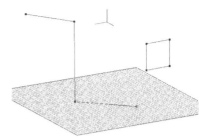

Figure 148. The square has been selected here as the cross section to be swept.

Figure 149. Choose **Sweep** from the **Selection** menu.

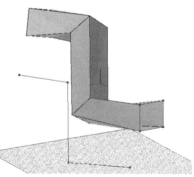

Figure 150. The square cross section has been swept along the "Z" shaped path.

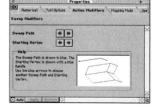

Figure 151. Use the Action Modifiers tab to select which selection is used as the sweep path and which as the cross section.

Sweep Command

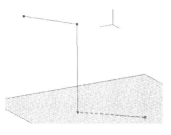

Figure 152. Select the target polyline.

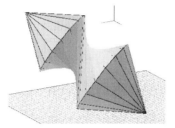

Figure 153. The target polyline has been lathed.

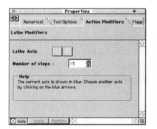

Figure 154. In the Action Modifiers tab, enter the number of steps that your target selection will take through the lathe.

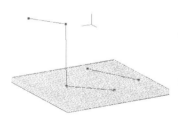

Figure 155. While holding Shift, select the cross section, shown here as a "Z" shaped polyline.

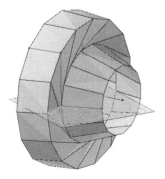

Figure 156. The cross section has been lathed around the selected edge.

To lathe a cross section around an implied lathing axis:

1. Deselect any selected items, and click the Selection tool.

2. Select the target polyline or polygon **(Figure 152)**.

3. Choose Lathe from the Selection menu to view the lathed object **(Figure 153)**.

4. In the Action Modifiers tab of the Properties window, enter the number of steps that your target polyline or polygon will take through the lathe **(Figure 154)**.

To lathe a cross section along an explicitly selected lathing axis:

1. Deselect any selected items, and click the Selection tool.

2. Select the edge that will serve as the lathing axis.

3. While holding the Shift key, select the cross section (i.e., the polygon or the open or closed 2D or 3D polyline) to be lathed **(Figure 155)**.

4. Choose Lathe from the Selection menu to view the lathe **(Figure 156)**.

5. If the Properties palette is not visible, choose Properties from the Windows menu.

6. Click on the Action Modifiers tab of the Properties palette.

7. If either selected object could serve as the lathe axis (e.g., if each selected object is an edge), a pair of blue arrow buttons labeled Lathe Axis can be pressed to toggle the cross sections' designation as the lathe axis (which is designated in blue in the Mesh Form modeling box) and the item being lathed.

8. Enter a higher or lower value in the Steps field to increase or decrease the smoothness of the lathed object.

Lathe Around Implied and Selected Axis

MODIFYING ACTIONS

Finally, the Mesh Form Modeler provides the ability to modify the action of many of the tools and commands you have just learned, such as:

Figure 157. Action Modifier tool.

- The numbers of polygons that comprise newly created sphere, cylinder, and mesh primitives.

- Vertex manipulations performed with the Sphere of Attraction tool.

- Objects created with the Boolean Operation command.

- Objects created with extrusions, sweeps, and lathes.

You can modify these actions in two different ways:

- By clicking the Action Modifier tools.

- By entering numerical values directly into the Action Modifier tab of the newly created object's Properties window.

Figure 158. The Action Modifier tab is shown for a Cylinder Modifier.

To use the Action Modifier tool:

1. Click the Plus and Minus keys on the toolbar until the desired effect is achieved **(Figure 157)**.

To use the Action Modifier tab:

1. Display the Properties Palette if it is not already displayed by choosing Properties from the Windows menu.

2. Enter the desired values in the appropriate fields **(Figures 158–159)**.

3. In order to display changes as they are made, make sure the Auto option is checked; otherwise, check the Apply button to update the object.

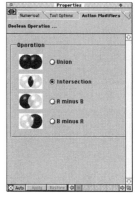

Figure 159. The Action Modifier tab is shown for Boolean Operation.

Congratulations! Now that you have mastered the Mesh Form Modeler, it is time to move onto another of our favorite parts of Ray Dream Studio 5: the Shaders.

Action Modifiers

Part III:
Finishing
3D Objects

Figure 1. The Checkers shader has been applied to this cube primitive.

Figure 2. Shaders are stored in Ray Dream's Browser window.

Figure 3. The current shader is visible and can be modified in the Current Shader Editor window.

Figure 4. A shader is a set of surface characteristics such as color and bump pattern, which are defined in either the Shader Document window or the Current Shader Editor window.

Shaders and 3D paint are used to apply colors, patterns **(Figure 1)**, textures, and other surface attributes to the 3D objects you build with Ray Dream Studio's modeling tools, such as the Free Form Modeler and the Mesh Form Modeler.

In this chapter you will learn how to:

- Differentiate between a stored shader **(Figure 2)**, an applied shader, and the current shader **(Figure 3)**.

- Browse, duplicate, apply, inspect, edit, customize, create, delete, and organize shaders.

- Use shaders and bitmap images as 3D Paint.

- Apply, layer, remove, and reposition 3D paint shapes.

SHADERS: A CONCEPTUAL OVERVIEW

Before working with shaders, we suggest that you master a few basic definitions and that you understand the difference between a "stored shader", an "applied shader", and the "current shader".

Key shader definitions and concepts

Let's begin by defining the terms shader, channel, and primer.

- A **shader** is a set of surface characteristics, such as color, shininess, and brightness. Ray Dream Studio lets you edit, create, and apply shaders to Free Form Modelers, Mesh Form Modelers, and certain other objects **(Figure 4)**.

- A **channel** is a specific characteristic of a shader. The overall visual "look and feel" of a shader is determined by the interplay of its channels **(Figure 5)**. Every shader has the following eight channels:

- **Color**—the base color of the shader.

- **Highlight**—the region of an object which reflects light into the current camera.

- **Shininess**—the size of the highlight region.

- **Bump**—variations in the reflective surface of an object that give the illusion of texture.

- **Reflection**—the degree to which the object reflects surrounding objects and colors.

- **Transparency**—the degree to which an object is translucent.

- **Refraction**—the bending of light when it passes through a transparent or translucent layer of refractive material, such as water.

- **Glow**—the luminance that emanates from an object.

- A **primer** is the base coat that covers a 3D object by default. The primer is a plain red shader by default **(Figure 6)**. When you apply a shader or 3D paint to an object, you can specify whether all of its channels, or only its non-empty channels, are substituted in place of the primer's channels.

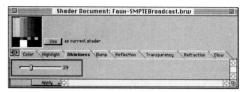

Figure 5. A shader has 8 channels, which collectively define its overall appearance when applied to objects.

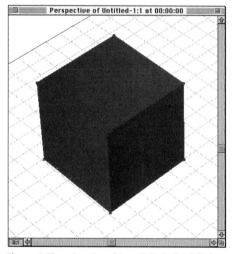

Figure 6. The primer is a plain red shader by default.

Differentiating shader types

Shaders, like other Ray Dream Studio documents, can appear in a number of different forms and locations throughout the Ray Dream Studio environment, such as on your system's hard disk, in Shaders tab of the Browser palette, and "on" 3D objects.

Figure 7. Stored shaders are selected from the Shaders tab of the Browser palette.

Figure 8. A Shader Document contains a stored shader's settings and is opened by double-clicking a shader in the Browser palette.

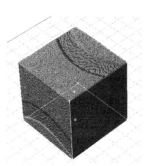

Figure 9. An applied shader is any shader that has already been applied to a 3D object in your scene (the tennis ball shader has been applied to this cube primitive).

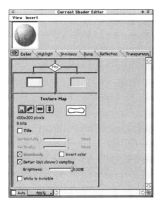

Figure 10. The current shader is edited and applied from the Current Shader Editor window.

Shader states

Functionally speaking, a shader can exist in four different states:

- A **stored shader** is any shader that has been saved on your system's hard disk and can be selected from the Shaders tab of the Browser palette. Stored shaders can be browsed, duplicated, or applied to a 3D object from the Browser palette **(Figure 7)**.

- A **Shader Document** is a disk file that contains a stored shader's settings and can be opened from the Shaders tab of the Browser palette and edited in the Shader Document window **(Figure 8)**.

- An applied shader is any shader that has already been applied to a 3D object that appears in a Scene file **(Figure 9)**.

- The **current shader** is the shader that is displayed in the Current Shader Editor window **(Figure 10)**. The current shader is the last shader that was either "grabbed" from a 3D object with the Perspective window's Eyedropper tool or selected in the Shaders tab of the Browser palette. The Current Shader can be edited, applied to a 3D Object, or saved to the Browser palette as a new stored shader.

WORKING WITH STORED SHADERS AND THEIR SHADER DOCUMENTS

In this section you will learn how to browse, duplicate, inspect, edit, and apply stored shaders.

Browsing stored shaders

Stored shaders can easily be browsed with the Browser palette.

To browse stored shaders with the Browser palette:

1. If it is not displayed, display the Browser palette by choosing Browser from the Windows menu **(Figure 11)**.

2. If the Shaders tab is not visible, click the left or right arrow to navigate the Browser palette's tabs.

3. Click the Shaders tab **(Figure 12)**.

4. Resize and scroll the Browser palette so that you can see all of the stored shaders' icons and names.

Duplicating stored shaders

It is a good idea to duplicate a stored shader and to use the duplicate rather than the original when experimenting with Ray Dream's shader editing and management tools.

To duplicate a stored shader:

1. If the Browser palette is not already displayed, choose Browser from the Windows menu.

2. Right-click/Ctrl-click on the stored shader to be duplicated to open a pop-up menu.

and

Choose Duplicate from the pop-up menu.

3. Note that the new stored shader appears in the Browser, sporting the icon of the original stored shader, and the name of the original shader, with the string "copy" appended to it **(Figure 13)**.

4. To rename the duplicate shader, follow the steps outlined in the following section on working with basic information about a stored shader's disk file.

Figure 11. Choose **Browser** from the **Windows** menu.

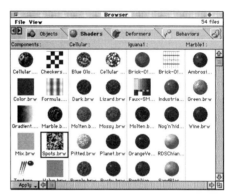

Figure 12. In the Browser palette, click the Shaders tab to display the stored shaders.

Figure 13. The duplicated shader appears in the Browser palette with the string "copy" appended to its name (this is the Text view of Browser palette).

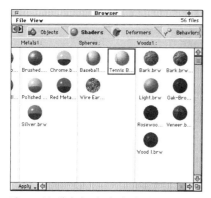

Figure 14. Click the shader in the Browser palette that you wish to apply to your 3D object.

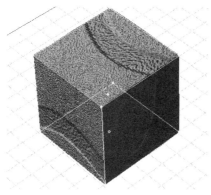

Figure 15. Drag the desired shader from the Browser onto the target object in the Perspective window.

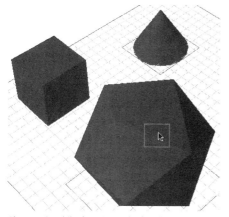

Figure 16. While dragging a shader, the cursor turns into an arrow symbol when positioned over a 3D object.

Applying a stored shader with the Browser palette

There are two ways of applying a stored shader to 3D objects: with a drag and drop operation and with the Apply button.

To apply a stored shader to a 3D object with the drag and drop method:

1. Make sure that both the Browser palette and the Perspective window are open and visible.

2. Click the desired stored shader in the Browser palette **(Figure 14)**.

3. Drag the stored shader onto the target object in the Perspective or Hierarchy window **(Figure 15)**, and release the mouse.

✔ Tips

■ The following tips relate to applying a shader with the drag and drop method when working with stored shaders, Shader documents, and the current shader as described later in this chapter.

■ With the drag and drop method, you can apply a shader only to one object at a time, and that object may but need not be selected as the current object.

■ When multiple 3D objects are selected, dragging the shader to the Perspective or Hierarchy window will apply it only to the object that is under the cursor when you release the mouse button, and not to the entire selection.

■ While it is being dragged, the cursor becomes a "can't drop" symbol until it is positioned over an object that can be shaded, where it becomes an arrow **(Figure 16)**.

Apply a Stored Shader with Drag/Drop

To apply a stored shader with the Apply button:

1. Select the 3D object or objects to be shaded in the Perspective or Hierarchy Window.

2. Select the desired shader and click the Apply button in the Browser palette **(Figure 17)**.

✔ Tip

■ Clicking any Apply button in the Browser palette (or in a Shader Document window or the Current Shader Editor window, as described below) has no effect unless one or more 3D objects are selected in either the Perspective or Hierarchy window.

The Shader Document

The information that makes up a stored shader—such as its name and channel settings—is stored in a disk file known as its Shader Document.

Inspecting and editing basic information about a Shader Document

You can use the Browser palette to access a stored shader's Shader Document. You can also use the Browser palette to access and edit certain basic information about the Shader Document file itself, including its name, path, and description.

To inspect and edit information about a stored shader's Shader Document disk file:

1. Right-click/Ctrl-click on the stored shader's icon in the Browser palette.

2. Choose Get Info from the pop-up menu **(Figure 18)**.

   or

   Choose Get Info from the File menu in the Browser palette.

3. Inspect the Name, Path, Type, and Comment fields in the Browser File Info dialog box **(Figure 19)**.

Figure 17. Select the desired shader and click the Apply button in the Browser palette.

Figure 18. Choose **Get Info** from the pop-up menu.

Figure 19. The **Browser File Info** dialog box displays a shader's Name, Path, Type, and Comment information.

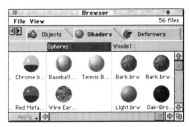

Figure 20. Click the name of the Browser directory in which the shader's icon is located to select that directory.

Figure 21. Choose **Update Selected Folder** from the **File** menu in the Browser palette.

Figure 22. You can apply a shader to an object from the Shader Document window by dragging the preview of the shader onto the object or by selecting the object and then clicking the Apply button.

4. If desired, you can edit the Name and Comment fields.

5. Click OK to close the dialog and save any changes.

Deleting a stored shader

Like any other object stored in the Browser palette, you cannot directly delete a stored shader from that palette. Instead, you must use your system's Explorer or Finder applet to delete the file and then refresh the Browser palette to reflect the deletion.

To delete a stored shader:

1. Follow the steps in the preceding information to get the file name and path of the stored shader's disk file (Shader Document).

2. Using the Windows File Manager or Explorer or the Mac Finder, delete the file.

3. Click the name of the Browser directory in which the shader's icon is located to select that directory **(Figure 20)**.

4. Choose Update Selected Folder from the File menu of the Browser palette **(Figure 21)**.

Applying a shader with the Shader Document

You can shade a 3D object from the Shader Document the same way you can with the Browser palette, as described above. The only difference is that you drag the shader preview **(Figure 22)** or click the Apply button that appears in the Shader Document instead of those that appear in the Browser palette.

Editing the Shader Document for a stored shader

Also as noted above, you can edit the eight channel settings that are contained in a stored shader's Shader Document.

To edit the Shader Document:

1. Double-click the target stored shader's icon in the Browser palette **(Figure 23)** to open its Shader Document **(Figure 24)**.

2. If the Shader Document's window is obscured by the Browser window or the Properties window, move the windows around until it is visible.

3. Navigate the Channels tabs with the horizontal arrow buttons.

4. While experimenting with the following channel settings, observe the effects instantly in the shader preview.

5. To set the Color channel, click the Color tab.

   and

   Double-click the color swatch to open the Color dialog box **(Figure 25)**.

   and

   Choose a color model (RGB or CMYK) from the dropdown list **(Figure 26)** and adjust the R,G, and B or C, M, Y, and K sliders or click the color selector to set the shader's base color **(Figure 27)**.

6. To set the Highlight, Shininess, Reflection, Transparency, and Refraction channels, click the corresponding tab.

   and

   Adjust the slider to the desired level.

7. To set the Bump channel, click the Bump tab.

   and

   Choose the bump pattern by Right-clicking/Ctrl-clicking on the bump box, and selecting Texture Map from the pop-up menu **(Figure 28)**.

Figure 23. Double-click the target stored shader in the Browser palette to open its Shader Document.

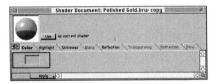

Figure 24. The Shader Document window.

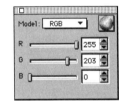

Figure 25. The Color dialog box.

Figure 26. Choose a color model from the dropdown list.

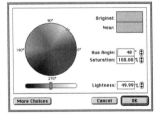

Figure 27. Use the color selector to set the shader's base color.

Figure 28. Choose **Texture Map** from the pop-up menu.

Figure 29. Change the orientation of the bump patterns by pressing the Shuffle buttons.

Figure 30. When you close the Shader Document window and have made changes to the shader, you are prompted with the option of saving the changes.

Figure 31. Choose **Save As** from the **File** menu.

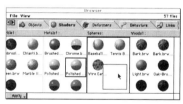

Figure 32. Drag the preview of the Shader Document to a directory in the Browser palette to save the shader as a new stored shader.

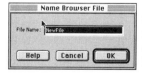

Figure 33. Enter the name for the new shader in the **Name Browser File** dialog box.

and

Change the orientation of the Bump patterns by pressing the Shuffle button as desired **(Figure 29)**.

and

Adjust the Amplitude and Brightness sliders as desired.

Saving edited Shader Documents to existing and new Shader Documents

When you have finished editing a Shader Document, you can simply save it back to disk or you can create a new stored shader by saving it under a different name.

To save (or discard) changes to a Shader Document:

1. Close the Shader Document window.

2. Click Yes or No in answer to the dialog box prompt asking whether you want to save your changes **(Figure 30)**.

or

1. Make sure the Shader Document window is the current window.

2. Choose Save As from the File menu **(Figure 31)**.

To save an edited Shader Document to a new stored shader:

1. Prepare the Browser palette by displaying it, clicking the Shaders tab, and scrolling it until the target shader directory is visible.

2. Click the shader preview in the Shader Document window, drag it to the target directory of stored shaders, and release the mouse when the cursor has turned to a pointer **(Figure 32)**.

3. In the Name Browser File dialog box, enter the name for the new shader **(Figure 33)**.

or

1. Choose Save As from the File menu.

2. In the Save As dialog box, specify the name and path for the new file and click Save.

You can also use the Shader Document to perform the advanced editing functions that are discussed below in the section dealing with the Current Shader Editor.

WORKING WITH THE CURRENT SHADER

The Current Shader Editor window can be used for the following operations, in any combination or order:

- Saving the current shader to the Browser palette as a stored shader.

- Applying the current shader to 3D objects.

- Inspecting and editing stored shaders and applied shaders.

Setting the current shader

Either a stored shader or an applied shader (i.e., a shader that has already been applied to a 3D object) can be made the current shader, opened in the Current Shader Editor window, customized with advanced options and then applied to a 3D object.

To make a stored shader the current shader:

1. If the Current Shader Editor window is not already open, choose Current Shader Editor from the Windows menu **(Figure 34)**.

2. Click the target stored shader in the Browser palette **(Figure 35)**.

3. Adjust all windows until the Current Shader Editor window is visible **(Figure 36)**.

Figure 34. Choose **Current Shader Editor** from the **Windows** menu.

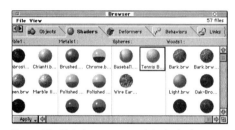

Figure 35. Click the target stored shader in the Browser palette.

Figure 36. You make a stored shader into the current shader by simply selecting it in the Browser palette. The current shader is visible in the Current Shader Editor window.

Figure 37. Eyedropper tool.

Figure 38. With the Eyedropper tool, click the 3D object containing the applied shader you wish to work with.

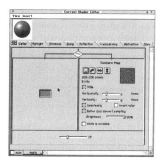

Figure 39. Make the Current Shader Editor window visible.

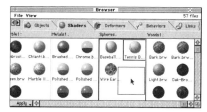

Figure 40. To save the current shader as a new stored shader, drag its preview to a directory in the Browser palette.

Figure 41. Enter a file name to save the current shader as a stored shader.

To make an applied shader the current shader:

1. Make the Perspective window the current window.

2. Click the Eyedropper tool **(Figure 37)**.

3. Click the 3D object containing the applied shader you wish to work with **(Figure 38)**.

4. Adjust the windows so that the Current Shader Editor window is visible **(Figure 39)**.

Applying the current shader to 3D objects

After a current shader is set in the Current Shader Editor window, you can shade 3D objects with it the same way you can with the Browser palette and Shader Document, as described above. The only difference is that you drag the shader preview or click the Apply button that appears in the Current Shader Editor window instead of those that appear in the Browser palette or Shader Document.

Saving the current shader as a stored shader

You can also save the current shader to new stored shader, just as you learned to do with edited Shader Documents earlier in this chapter. To do so, you drag and drop the current shader's preview to a target directory of the Browser palette **(Figure 40)**, and enter a file name in the Name Browser File dialog box **(Figure 41)**.

Make an Applied Shader the Current Shader

Editing the current shader's channels

The process of editing the current shader's eight channel settings in the Current Shader Editor window is similar to editing a stored shader's channel settings by opening its Shader Document, as explained above.

Figure 42. Click the default shader in the Browser palette.

The Current Shader Editor window, however, offers various menu options that are not available with the Shader Document window. You will learn about these options after you learn how to build a custom, compound shader.

Figure 43. Choose **Operators** from the **Insert** menu and select **Mix** from the submenu.

Building a shader with the Current Shader Editor window

To build a simple shader that combines a color and a texture map:

1. Click the default shader in the Browser palette **(Figure 42)**.

2. In the Current Shader Editor window, click the Color tab.

3. Choose Operators from the Insert menu, and click Mix from the submenu **(Figure 43)**.

4. Right-click/Ctrl-click the rectangle labeled "Drop first shader here", and choose Color from the pop-up menu **(Figure 44)**.

Figure 44. Right-click/Ctrl-click the rectangle labeled "Drop first shader here", and choose **Color** from the pop-up menu.

5. Double-click the red square that opened up in that rectangle to open the Color Dialog box **(Figure 45)**.

6. Specify a color with the sliders.

   or

   Click the Color Picker icon to select a color.

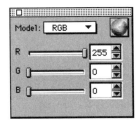

Figure 45. The Color dialog box.

7. Right-click/Ctrl-click the rectangle labeled "Drop second shader here", and choose Texture Map from the pop-up menu **(Figure 46)**.

8. Double-click the right rectangle to open the Texture Map box, and click the disk icon to open an image file.

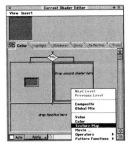

Figure 46. Right-click/Ctrl-click the rectangle labeled "Drop second shader here", and choose **Texture Map** from the pop-up menu.

Figure 47. Choose **Value** from the pop-up menu.

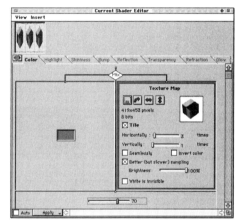

Figure 48. Adjust the slider bar under the Color tab of the Current Shader Editor window to blend the color and the texture map as desired.

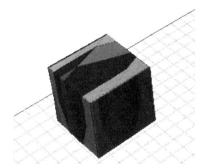

Figure 49. The shader has been applied to a cube primitive.

9. Right-click/Ctrl-click the rectangle labeled "Drop function here", and choose Value from the pop-up menu **(Figure 47)**.

10. Adjust the slider to blend the color and the texture map as desired **(Figure 48)**.

11. In the texture map rectangle, click the Orientation buttons to adjust the position of the bitmap on the surface of the shader.

12. Configure the shader's integration of the texture map by setting the following options in the Texture Map rectangle:

- To reorient the image on the shader's surface, click the Orientation buttons.

- To tile the image throughout the shader, place a check in the Tile checkbox and adjust the Horizontal and Vertical frequency sliders, the Seamlessly tile checkbox and the Invert Color option, the Better Sampling checkbox, the Brightness slider, and the White is invisible checkbox **(Figure 48)**.

13. Apply the shader to an object in your scene as described above **(Figure 49)**.

or

Save the shader to the Browser palette as described above.

Editing complex shaders

Frequently, a shader's channel setting is composed of a single element, such as a color, a bitmap image, or a value. But just as frequently, a channel can be comprised of a mixture of multiple elements, such as a blend between two colors, or a color and an image, or between a color and another shader. The Current Shader Editor window's View menu options, One Level, All Levels, Next Level, and Previous Level are used to display, hide, and navigate those levels.

To display single or multiple levels of the current shader's channel elements:

1. Click the tab of the channel that contains multiple levels of information (e.g., the Color tab for the Tennis Ball shader).

2. Choose One Level from the View menu **(Figures 50–51)**.

or

Choose All Levels from the View menu **(Figures 52–53)**.

To navigate the current shader's levels:

1. Choose Next Level from the View menu.

or

Choose Previous Level from the View menu.

The 3D objects to which shaders are applied can, of course, vary in shape and depth. You can visualize how a shader might appear if applied to a relatively flat object or a more volumetric object without spending the time needed to apply the shader and to preview the object. To do so, toggle the Current Shader Editor window's View window between its flat and spherical modes.

To preview the current shader as a flat square or sphere:

1. Choose Flat Preview from the View menu **(Figure 54)**.

or

Choose Sphere Preview from the View menu.

Figure 50. Choose **One Level** from the **View** menu.

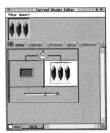

Figure 51. The One Level view of the current shader.

Figure 52. Choose **All Levels** from the **View** menu.

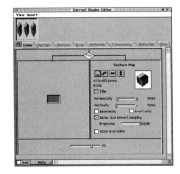

Figure 53. The All Levels view of the current shader.

Figure 54. Choose **Flat Preview** from the **View** menu.

Navigate the Current Shader's Levels

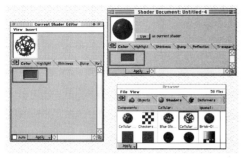

Figure 55. You can have the Browser palette, the Current Shader Editor window, and multiple Shader Document windows open all at once.

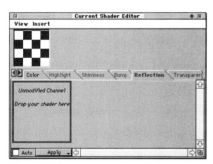

Figure 56. The stored or current shader used to replace the primer shader may contain some empty "unmodified" channels.

ADVANCED SHADER TOPICS

Managing multiple shader windows

It is possible to have all shader-related windows open at one time—e.g., the Browser palette, the Current Shader Editor window, and one or more Shader Document windows **(Figure 55)**.

Thus, the current shader (i.e., the shader that is displayed in the Current Shader Editor window), is not necessarily the shader that will be used in the next shader application. For example, clicking the Apply button in a particular window (e.g., in the Browser palette) applies the shader that is previewed in that window, even if a different shader is displayed in the Current Shader Editor window.

Primers and shaders

In the first section of this chapter, you learned that every 3D object is coated with a default "primer" shader, which has the same number of channels as any other shader.

The stored or current shader that is used to replace the primer shader may contain some empty "unmodified" channels (i.e., channels for which no value has been set) **(Figure 56)**. Ray Dream Studio gives you the option of controlling whether only the non-empty channels of the shader are used to replace the corresponding channels of the primer or whether all of the shader's channels (including the empty ones) are used to replace the primer's channels.

You can specify the default behavior (non-empty vs all channels) by specifying your choice in the Preferences area. The specified default preference is used whenever you shade a 3D object by dragging the shader's preview icon from, or clicking the Apply button in, either the Browser palette or the Current Shader Editor window.

Multiple Shader Windows

To specify the default apply behavior for the Shader Editor:

1. Choose Preferences from the File menu **(Figure 57)**.

2. Click Shader Editor from the drop-down list **(Figure 58)**.

3. In the Default Apply Mode area of the dialog box, check Apply Non-Empty Channels **(Figure 59)**.

   or

   Check Apply All Channels.

You can also override the default (or specify a particular method if you can't remember the default) when you operate the Apply button in either the Browser palette or the Current Shader Editor window.

To specify the apply behavior for a specific shader application:

1. In either the Browser palette or the Current Shader Editor window, click and hold the Apply button until a pop-up menu appears **(Figure 60)**.

2. Choose Apply Non-Empty Channels or Apply All Channels from the pop-up menu.

WORKING WITH 3D PAINT

Ray Dream's shader tools and techniques are a great way of applying surface characteristics to an entire 3D object.

But you can also apply a shader (or a series of shader layers) to only a portion of a 3D object, thanks to Ray Dream's 3D Paint tools.

Figure 57. Choose **Preferences** from the **File** menu.

Figure 58. Choose **Shader Editor** from the dropdown list.

Figure 59. Check Apply Non-Empty channels in the Default Apply Mode area of the **Preferences** dialog box.

Figure 60. Click and hold the Apply button in the Browser palette or Current Shader Editor window until a pop-up menu appears.

Specify the Apply Behavior for a Shader

Figure 61. Paint Shape Selection tool.

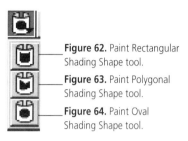

Figure 62. Paint Rectangular Shading Shape tool.

Figure 63. Paint Polygonal Shading Shape tool.

Figure 64. Paint Oval Shading Shape tool.

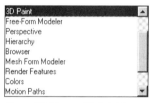

Figure 65. 3D Paint Brush tool.

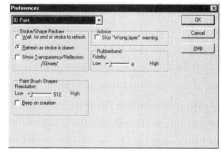

Figure 66. Choose **3D Paint** from the dropdown list.

Figure 67. In the **Preferences** dialog box, choose either "Wait to end of stroke refresh" or "Refresh as stroke is drawn".

Ray Dream offers five 3D paint tools:

- The Paint Shape Selection tool lets you select and navigate different 3D paint shapes **(Figure 61)**.

- The Paint Rectangular Shading Shape tool lets you apply 3D paint in a rectangular shape that you define with the mouse **(Figure 62)**.

- The Paint Polygonal Shading Shape tool lets you apply 3D paint in a polygonal shape that you define with the mouse **(Figure 63)**.

- The Paint Oval Shading Shape tool lets you apply 3D paint in an oval or circular shape that you define with the mouse **(Figure 64)**.

- The 3D Paint Brush tool lets you apply 3D paint with individual brush strokes that you define with the mouse **(Figure 65)**.

Before using these tools, it is a good idea to set some preferences to balance preview quality and drawing precision with preview speed.

To set preferences for 3D paint operations:

1. Choose Preferences from the File menu.

2. In the dropdown list box, choose 3D Paint **(Figure 66)**.

3. In the Preferences dialog box, choose "Wait to end of stroke to refresh" to increase preview speed.

or

Choose "Refresh as stroke is drawn" to increase preview quality **(Figure 67)**.

4. Place a check in the Show Transparency/Reflection (Slower) checkbox to increase preview quality.

or

Remove the check from that box to improve preview speed.

5. Increase the Paint Brush Shapes Resolution slider and the Rubber Band Fidelity slider settings to increase painting precision.

or

Decrease those slider settings to increase preview speed.

Applying preset 3D paint shapes

The Rectangular, Polygonal, and Oval shader shape tools work similarly to each other.

To apply a rectangular, polygonal, or oval 3D Paint shape to a 3D object:

1. Make sure that the 3D object to which the 3D paint shape will be applied is visible in the Perspective window.

2. Set the current shader to be applied as 3D paint with one of the following methods:

Click a stored shader in the Browser palette.

or

Click the "Use as current shader button" in any displayed Shader Document window.

or

Grab any applied shader from any 3D object displayed in the Scene with the Eyedropper tool.

3. Click the currently visible 3D paint shape tool repeatedly until the desired tool appears.

or

Click and hold the currently visible 3D paint shape tool until a pop-up toolbar appears, and drag the mouse to the desired tool **(Figure 68)**.

4. To shade the area that will be enclosed by the selection you draw, click the mouse in the top-left corner of the area to be shaded.

Figure 68. Select the desired tool from the **Paint Shape** pop-up toolbar.

Apply a 3D Paint Shape to a 3D Object

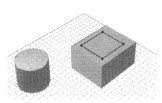

Figure 69. Drag the mouse on a surface of an object to draw the outline of the selected paint shape (rectangle in this case).

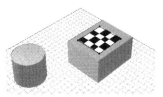

Figure 70. Release the mouse to shade the surface (in this case, the Checkers shader is used).

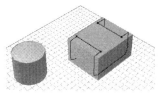

Figures 71–72. Hold the Alt/Option key while dragging to draw the paint shape as if it were connected around the back of the object.

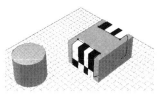

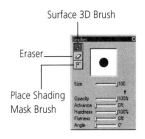

Surface 3D Brush

Eraser

Place Shading Mask Brush

Figure 73. 3D Paint Brush tool.

Figure 74. The **3D Paint Brush tool** dialog box.

and

Drag the mouse to the bottom right corner of the area to be shaded **(Figure 69)**.

and

Release the mouse **(Figure 70)**.

5. To shade the area that would be enclosed if the starting and ending points of the selection you draw were connected around the "back" of the 3D object, repeat Step 4, and hold the Alt/Option key while dragging the mouse **(Figures 71–72)**.

The 3D Paint Brush tool

The 3D Paint Brush tool **(Figure 73)** works quite differently than do the preset paint shape tools.

This tool lets you:

- Select from the following options:

  - The Surface 3D Brush, which applies the current shader to a 3D object the way a regular paint brush applies paint.

  - The Eraser **(Figure 74)**, which removes existing layers of 3D paint that were originally applied with the Surface 3D Brush, or were applied with a another 3D paint tool and then later converted to a brushed 3D paint shape.

  - The Place Shading Mask Brush, which imports a 2D image file that you specify as a mask, and applies the current shader to the darker areas of the image to the surface of the 3D object.

  - Adjust the following settings for Surface 3D Brush and the Eraser:

3D Paint Shapes, 3D Paint Brush Tool

- The Size of the brush.
- The Opacity with which the current shader will be applied or removed **(Figure 75)**.
- The Advance—i.e., the tendency of the brush or eraser to "skip" as it is dragged along the 3D object's surface.
- The Flatness of the brush or eraser, from perfectly flat, like a house painter's brush, to perfectly round, like an artist's paint brush.
- The Angle of the stroke, relative to the direction of the stroke, to make it act like a calligraphy pen or eraser.
- The Hardness—i.e., the pressure with which the Surface 3D Brush, the Eraser, or the imported 2D image brush shape is applied to the 3D object.

Figure 75. Set the Opacity setting in the **3D Paint Brush tool** dialog box with which the current shader will be applied or removed.

Using the Surface 3D Brush

To apply a 3D paint shape to a 3D object with the 3D Paint Brush tool:

1. Display the target 3D object in the Perspective window **(Figure 76)**, and set the current shader as described in Step 2 of the preceding section.
2. Click the 3D Paint Brush tool.
3. In the Brushes dialog box, click the Surface 3D Brush button.
4. Adjust the Size, Opacity, Advance, Hardness, Flatness, and Angle sliders as desired.
5. Click and drag the mouse over a 3D object to apply the paint, eraser, or masking strokes as desired **(Figure 77)**.

✔ **Tip**

■ A 3D paint shape may contain only one shader.

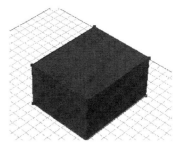

Figure 76. Display the object in the Perspective window that you wish to paint with the 3D Paint Brush tool.

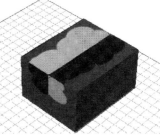

Figure 77. Drag over the 3D object in the Perspective window to apply the paint with the 3D Paint Brush tool (the Checkers shader is the current shader here).

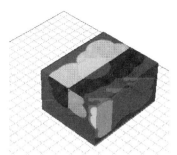

Figure 78. You can apply additional brush strokes outside the original area with the Surface 3D Brush.

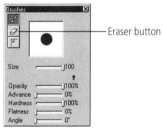

Eraser button

Figure 79. Click the Eraser button in the **3D Paint Brush tool** dialog box.

To add more 3D paint to an existing 3D paint shape created with the Surface 3D Brush:

1. Set the current shader to the shader of the 3D paint shape by clicking the 3D paint shape with the Eyedropper tool.

2. Click the 3D Paint Brush tool, select the Surface 3D Brush, and adjust its settings as described above.

3. Click within the area of the 3D paint shape.

4. Apply strokes as described above.

5. Brush strokes can be applied outside the original area of the 3D paint shape to expand its size **(Figure 78)**.

Using the Eraser

The Eraser is used to remove a painted shape.

1. Click the 3D Paint Brush tool.

2. In the Brushes dialog box, click the Eraser button **(Figure 79)**.

3. Adjust the Size, Opacity, Advance, Hardness, Flatness, and Angle sliders as desired.

4. Click and drag the mouse over a 3D object to apply the paint, eraser, or masking strokes as desired.

✔ Tip

■ The Eraser tool can be applied only to brushed paint shapes. To use this tool on shapes created with other tools, follow the steps described below to select and convert the shape to a brushed shape.

Using an imported brush shape

You can also import a 2D image file to serve as a brush shape. The imported brush shape feature acts like a painting mask. The colors of the image are ignored. The relative darkness and lightness of different areas of the image act like the cut-out areas of the mask that will permit the current shader to soak through to the surface of the 3D object.

Figure 80. Click the Place Shading Mask button in the **3D Paint Brush tool** dialog box.

To use an imported brush shape:

1. Display the target 3D object in the Perspective window and set the current shader as described in Step 2 on page 184.

2. Click the 3D Paint Brush tool.

3. In the Brushes dialog box, click the Place Shading Mask button **(Figure 80)**.

4. Click and drag the mouse to define the area to which the mask will be applied **(Figure 81)**.

5. In the Open dialog box, select the 2D bitmap image file to be used for the mask **(Figure 82)**.

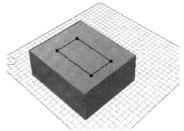

Figure 81. Drag to define the area to which the mask will be applied.

Working with 3D paint shapes and layers

You can perform the following types of operations with 3D paint shapes and layers:

- Select, move, resize, delete, and convert 3D paint shapes.

- Select, move, resize, delete, and rearrange 3D paint shape layers.

You can perform these operations on a 3D shape either by acting on it directly with the mouse and keyboard, or by adjusting its specific settings in the Shaders tab of the Properties palette.

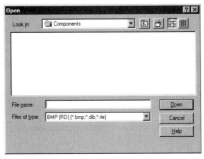

Figure 82. Select the 2D bitmap image file to be used as the mask.

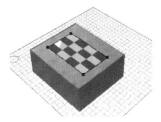

Figure 83. Paint Shape Selection tool.

Figure 84. Click the target 3D paint shape to select it.

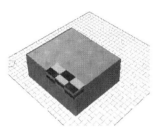

Figure 85. Move the 3D paint shape by dragging it.

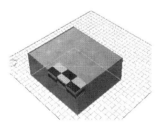

Figure 86. Click the object that contains the paint shapes on which you wish to operate.

Figure 87. Display the settings for each 3D paint shape by clicking the plus symbol (arrow on the Mac).

To manage 3D paint shapes with the mouse and keyboard:

1. Click the Paint Shape Selection tool **(Figure 83)**.

2. Click the target 3D paint shape to select it **(Figure 84)**.

3. To move the selected shape manually, drag it with the mouse **(Figure 85)**.

4. To resize the selected shape, reposition the handles on its bounding box.

5. To move a paint shape to the top layer or the bottom layer, choose Paint Shapes from the Arrange menu and click To Front or To Back on the submenu.

6. To delete the selected shape, press the Delete key.

or

Choose Cut from the Edit menu.

To manage 3D paint shapes and layers with the Properties palette:

1. Click the Selection tool.

2. Click the 3D object that contains the paint shapes on which you wish to operate **(Figure 86)**.

3. Display the Properties palette by choosing Properties from the Windows menu.

and

Click the Shading tab of the Properties palette.

4. To display the settings for each 3D paint shape, click the yellow plus symbol (arrow on the Mac) that appears to the left of each "element" label **(Figure 87)**.

5. Compare the shader and shape of each paint shape on the 3D object with the shader and shape of each element in the Properties palette to determine which shape on the object corresponds to which element in the palette.

Manage 3D Paint Shapes

6. To reposition a shape, change the values in its h and v fields.

7. To resize a shape, change the values in its width and height fields.

8. To delete a shape, click its element label.

and

Press the Delete key.

or

Choose Cut from the Edit menu.

9. To adjust a paint shape's opacity, adjust the Opacity slider.

10. To change the layering order of two or more 3D paint shapes, collapse any element levels that are expanded by clicking its Minus sign.

and

Click the element label of a shape to be moved to a new layer position.

and

Drag it up or down to its new position.

11. To convert a paint shape's type, click the button in the Shape dropdown list and select a different type of shape **(Figures 88–89)**.

12. To edit the shader used to shade the paint shape in the Current Shader Editor window, set the current shader to the shape's shader with the Eyedropper tool as described earlier in this chapter.

and

Edit the shader in the Current Shader Editor window as desired.

and

Click the Apply button in the Current Shader Editor window.

or

Drag the shader preview from the Current Shader Editor window to the shader preview in the paint shape's element detail in the Properties palette.

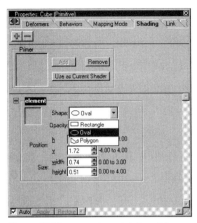

Figure 88. You convert a paint shape's type by clicking and selecting a new type from the **Shape** dropdown list.

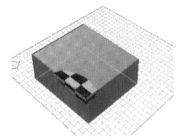

Figure 89. The rectangular paint shape has been converted to an oval shape.

✔ **Tip**

■ If you encounter an error message when attempting to undo the editing of an element's shader, try repeating the undo operation a second time.

PREVIEWING AND RENDERING THE EFFECTS OF SHADERS AND 3D PAINT

Obviously, a Wireframe preview does not display the effects of a shader, since the Wireframe view temporarily makes all surfaces transparent. One of the other preview modes—Fast Preview, Shaded Preview, or Better Preview—is required to display the entire scene or to render a selection from the scene.

✔ **Tips**

■ Performance can be improved by working in Wireframe mode whenever possible.

■ 3D paint performance can be improved by using the 3D paint preferences that optimize performance over preview quality and shading precision, as outlined earlier in this chapter.

■ Certain operations, such as the application of brushed 3D paint shapes with the Surface 3D Brush option for the 3D Paint tool, require the use of the Better Preview mode and prompt you to switch to that mode.

Preview and Render Shaders, 3D Paint

Using the Render Area tool

Another way to save rendering time is to render selected areas of an object or scene with the Render Area tool **(Figure 90)**.

To use the Render Area tool:

1. Make the Perspective window the current window.

2. Click the Render Area tool.

3. Click and drag the mouse to define the rectangular area to be rendered **(Figures 91–92)**.

✓ Tips

■ The selected area will be previewed in a view that is slightly better than the Better Preview.

■ Dragging a window (such as the Properties palette) over the rendered area and then moving the window away may have the effect of wiping out the rendering and restoring it to the current default preview level.

Figure 90. Render Area tool.

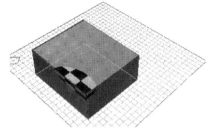

Figure 91. An oval paint shape on a rectangle is shown before using the Render Area tool.

Figure 92. After using the Render Area tool.

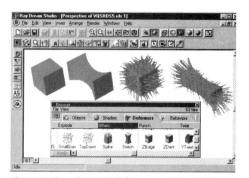

Figure 1. The cube on the left was created with the Mesh Form Modeler and then duplicated three times in the Perspective window. A Stretch type deformer was applied to the second cube. A Spike type deformer was applied to the third cube. The fourth cube was deformed with the same Stretch deformer and then placed into a group by itself. A Spike deformer was then applied to the group.

A deformer can be defined as a set of characteristics that you can apply to a 3D object to alter the appearance of its geometric shape **(Figure 1)**.

Although the application of a deformer may appear to alter the actual shape of an object or to convert it into multiple objects, it does not alter the actual geometry of the target object. You can verify this by inspecting an object with its native modeling tool before and after the application of a deformer.

Comparing deformers with shaders

The selection, editing, application, and management of deformers is similar, but not identical, to the selection, editing, application, and management of shaders. If you have already worked through the shaders chapter, you will recognize many familiar themes, and as you work through this chapter, you will learn the deformers' variations on those themes.

Deformer states

Like shaders, deformers can exist in several different states. A deformer's state determines what Ray Dream permits you to do with it.

- A stored deformer is one that you access through the Deformers tab in the Browser palette. Stored deformers are "housed" in different families of deformers that correspond to different directories on your system's hard disk **(Figure 2)**.

Figure 2. The Deformers tab of the Browser palette.

- A Deformer document is the disk file that contains a stored deformer's settings. Deformer documents can be accessed via the Browser palette **(Figure 3)**.
- An applied deformer is a deformer that has already been applied to an object **(Figure 4)**.

✔ Tip

- There is no deformer state that is equivalent to the current shader state. This is because there is no deformer analog to the Current Shader Editor window.

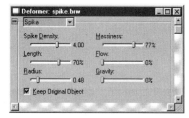

Figure 3. The Deformer Document window for a Spike deformer named "spike.brw."

Also like shaders, deformers can be applied and managed with several different techniques, depending upon their state:

- Stored deformers can be browsed, inspected, edited, applied, duplicated, and deleted with the Browser palette.
- Deformer documents can be created or accessed with the Browser palette, edited, saved, applied to objects, and used to create new stored deformers.
- Applied deformers can be edited, applied to other objects, and used to create new stored deformers.

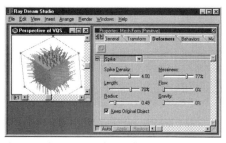

Figure 4. The applied deformer for the currently selected object.

How deformers and shaders differ

Some differences between shaders and deformers are worth noting:

- Deformers cannot be applied in layers in the way that shaders can be applied in layers with 3D paint.
- A single, ungrouped object can be deformed with only one deformer at a time **(Figure 5)**.

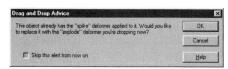

Figure 5. When you try to add a second deformer to an object that already has already been deformed, Ray Dream prompts you to replace the original applied deformer or to cancel the operation.

Figure 6. To add a second deformer to an already deformed object, group the object by itself with the **Arrange/Group** menu command and then apply the deformer to that group.

Figure 7. A cube deformed with an Atomize type of deformer.

Figure 8. A cube deformed with a Bend and Twist type of deformer.

Figure 9. A cube deformed with a Black Hole type of deformer.

Figure 10. A cube deformed with a Dissolve type of deformer.

Figure 11. A cube deformed with an Explode type of deformer.

Figure 12. A cube deformed with a Formula type of deformer.

Figure 13. A cube deformed with a Punch type of deformer.

Figure 14. A cube deformed with a Shatter type of deformer.

- A single object can, however, be placed in a group, to which a second deformer can be applied **(Figure 6)**.

- Multiple deformers cannot be mixed to create a new deformer, as can be done with shaders.

- Unlike shaders, which are all of a single type, there are many different types of deformers, as detailed below.

Deformer types

Ray Dream Studio 5 supports 13 different types of deformers. Each type represents a specific visual, volumetric characteristic, such as a twist, a stretch, or a squash.

- The Atomize type of deformer replaces an object's surfaces with tiny spheres that can be thought of as atoms or droplets **(Figure 7)**.

- The Bend and Twist type of deformer twists an object around an axis and bends the object away from that axis **(Figure 8)**.

- The Black Hole type of deformer transforms an object into a swirling vortex, like that of draining water or funnel cloud **(Figure 9)**.

- The Dissolve type of deformer makes an object disappear by transforming it into polygons and then reducing those polygons until they disappear **(Figure 10)**.

- The Explode type of deformer transforms an object into a number of smaller pieces, as if they had exploded **(Figure 11)**.

- The Formula type of deformer deforms an object according to a mathematical formula that you supply **(Figure 12)**.

- The Punch type of deformer places a dent in the object **(Figure 13)**.

- The Shatter type of deformer breaks objects created with the Mesh Form Modeler along their edges **(Figure 14)**.

Deformer Types

- The Spherical Morph type of deformer rounds the edges of an object to make it more sphere-like **(Figure 15)**.
- The Spike type of deformer adds conical protrusions to the surface of an object **(Figure 16)**.
- The Stretch type of deformer elongates and buckles an object to simulate stretching, or shortens and bulges an object to simulate squashing **(Figure 17)**.
- The Warp type of deformer expands an object's outer regions and compresses its inner regions to simulate the shrinkage and expansion of moisture-induced warping **(Figure 18)**.
- The Wave type of deformer introduces planar, radial, or cylindrical waves into an object **(Figure 19)**.

In the next three sections of this chapter, you will learn how to browse, inspect, duplicate, move, delete, apply, edit, remove, and create deformers. In the last section of this chapter, you will learn how to configure the settings for each of the different types of deformers.

WORKING WITH STORED DEFORMERS

Ray Dream Studio 5 ships with dozens of preconfigured stored deformers. These "stock" deformers provide an excellent way to learn how to use and manage deformers.

Browsing stored deformers

You can easily browse stored deformers with the Browser palette.

Figure 15. A cube deformed with a Spherical Morph type of deformer.

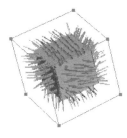

Figure 16. A cube deformed with a Spike type of deformer.

Figure 17. A cube deformed with a Stretch type of deformer.

Figure 18. A cube deformed with a Warp type of deformer.

Figure 19. A cube deformed with a Wave type of deformer.

Figure 20. Scroll the tabs with the arrow buttons, and scroll the deformer families with the horizontal scroll bar at the bottom of the Browser palette.

Figure 21. Right-click/Ctrl-click a deformer's icon, and choose **Get Info** from the pop-up menu.

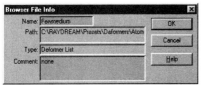

Figure 22. Inspect and edit basic information about a stored deformer with the **Browser File** dialog box.

Figure 23. Select the deformer to be duplicated.

Figure 24. The **Duplicate** command is in the **File** menu of the Browser palette.

To browse the stored deformers:

1. If it is not already visible, display the Browser palette by choosing Browser from the Windows menu.

2. Click the tab arrows to navigate the Browser palette's tabs.

3. Click the Deformers tab.

4. Widen and scroll the window to see the various deformer families and the deformers they contain **(Figure 20)**.

Getting basic information about a stored deformer

As is the case with shaders, you may need to retrieve or edit information about a stored deformer or its corresponding Deformer document disk file.

To get basic information about a stored deformer:

1. Right-click/Ctrl-click the deformer's icon in the Browser palette.

2. Choose Get Info from the pop-up menu **(Figure 21)**.

3. Inspect and edit the name and comment fields, and inspect the file name and path fields for the deformer **(Figure 22)**.

4. Click OK to save the changes.

or

Click Cancel to discard any changes.

Duplicating a stored deformer

Like shaders, deformers can be duplicated from within the Browser palette.

To duplicate a stored deformer:

1. Click the stored deformer's icon in the Browser palette **(Figure 23)**.

2. Choose Duplicate File from the File menu in the Browser **(Figure 24)**.

or

Right-click/Ctrl-click the stored deformer's icon, and choose Duplicate File from the pop-up menu.

3. Note the name that was automatically supplied by Ray Dream for the new stored browser **(Figure 25)**.

4. If you wish to change that name, use the "Get basic information" procedure described above to inspect and replace the name.

5. If you wish to relocate the new stored browser to a different family, use the procedure described below for moving stored deformers.

Moving a stored deformer to another family

Stored deformers are organized in families whose names appear directly under the main tabs of the Browser palette. The name for each family of deformers is derived from the disk directory in which its member Deformer documents are located. The names of these families generally correspond to the different types of deformers. However, you can store any type of deformer in any deformer family you wish.

You can scroll these families with the horizontal scroll bar located at the bottom of the Browser palette. Moving a stored deformer from one family also moves the stored deformer's Deformer document to the disk directory that corresponds to the new host family.

To move a stored deformer to another family of stored deformers:

1. Display and size the Deformers tab of the Browser palette as described above.

2. Scroll the Browser palette window with the vertical scroll bar and with the horizontal scroll bar at the bottom of the palette until both the stored deformer to be moved and the family to which it is to be moved are both visible.

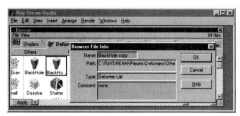

Figure 25. Ray Dream automatically adds "copy" to the name of the new deformer.

Figure 26. Drag the icon of the deformer to be moved to a new deformer family in the Browser palette.

Figure 27. The Browser palette automatically updates to show the deformer in its new family.

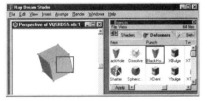

Figure 28. Drag the stored deformer to an object.

Figure 29. The deformer is applied when the mouse is released.

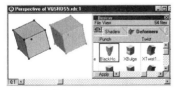

Figure 30. Select one or more objects in the Time Line or Perspective window to which the currently selected stored deformer will be applied.

3. Click the icon or name of the stored deformer to be moved.

4. Without releasing the mouse, drag the icon to the new family **(Figure 26)**.

5. Release the mouse button **(Figure 27)**.

Applying a stored deformer to an object

You can apply a stored deformer to a 3D object in your scene with either the drag and drop technique or the Apply button technique.

To apply a stored deformer to an object with the drag and drop method:

1. Click the preview icon for the desired deformer in the Browser palette.

2. Without releasing the mouse, drag the deformer's icon onto the target object or group in the Perspective window or in the Objects tab of the Time Line window **(Figure 28)**.

3. Release the mouse to apply the deformer **(Figure 29)**.

✔ Tip

■ Use the No Preview or Wireframe preview to accelerate screen redraws.

To apply a stored deformer to an object:

1. Select single or multiple target objects or groups in the Perspective window or in the Objects tab of the Time Line window **(Figure 30)**.

2. Click the icon for the desired deformer in the Browser palette.

3. Click the Apply button in the Browser palette.

Apply a Deformer to an Object

Applying a second deformer to an object

If you attempt to apply a second deformer to an ungrouped object or objects, you will be prompted either to cancel the operation or to replace the existing deformer.

You can, however, apply two deformers to one or more objects if you first group them together.

To apply a second deformer to one or more objects:

1. Select the object or objects in the Perspective window or in the Objects tab of the Time Line window (**Figure 31**).

2. Choose Group from the Arrange menu.

3. Select the second deformer to be applied in the Browser palette.

4. Apply the second deformer to the new group with either the drag and drop method or the Apply button method outlined above (**Figure 32**).

Creating a new stored deformer from scratch

A new stored deformer can easily be created from scratch within the Browser palette.

To create a new stored deformer:

1. Click the Deformers tab of the Browser palette.

2. Choose New Document from the File menu of the Browser palette (**Figure 33**).

3. Adjust the windows on your screen so that you can see the Deformer document that was just opened (**Figure 34**).

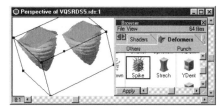

Figure 31. Select multiple objects by holding the Shift key while clicking them in the Perspective window or the Time Line window, and select the second deformer to be applied in the Browser palette.

Figure 32. These cubes have now been deformed with both a Black Hole type of deformer and a Spike type of deformer.

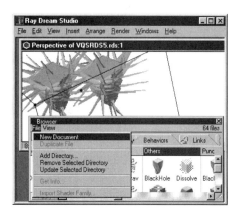

Figure 33. Choose **New Document** from the Browser palette's **File** menu.

Figure 34. The Deformer Document window.

Apply a Second Deformer to an Object

Figure 35. Specify the new deformer's type and adjust its settings.

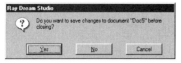

Figure 36. Click Yes to save the new document to the deformer family that is currently selected in the Browser palette.

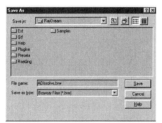

Figure 37. In the **Save As** dialog box, select the directory that corresponds to the deformer family that will host the new stored deformer.

Figure 38. The target deformer family is automatically updated with information about its latest addition.

Figure 39. To open a stored deformer's Deformer document, double-click its icon in the Browser palette.

Figure 40. The Deformer Document window.

4. Specify the deformer type from the 13 types listed in the dropdown list box, and adjust the sliders and field entries as desired, using the guidelines set forth in the last section of this chapter **(Figure 35)**.

5. Close the Deformer Document window.

6. In the dialog box that appears, click Yes to save the new deformer **(Figure 36)**.

7. In the Save As dialog box, navigate to the disk folder that corresponds to the family of deformers in the Browser palette which will host the new stored deformer **(Figure 37)**.

8. In the Browser palette, navigate to and scroll the target deformer family to verify that the new stored browser appears there **(Figure 38)**.

WORKING WITH DEFORMER DOCUMENTS

As noted earlier this chapter, a stored deformer's settings are saved in a disk file. Ray Dream refers to this file as a Deformer document. As described below, you can access, edit, save, and copy Deformer documents and apply their settings to 3D objects in scenes.

Browsing and editing Deformer documents

Deformer documents are accessed with the Deformers tab of the Browser palette.

To open and edit a stored deformer's Deformer document:

1. Double-click the deformer's icon in the Browser palette **(Figure 39)**.

2. Adjust the windows on your screen so that the Deformer document window is visible **(Figure 40)**.

3. Specify the deformer type from the 13 types listed in the dropdown list box **(Figure 41)**.

4. Adjust the sliders and field entries as desired, using the guidelines set forth in the last section of this chapter **(Figure 42)**.

5. Close the window and specify whether to save any changes made to the settings **(Figure 43)**.

✔ Tips

■ Unlike changes to shader documents, changes to Deformer documents cannot be previewed in the Deformer Document window.

■ The only way to observe the effects of editing a deformer's settings is to apply it to an object (a dummy object, if necessary), and to perform the edits in the Deformers tab of the object's Properties palette, as discussed below.

■ If you change the deformer type specified in a Deformer document, it is a good idea to move the icon for its corresponding stored deformer to the appropriate deformer family in the Browser palette.

Applying a Deformer document's settings to an object

Unlike the Shaders Document window, the Deformer Document window contains no Apply button. Thus, only the drag and drop method can be used to apply a deformer contained in a Deformer document to an object.

To apply a Deformer document's deformer to an object:

1. If it is collapsed, expand the rectangular deformer settings area by clicking the plus sign (arrow on the Mac) next to the deformer type field.

2. Click any empty portion of the settings area **(Figure 44)**.

Figure 41. Change the deformer's type, if desired.

Figure 42. Adjust the deformer's settings.

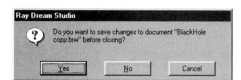

Figure 43. Save or discard your changes to the Deformer document.

Figure 44. Clicking within the settings area and holding the mouse down creates a selection outline around the selection area, indicating that it can be dragged and dropped.

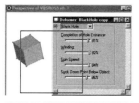

Figure 45. Drag the outline to the target object and release the mouse when the pointer turns to an arrow.

Figure 46. Setting the Completion of Hole Entrance slider to a high value causes this cube to nearly disappear.

Figure 47. Double-click the stored deformer's icon in the Browser palette to open its corresponding Deformer document.

Figure 48. Click the plus sign (arrow on the Mac) to expand the settings area.

Figure 49. Drag the Deformer document's settings area to family of stored deformers.

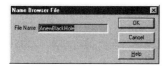

Figure 50. Name the new stored deformer.

3. Without releasing the mouse, drag the entire rectangle onto the target object in either the Perspective window or the Hierarchy window **(Figure 45)**.

4. Release the mouse **(Figure 46)**.

Creating a new stored deformer from an existing Deformer document

Any opened Deformer document can be used to create one or more new stored deformers.

To create a new stored deformer from a Deformer document:

1. Open the source Deformer document by double-clicking the icon in the Browser palette for its corresponding stored browser **(Figure 47)**.

2. Click the Browser palette's Deformers tab.

3. If the rectangular deformer settings area is collapsed, expand it by clicking the plus sign (arrow on the Mac) next to the deformer type field **(Figure 48)**.

4. Click on any empty portion of the settings area.

5. Without releasing the mouse, drag the entire rectangle into the deformer family in the Deformers tab of the Browser palette that will host it **(Figure 49)**.

6. Release the mouse button.

7. In the Name Browser File dialog box, enter the name of the new stored browser, and click OK **(Figure 50)**.

8. Verify the creation of the new stored deformer by scrolling the Browser palette to display the host family and its new member.

✔ Tip

■ The host family can be either the same family as the original stored deformer or a different one.

Create a New Stored Deformer

WORKING WITH APPLIED DEFORMERS

Applied deformers, like applied shaders, can be accessed, edited, and reapplied to other objects with a number of different techniques.

Inspecting and editing applied deformers

Just as an applied shader can be edited in the Current Shader Editor window, an applied deformer can be edited in the Deformers tab of the object's Properties palette.

Unlike the Shaders tab, the Deformers tab does not provide a preview. To see what a deformer actually looks like, you must apply it to the object itself.

To edit an applied deformer with the Properties palette:

1. Select the host object in either the Perspective window or the Hierarchy window.

2. If it is not already displayed, display the object's Properties palette by choosing Properties from the Windows menu.

3. Click the Deformers tab in the Properties palette **(Figure 51)**.

4. To observe the effects on the object immediately after a change is made, place a check mark in the Auto checkbox at the bottom of the Properties palette.

or

To apply changes manually with the Apply button, remove the check mark from the Auto option and click Apply.

5. If it is collapsed, expand the deformer settings region by clicking the plus sign (arrow on the Mac) next to the deformer type field.

Figure 51. Click the Deformers tab in the **Properties** palette.

Figure 52. Choose the deformer type.

Figure 53. Adjust the settings for the deformer.

Figure 54. The Show-Hide Direct Manipulation button.

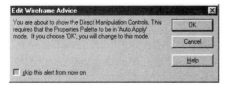

Figure 55. The **Edit Wireframe Advice** dialog box.

6. Specify the deformer type from the 13 types listed in the dropdown list box **(Figure 52)**.

7. Adjust the sliders and field entries as desired, using the guidelines set forth in the last section of this chapter **(Figure 53)**.

8. If the Auto checkbox is not checked, click the Restore button to undo all settings made since you last pressed the Apply button.

9. If the Auto checkbox is not checked, click the Apply button to apply the changes to the object.

You can also manipulate certain types of applied deformers more directly with bounding box handles. The following types of applied deformers can be directly manipulated:

- Bend and twist
- Punch
- Shatter
- Stretch
- Wave

✔ **Tip**

- When editing any of these types of deformers, the Show-Hide Direct Manipulation toggle button becomes enabled **(Figure 54)**.

To edit an applied deformer's settings directly:

1. Access the Deformers tab of the host object's Properties palette, as described in Steps 1-6 in the preceding procedure for editing an applied deformer.

2. Click the Show-Hide Direct Manipulation button.

3. If the Edit Wireframe Advice dialog box appears, click OK to place the Properties palette into Auto apply mode **(Figure 55)**.

4. Click and adjust the bounding box handles that are displayed on the host object to customize the deformer's settings **(Figure 56)**.

5. Click the Show-Hide Direct Manipulation button to close the deformer's bounding box handles.

Applying an applied deformer to another object

You can directly apply one object's applied deformer to another object with the drag and drop method.

To apply one object's applied deformer to another object:

1. Select the source object in the Perspective or Hierarchy window.

2. Display the Deformers tab of the object's Properties palette.

3. Size or scroll the Perspective or Time Line window so that the object to be deformed is visible, but do not select that object.

4. Click any empty section of the deformer settings area.

or

If the settings are collapsed, click between the plus button (arrow on the Mac) and the deformer type field.

5. Without releasing the mouse, drag the entire rectangle onto the target object **(Figure 57)**.

6. Release the mouse button.

7. Verify the application by selecting only the target object in the Perspective or Hierarchy window and inspecting the deformer settings in the Deformers tab of its Properties palette **(Figure 58)**.

✔ Tip

■ You can, of course, edit the just-applied settings without disturbing the deformer settings in the source object.

Figure 56. To adjust a Punch type deformer, drag the outer handles to adjust the radius of the punch and drag the center handle left or right to punch inward or outward.

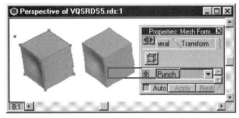

Figure 57. The left cube's applied deformer is dragged to the cube on the right.

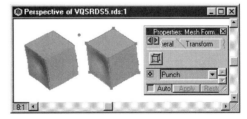

Figure 58. The right cube is selected to display its newly applied deformer.

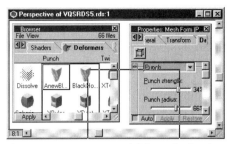

Figure 59. Create a new stored deformer by dragging the applied deformer's settings area to the desired deformer family in the Browser palette.

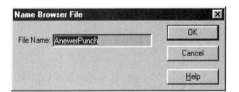

Figure 60. Name the new stored browser.

Creating a new stored deformer from an applied deformer

Once you have edited an applied deformer, you can save it to a new stored deformer for reuse with other objects in the present scene or in other scenes.

To create a new stored deformer from an applied deformer:

1. Select the host object in the Perspective or Hierarchy window.

2. Display the object's Properties palette, and click the Deformers tab.

3. Click any empty section of the deformer settings area.

or

If the settings are collapsed, click between the plus button (arrow on the Mac) and the deformer type field.

4. Click on any empty portion of the settings area.

5. Without releasing the mouse, drag the entire rectangle into the target directory in the Deformers tab of the Browser palette **(Figure 59)**.

6. Release the mouse button.

7. In the Name Browser File dialog box, enter the name of the new stored deformer and click OK **(Figure 60)**.

Removing an applied deformer

Removing an applied deformer from an object is simply a matter of changing the deformer type specified in the Deformers tab of the object's Properties palette to "None".

To remove an applied deformer:

1. Select the object in either the Perspective or Time Line window.

2. Display the Deformers tab of the object's Properties palette.

3. Click the button in the dropdown list of deformer types to open the list.

4. Click "None" and release the mouse **(Figure 61)**.

Guidelines for editing deformers

In a moment you will learn a number of guidelines that will help you understand and adjust the specific settings for each of the 13 different types of deformers.

To follow along on your system, make the following preparations.

Before using the guidelines below, we suggest that you make these preparations **(Figure 62)**:

1. Create a cube primitive called "Left Cube" with a deformer type of None, and copy it to form a second object called "Right Cube."

2. Using the Wireframe or Fast Preview, align the objects in the Perspective window and size that window as shown.

3. Display and position the Objects tab of the Time Line window as shown.

4. Display, size, and position the Deformers tab of the Properties palette as shown.

5. Select the left cube by clicking on its name in the Time Line window.

6. Set the Left Cube's deformer type to the type you want to learn, and click the Apply button.

7. Adjust the slider or enter the value for the first setting you want to learn, and click the Apply button again.

8. Apply the Left Cube's applied deformer to the Right Cube by dragging the Left Cube's settings area to the Right Cube's name in the Time Line window.

9. Select the Right Cube by itself by clicking on its name in the Time Line window.

Figure 61. To remove an applied deformer from the currently selected object, set its deformer type to None.

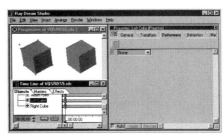

Figure 62. Preparing the A-B comparison work space for exploring the interaction of various deformer settings.

Guidelines for Editing Deformers

Figure 63. The Left Cube uses a high Particle Density setting of 8.1 (resulting in coverage of most of the cube's surface with atoms) and a low Size of Particles setting of 1.0 (resulting in usage of a small atom size). The Right Cube uses "opposite" settings, as shown in the illustration, which result in reduced surface coverage, enlarged atoms, and a greatly enlarged bounding box.

10. Increase the setting you are learning, click the Apply button, and notice how the Left Cube now differs in appearance from the Right Cube.

11. If necessary, use the Better Preview to visualize the differences.

12. To experiment with a different setting, set the deformer type and repeat Steps 5-11.

✔ Tips

■ The Time Line window is useful because it makes it easier to change the currently selected object and to access a target object in a drag and drop procedure.

■ When alternating between preview qualities, click the title bar of the Perspective window to access its View menu. After setting the preview quality, redisplay the Time Line window by choosing Time Line from the Windows menu.

■ For many settings, using the highest or lowest possible values—e.g., a 0% Completion of Explosion for an Explode type of deformer, or a 100% Particle Density for an Atomize type of deformer—may produce nondetectable changes. This problem is solved by avoiding the use of maximum and minimum values.

■ You will also benefit by adjusting the settings for any given deformer type in the order set forth below, rather than in the order in which they appear in the settings area of the Properties palette or Deformer Document window.

To adjust the settings of an Atomize deformer:

1. Set the Particle Density slider **(Figure 63)** to a setting between 10 (which covers the entire surface of the object with atoms) and 0 (which prevents any part of the surface from being covered with atoms).

2. Set the Size of Particles slider to a set-ting between 10 (which maximizes the size of the atoms) and 0 (which minimizes the size of the atoms).

3. When animating the Atomize deformer, increase or decrease the Completion of Wiggle Effect slider between 0% and 600% at different points in the timeline to control the motion of the atoms. For example, to animate the complete range of motion, set a 0% completion value for the first frame, and a 100% value for the final frame.

✔ **Tip**

■ Using large Size of Particle settings can cause the object's apparent vol-ume to increase dramatically.

To adjust the settings of a Bend and Twist deformer:

1. Select the axis around which the object will be twisted.

2. Adjust the Twist Start slider **(Figure 64)** to set the position along the spec-ified axis at which the twisting or bending should begin. This position is expressed as a percentage of the object's length, depth, or height along the specified axis. For example, to start the twist at the midpoint of the object's "height" along the Z axis, enter 50%.

3. Adjust the Twist slider to a setting between 0 and 180 degrees to twist the object in one direction (e.g., clockwise around the Z axis) or between 0 and –180 degrees to twist it in the opposite direction.

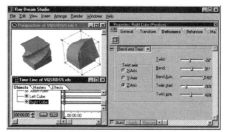

Figure 64. The Left Cube is twisted around the Z axis. Its twist begins one-third of the way "up" its height (Twist start = 33%), and spans the remainder of the cube's height (Twist size = 100%). It has a 0 Bend degree, making its Bend axis irrelevant. The Right Cube, whose settings are shown in the illustra-tion, also twists around the Z axis, but in the oppo-site direction and to a lesser degree (Twist = –28 degrees). It also features a deep bend of 91 degrees to the right (Bend axis of 180 degrees). Both the twist and the bend begin about a quarter of the way up the cube's height (Twist start = 26%) and con-tinue over 46% of the cube's remaining height.

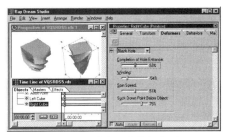

Figure 65. A quarter of the Left Cube has been devoured by the black hole (Completion of Hole Entrance = 25%), winds moderately to the right (Winding = 24%), and spins at less than a quarter of its maximum possible speed (Spin Speed = 20%) toward a point that's half the maximum possible distance below the object (Suck Down Point = 50%). The Right Cube, whose settings are shown, is over half devoured by the black hole, and spins more frequently in the opposite direction, and at a higher rate of speed, toward an object that is three quarters the maximum possible distance below the object.

4. Adjust the Twist Size slider to specify the percentage of the object's dimension along the specified axis that falls between the Twist start position and the end of the object that will be twisted. For example to twist along the entire length of this segment, enter 100%, and to twist along only half the length of the segment, enter only 50%.

5. Adjust the Bend slider to specify the number of degrees (between 0 and 180) that the object will be bent around the specified axis. For example, a value of 90 degrees will bend an object so that it appears to be making a bow.

6. Finally, adjust the Bend Axis to a value between −180 and 180 degrees to specify the "direction" of the bend relative to the specified axis.

✔ **Tip**

■ An object can be either twisted or bent, or bent and twisted.

To adjust the settings of a Black Hole deformer:

1. Adjust the Completion of Hole Entrance slider **(Figure 65)** to set the percentage of the object's volume that appears to have been sucked down the hole. When animating this type of deformer, use progressively larger percentages along the timeline to give the impression that more and more of the object has been "drained away."

2. Adjust the Winding slider to specify what percentage of maximum revolution the object has undergone during the "draining" motion. Enter a positive or negative number to specify a clockwise or counterclockwise direction, respectively.

3. Adjust the Spin Speed slider to specify the percentage of maximum speed at which the vortex is spinning.

4. Adjust the Suckdown Point Below Object slider to specify the percentage of maximum distance the suckdown point is located below the object.

To adjust the settings of a Dissolve deformer:

1. Adjust the Completion slider **(Figure 66)** to set the percentage of the dissolve that has occurred. When animating this type of deformer, use progressively larger percentages along the timeline to give the impression that more and more of the object has been dissolved.

2. Adjust the Size of Pieces to specify the size of the fragments that result from the dissolve.

✔ Tip

■ As the Size of Pieces setting increases, the number of pieces decreases.

To adjust the settings of an Explode deformer:

1. Adjust the Completion slider **(Figure 67)** to set the percentage of the explosion that has occurred. When animating this type of deformer, use progressively larger percentages along the timeline to give the impression that more and more of the object has been exploded.

2. Adjust the left and right Size of Pieces slider controls to set the range of pieces.

3. Adjust the left and right Speed slider controls to set the range of speed with which the pieces are blown away from the original object.

4. Adjust the Gravity slider to specify how quickly the exploded pieces fall downward.

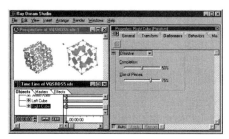

Figure 66. Both the Left Cube and the Right Cube have been half dissolved (Completion = 50%). But the Left Cube uses a smaller fragment size (Size of Pieces = 25%) than the Right Cube (Size of Pieces = 75%).

Figure 67. The Left Cube is about one-third through its explosion (Completion of Explosion = 32%), uses fragments that range in size from small to medium (Size of Pieces approximates 30% to 50% of maximum possible size), and travels and rotates at relatively low speeds (Speed ranges from about 5% to 40% of the maximum possible speed, and Rotational Speeds range from 5% to 10% of the maximum possible speed). The Right Cube, whose settings are shown, is three quarters through its explosion, uses smaller pieces traveling at higher speeds. Both cubes use identical Gravity, Slow Down at End, and Rotational Speed settings.

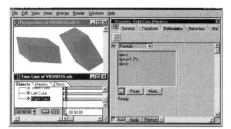

Figure 68. The Left Cube's formula is: dx = –x; dy = –y + 1.2 * x; dz = –z. The Right Cube's formula is: dx = –x; dy = –y + 1.2 * z; dz = –z.

5. Adjust the Slow Down at End slider to control the ratio at which the speed of a fragment decreases as the fragment's distance from the original object increases.

6. Adjust the left and right Rotational Speed slider controls to set the range of speed at which the exploded pieces can rotate.

7. Place a check in the Large Pieces Move Slower checkbox if you want fragment speed to decrease as fragment size increases.

8. Place a check in Pieces Stop At Bottom checkbox if you want the pieces to stop falling once they have reached the bottom of the original object's bounding box.

9. Place a check in the Explode from Top Down checkbox if you want the object to explode from the top down.

✔ Tips

■ To maximize the range of the Size of Pieces setting, the Speed setting, the Slow Down At End setting, or the Rotational Speed setting, move the left slider control to the left extreme of the slider, and move the right slider control to the right extreme of the slider.

■ To minimize the range of any of these settings, move both of its sliders against each other at the desired value.

To adjust the settings of a Formula deformer:

1. Load a formula, if desired, by clicking the disk icon, choosing Open from the pop-up menu, and opening the text file that contains the formula.

2. To edit a loaded formula, or to enter a new formula, enter lines of text in the text field **(Figure 68)**.

3. To automate the construction of advanced formulas, click the More button.

and

Click the Operators, Input Variables, and Output Variables buttons to insert operators and variables directly into the formula.

and

Adjust the Animatable Parameter sliders to values between –1 and 1 for each animatable parameter.

and

Click OK to return to the Properties palette.

4. Test the formula by pressing the Parse button.

5. Save the formula, if desired, to a text file by clicking the disk icon and choosing Save as from the pop-up menu.

✔ Tips

■ Although Formula deformers are an advanced topic, you can create some interesting effects simply by experimenting with different formulas.

■ The Ray Dream Studio 5 distribution CD-ROM contains additional information on using formulas.

To adjust the settings of a Punch deformer:

1. Adjust the Punch Strength slider **(Figure 69)** to specify what percentage of maximum punch strength has been applied to the object. Use a positive value to specify an external punch that dents the object inward, toward its center. Use a negative value to specify an internal punch that dents the object outward, away from its center.

2. Specify the Orientation of the punch for the axis (X, Y, or Z) along which the force of the punch is delivered.

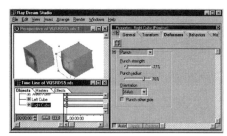

Figure 69. The Left Cube received a strong external punch (Punch strength = 74% of maximum possible strength) to a narrow radius (Punch radius = 25%) along the X axis. The Right Cube, whose settings are shown, received a strong internal punch (Punch strength = –77% of maximum possible strength) to a much wider radius (Punch radius = 76%) along the same axis.

Figure 70. The Left Cube shatters to a Scale of 49%. The Right Cube shatters to a Scale of 110%.

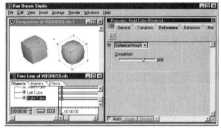

Figure 71. The Spherical Morph of the Left Cube has a 33% Completion setting. The Spherical Morph of the Right Cube has a 66% Completion setting.

3. Toggle the "Side" of the object to be punched by checking or unchecking the "Punch other side" checkbox.

- If the punch's Orientation is along the X axis, the punch will be toggled between the left side and the right side of the object.

- If the punch's Orientation is along the Y axis, the punch will be toggled between the front side and the back side of the object.

- If the punch's Orientation is along the Z axis, the punch will be toggled between the top side and the bottom side of the object.

4. Adjust the Radius of the punch to specify what percentage of the side to be punched is dented by the punch. A value of 100% will dent the affected side throughout its entire dimension, while a value of 50% will dent the side along only half of its dimension.

✔ Tip

■ The Radius of the punch is measured from the center of the affected Side.

To adjust the settings of a Shatter deformer:

1. Adjust the Scale slider **(Figure 70)** to specify a percentage by which the object is increased in scale as it is shattered.

2. The maximum increase is 300%.

To adjust the settings of a Spherical Morph deformer:

1. Adjust the Completion slider to set the percentage of the spherical morphing that has occurred **(Figure 71)**.

2. When animating this type of deformer, use progressively larger percentages along the timeline to give the impression that more and more of the object has been morphed.

To adjust the settings of a Spike deformer:

1. Adjust the Spike Density slider **(Figure 72)** to set the number of spikes that emanate from the object. Higher values generate more spikes.

2. Adjust the Length slider to set the spikes' percentage of their maximum possible length. Higher values generate longer spikes.

3. Adjust the Radius slider to set the width of the spikes. Higher values generate wider spikes.

4. Adjust the Messiness slider to set the spikes' percentage of their maximum possible directional randomness. Higher values generate messier spikes.

5. Adjust the Flow slider to set the spikes' percentage of their maximum possible movement during animation. Together, higher Messiness and Flow values generate messier, faster-moving spikes.

6. Adjust the Gravity slider to set the spikes' percentage of their maximum possible influence by gravity. Higher values generate spikes that droop like dew-laden blades of grass.

7. Check the Keep Original Object checkbox to continue displaying the original shape along with its new spikes. Uncheck the box to hide the original shape and to display only the new spikes.

To adjust the settings of a Stretch deformer:

1. Specify the axis along which the stretch (or press) will occur.

2. Adjust the Stretch slider **(Figure 73)** to a value greater than its default 100% setting (up to a maximum of 300%) to stretch the object from its center by an equal amount along both directions of the specified axis.

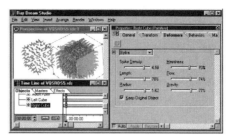

Figure 72. The Left Cube discards its original cube shape, and its Spike Density, Length, Radius, Messiness, Flow, and Gravity settings are all about one third of their maximum possible values. The Right Cube retains its original cube shape, and its Spike Density, Length, Radius, Messiness, Flow, and Gravity settings are all about two-thirds of their maximum possible values.

Figure 73. The X dimension of the Left Cube is stretched to 174% of its original length. The Z dimension of the Right Cube is stretched to only 22% of its original height and therefore appears "squashed".

Adjust Settings of a Stretch Deformer

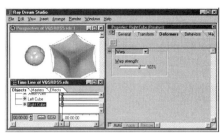

Figure 74. The Left Cube's Warp strength value of −103% collapses the corners and bulges the centers of its surfaces. The Right Cube's Warp strength collapses the centers and bulges the corners of its surfaces.

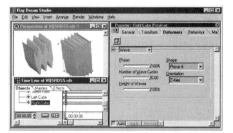

Figure 75. The Left Cube's Phase, Number of Wave Cycles, and Height of Waves are all set to 50% of their maximum possible values, while the Right Cube's values are all set to 100% of their maximum possible settings. Both cubes use a Planar Shape setting and an Orientation along the Z axis.

Figure 76. For both cubes, the Phase, Number of Wave Cycles, and Height of Waves are all set to 50% of their maximum possible values, and the Orientation is set to the Z axis. The Left Cube uses a Radial Shape setting, while the Right Cube uses a Cylindrical Shape setting.

3. Adjust the Stretch slider to a value less than its default 100% setting (down to a minimum of 1%) to compress the object toward its center by an equal amount along both directions of the specified axis.

To adjust the settings of a Warp deformer:

1. Adjust the Warp slider **(Figure 74)** to a value greater than its default 100% setting (up to a maximum of 200%) to stretch the object's corners away from its center and to compress the centers of its surfaces toward its center.

2. Adjust the Warp slider to a value less than its default 100% setting (down to a minimum of −199%) to compress the object's corners toward its center and to stretch the centers of its surfaces away from its center.

To adjust the settings of a Wave deformer:

1. Adjust the Phase slider to set the percentage of the wave cycle that has been completed. Higher values generate a wave that is further along in its cycle. A value of 100% generates a wave that has fully cycled back to its starting position **(Figures 75–76)**.

2. Adjust the Number of Wave Cycles slider to specify the number of complete wave cycles that appear over the object's length over the axis along which the wave is traveling. A minimum of one quarter of one cycle, and a maximum of five complete cycles can be specified.

3. Adjust the Height of Waves slider to specify the percentage of the maximum possible wave height to which the waves will actually rise. Higher values generate higher waves.

Settings of a Warp and Wave Deformer

4. Select the Orientation from the drop-down list of axes (X, Y, or Z) to specify the axis along which a planar wave would travel. For example, choose the Z axis to display a typical, vertically-undulating wave.

5. Select the Shape from the dropdown list box. For example, if the Orientation has been set to the Z axis:

- Choose a Planar A shape for a wave that moves along the X axis, and choose a Planar B shape for a wave that moves along the Y axis.

- Choose a Radial shape for a wave that moves along the Z axis.

- Choose a Cylindrical shape for a wave that looks like a bellows.

Part IV

Producing Scenes

Figure 1. A distant light and a bulb light illuminate this daytime interior scene.

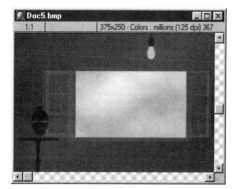

Figure 2. In this scene, the intensity of both the distant light and the bulb light has been reduced substantially.

SCENE PRODUCTION: AN OVERVIEW

Not long ago, the phrase, "Lights! Cameras! Action!" was the exclusive domain of the Hollywood director. But in today's world of desktop publishing, CD-ROMs and the Internet, our business, academic, and other audiences increasingly demand first-class multimedia communications that are stuffed to the gills with high production values. Ray Dream Studio makes it easy to meet these demands.

In the final four chapters of this book, you will learn how to use Ray Dream's lights, cameras, filters, effects, behaviors, animation, previews, and other features to produce engaging scenes quickly and easily. In the last chapter, you will learn how to render still images and movies from your scene.

LIGHTING THE SCENE

The backdrop and background settings that are set in the Effects tab of the Current Scene Settings window immediately set the tone of your scene. Lights and lighting effects, however, also play a major role in this regard. Spot, distance, and bulb lights, and special effects like multimedia gels, can greatly improve the impact of any scene **(Figures 1–2)**.

Lights are created so that they can be placed in a particular location and aimed at a particular object to provide direct illumination, indirect illumination, reflection, silhouette, lens glare, shadow, and other effects.

Ambient light

The first light source to consider is the scene's ambient light. Ambient light is a render setting that is accessed with the Effects tab of the Current Scene Settings window.

To inspect and edit the scene's ambient light:

1. Choose Current Scene Settings from the Render menu **(Figure 3)**.

2. Click the Effects tab.

3. Expand the ambient light area by clicking on the plus sign (arrow on the Mac) **(Figure 4)**.

4. To change the color of the ambient light, double-click the color preview swatch and select a color with your system's Color Picker dialog box.

5. To increase or decrease brightness, adjust the slider control.

6. To view the result, choose the Shaded Preview or Better Preview from the View menu.

or

Render the scene using the current render settings by choosing Use Current Settings from the Render menu **(Figure 5)**.

or

Click the Render tool and draw a marquee around the portion of the scene to be rendered **(Figure 6)**.

✔ Tip

■ Ambient light is uniform throughout the scene and casts no shadows.

The default light

Whenever a new, empty scene is created, a single light, called Light 1, is added to the scene. It is placed at the top-left corner of the Perspective window and is pointed at the point of origin **(Figure 7)**.

The default light is a good vehicle for learning about light types and uses.

Figure 3. Choose **Current Scene Settings** from the **Render** menu.

Figure 4. The ambient light setting area of the **Current Scene Settings** tabbed window.

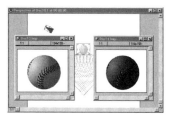

Figure 5. The brightness setting of the ambient light is greater in the left image (100%) than that in the right image (20%). In both of these images, the brightness level of the default light was reduced from its default setting of 100% to 0%, to isolate the effect of the ambient light setting.

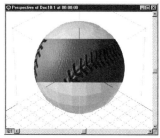

Figure 6. Preview the effects of different ambient light settings by rendering a portion of the scene.

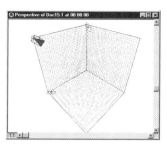

Figure 7. The default light in a new scene and its bounding box and projections.

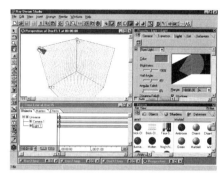

Figure 8. Arrange the windows as shown, and click the Show-Hide Direct Manipulation button at the top-left corner of the Properties palette.

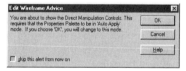

Figure 9. If this dialog box appears, click OK to enter Auto apply mode.

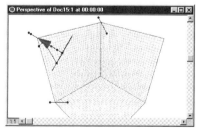

Figure 10. The direct manipulation handles for a Spot light.

To select and inspect the default light:

1. Create a new, empty scene by choosing New from the File menu and, if the New dialog box opens, clicking the Create Empty Scene button.

2. Choose Workspace from the Windows menu and select a setting from the submenu (e.g., the 800x600 Illustration) to arrange Ray Dream Studio's windows.

3. Click the Selection tool.

4. Click the light to select it.

5. If the Properties palette is not displayed, choose Properties from the Windows menu.

6. Reposition the Properties palette so that it is in full view but does not obscure the light in the Perspective window.

7. Click the Light tab in the Properties palette.

8. Click the Show-Hide Direct Manipulation button to display the light's bounding box and handles (**Figure 8**).

9. If the Edit Wireframe Advice dialog box appears, click OK to place the Properties palette into Auto apply mode (**Figure 9**).

10. Verify that the light's bounding box and handles are displayed (**Figure 10**).

✔ Tip

■ Setting the Show-Hide Direct Manipulation button to the Show (pressed-in) setting causes the bounding box handles' positions and the Properties palette's settings to update each other in real time.

Inspect and Select the Default Light

AIMING AND DISTANCING LIGHTS

Lights work best when you place and aim them with care.

To prepare to follow along with the steps below:

1. Make the Perspective window the current window.

2. Add a sphere primitive to the origin point of your scene by choosing Sphere from the Insert menu.

3. Apply the Baseball shader (located in the Metals1 directory of the Shaders tab in the Browser palette).

To aim a light at a 3D object in the scene:

1. Click the Selection tool.

2. Click the light to select it.

3. While holding down the Shift key, click the target object **(Figure 11)**.

4. Choose Point At in the Arrange menu **(Figure 12)**.

If a light is too close or too far from its target object, you can easily reset the distance between them.

To adjust the distance between a light and an object:

1. Select both the light and the object in the Perspective window.

2. Choose Properties from the Windows menu.

3. To anchor the object and reposition the light to the new distance, select the object from the Lock dropdown list.

or

To anchor the light and reposition the object to the new distance, select the light from the Lock dropdown list.

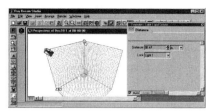

Figure 11. Select the light and the object at which the light will be pointed. The order of selection is not important.

Figure 12. Choose **Point At** in the **Arrange** menu.

Aim a Light at a 3D Object

Figure 13. Inspecting and editing the distance between a light and an object.

Figure 14. Select the type of light.

and

Edit the value and unit of measurement for the Distance, if desired.

and

If the Auto checkbox is not checked, click the Apply button or place a check in the Auto checkbox **(Figure 13)**.

✔ **Tip**

■ This technique is also useful for positioning a camera more closely to an object.

SETTING A LIGHT'S PROPERTIES

You can configure a light's general and special settings in the various tabs of its Properties palette.

For example, you can specify a light's type and adjust its type-specific settings in the Light tab of the Properties palette. And, you can select and configure its Gel settings in the Gel tab.

To select and configure a light's type:

1. Click the dropdown list button in the Light tab of the light's Properties palette **(Figure 14)**

and

Select the type of light: bulb, spot, or distant.

2. Adjust the following settings for each type of light:

• Set the color by double-clicking the preview swatch and choosing a new color with your system's Color Picker dialog box.

• Adjust the light's Brightness to set its intensity.

• Place or remove a check in the Shadows checkbox to permit or prevent the light from producing shadows.

and

Select and Configure a Light's Type.

Adjust the slider to specify the strength of the shadows created by the light.

3. For spot lights and bulb lights **(Figure 15)**, adjust the following settings:

* Adjust the Distance Falloff to specify the percentage of intensity that is lost as an object's distance from the light is increased.

* Specify the value and unit of measure for the light's Range.

4. For spot lights, also adjust the following settings:

* Half Angle is the angle of the cone of illumination that the light produces.

* Angular Falloff is the percentage of intensity that is lost as an object is moved away from direct alignment with the light.

5. For distant lights, also adjust the direction setting by clicking the Front or Back radio button **(Figure 16)**.

6. If the Auto checkbox is not checked, click the Apply button or place a check in the Auto checkbox.

✔ **Tip**

■ Unlike the spot light and the bulb light, the distant light does not "appear" in the scene as a selectable object. You must click a distant light's name in the Objects tab of the Time Line window to select it.

Selecting and configuring light gels

Gels are objects or substances that are placed between a light and the illuminated object to create different shades or patterns.

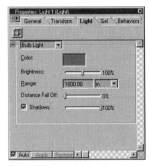

Figure 15. Bulb light settings.

Figure 16. Distant light settings.

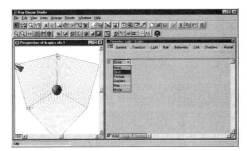

Figure 17. The Gel settings tab.

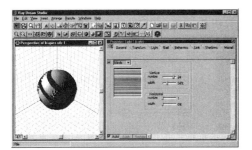

Figure 18. These Blinds Gel settings simulate light passing through window blinds.

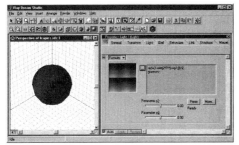

Figure 19. The default settings of the Formula Gel produce a reddish tint on the baseball's small surface.

To select and configure a gel for the currently selected light:

1. Click the Gel tab of the light's Properties palette **(Figure 17)**.

2. Click the list dropdown button, and select and configure one of the following gels.

The Blinds gel

Use the Blinds gel to simulate light passing through horizontal, vertical, or combined blinds.

To configure the Blinds gel:

1. Adjust the Number and Width of the Horizontal blind sliders to values greater than zero **(Figure 18)**.

2. To use a vertical blind gel, adjust the Number and Width of the Vertical blind sliders to values greater than zero.

3. Use the Formula gel to produce a mathematically described light.

and

Configure its settings by adjusting the P1 and P2 Parameter sliders.

The Formula gel

To configure a Formula gel:

1. Enter a formula in the text field **(Figure 19)**.

or

Load a formula from disk by clicking the disk icon and selecting the host file.

2. Click the More button to access the Formula Editor window, if desired, and click OK.

3. Click the Parse button to test the formula.

4. Adjust the Parameter p1 and p2 adjusters while viewing the preview area.

Select and Configure a Gel

The Gradient gel

Use the Gradient gel to simulate light passing through horizontal, vertical, or combined blinds.

To configure the Gradient gel:

1. Click the Horizontal or Circular radio button to build, respectively, a horizontal or circular gradient gel **(Figure 20)**.

2. To set the Start and Finish colors, double-click their swatch previews and select a color with the Color Picker.

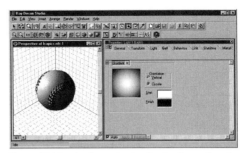

Figure 20. The circular option for the Gradient gel works best for spherical objects.

The Map gel

The Map gel is a bitmap image that can be tiled or inverted across the light so that it is projected like a slide.

To configure the Map gel:

1. Click the disk icon to launch, and select Open from the pop-up menu **(Figure 21)**.

2. Use the resulting Open dialog box to locate and select the desired bitmap image file.

3. Click the three directional buttons while viewing the preview area to experiment with different orientations of the bitmap.

4. To tile the image, click the Tile button.

and

Specify the horizontal and vertical frequency of the tiling effect by adjusting the Horizontally and Vertically slider controls.

5. If desired, invert the image's colors by placing a check in the Invert color checkbox.

6. To maximize image quality, place a check in the Better (but slower) sampling checkbox.

7. Set the image's brightness with the Brightness slider.

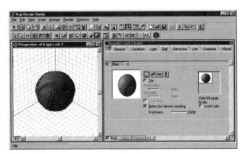

Figure 21. This bitmap gel is a picture of a baseball. When projected onto an object that is itself a baseball, the gel produces the effect of motion.

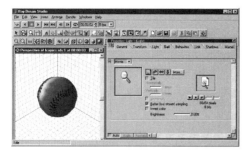

Figure 22. The AVI file used in this Movie gel shows a magnifying glass that reveals a document icon as it rotates. To play the movie, display the Time Controller toolbar and click the Play button. The scene "plays" for the default animation period called the Render Range, which is discussed in Chapter 14.

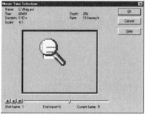

Figure 23. The **Movie Time Selection** dialog box.

To configure the Movie gel:

The Movie gel is a bitmap image that can be tiled or inverted across the light so that it is projected like a video.

1. Click the disk icon to launch and select Open from the pop-up menu **(Figure 22)**.

2. Use the resulting Open dialog box to locate and select the desired movie image file.

3. Click the three directional buttons while viewing the preview area to experiment with different orientations of the movie.

4. To tile the image, click the Tile button.

and

Specify the horizontal and vertical frequency of the tiling effect by adjusting the Horizontally and Vertically slider controls.

5. If desired, invert the movie's colors by checking the Invert color checkbox.

6. To maximize image quality, place a check in the Better (but slower) sampling checkbox.

7. Set the image's brightness with the Brightness slider.

8. Click the More button to open a dialog box that displays the following information about the movie file **(Figure 23)**:

- File name and path
- File size
- Movie duration
- Scale of the preview area
- File color depth
- Movie frame rate (frames per second)

and

Use the Play, Stop, Loop, and Scrub controls to preview the movie.

and

Click OK or Cancel to return to the movie area of the Gel tab.

Movie Gel

✓ **Tip**

- ■ The aspect ratio of a movie to be used with a bulb light should be 2:1.
- ■ The aspect ratio of a movie to be used with a distance or spot light should be 1:1.

Applying the gel

If the Auto apply checkbox does not contain a check mark, you must click the Apply button at the bottom of the Properties palette to apply the Gel to the selected light.

ADDING LIGHTS TO THE SCENE

To add a light to a scene:

1. Choose Light from the Insert menu to add a light at the point of origin **(Figure 24)**.

or

1. Click the Create Light tool in the Tools toolbar for the Perspective window **(Figure 25)**.

and

Click and drag at the location in the scene where the light is to be placed, and release the mouse button.

Lights, of course, can be positioned with the Transformation tab of their Properties palette **(Figure 26)**.

Figure 24. Choose **Light** from the **Insert** menu to add a new light to your scene.

Figure 25. The Create Light tool.

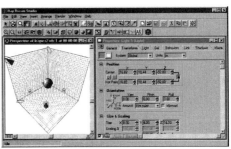

Figure 26. A light's position can be set in the Transform tab of its Properties palette.

Figure 27. Set a light's Shadow features in the Shadows tab of the light's Properties palette.

MANAGING SHADOWS

At the beginning of this chapter you learned that ambient light cannot create shadows, and that bulb, distant, and spot lights can create shadows.

It is sometimes useful to configure a light or object so that it does not create or cast a shadow. It is also sometimes useful to render a scene without shadows—e.g., to reduce the render time, or to achieve a particular visual effect.

The creation, suppression, or suspension of shadows is controlled by adjusting certain settings for the light in question, the 3D objects illuminated by that light, and the Current Scene's Renderer settings.

Because the instructions for adjusting these light, object, and render settings are spread throughout this book, we thought it would be helpful to summarize the shadow settings in a single section.

Setting a light's shadow features

To specify the shadow features for a bulb, spot, or distant light:

1. Select the light by clicking it in the Perspective or Time Line window.

2. Display the light's Properties palette by choosing Properties from the Windows menu.

3. Click the Shadows tab of the Properties palette.

4. Expand the Shadow Features settings area by clicking the Plus sign.

5. Choose No Shadows, Ray-Traced Shadows, or Soft DRT Shadows from the dropdown list box to specify the type of shadow, if any, that will be cast by objects that block light emitted by the selected light object **(Figure 27)**.

6. If the Auto checkmark is not checked, click the Apply button.

Enabling a light's shadow features

To enable or disable a light's shadow features:

1. Select the light by clicking it in the Perspective or Time Line window.

2. Display the light's Properties palette by choosing Properties from the Windows menu.

3. Click the Light tab of the Properties palette.

4. Place or remove a check mark in the Shadows checkbox to enable or disable the shadow feature set in the Shadows tab **(Figure 28)**.

5. If shadow casting is enabled, adjust the slider to specify the shadow strength.

6. If the Auto check mark is not checked, click the Apply button.

Overriding shadows for individual 3D objects

To permit or prevent a 3D object from casting a Soft DRT shadow:

1. Select the 3D object by clicking it in the Perspective or Time Line window.

2. Display the object's Properties palette by choosing Properties from the Windows menu.

3. Click the General tab of the Properties palette.

4. Place or remove a check mark in the Shadows checkbox to permit or prevent the object from casting a shadow **(Figure 29)**.

5. If the Auto check mark is not checked, click the Apply button.

Figure 28. Enable, disable, and adjust the light's Shadow features in the Light tab of the Light's Properties palette.

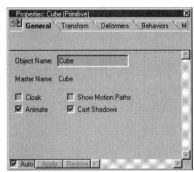

Figure 29. The General tab of a 3D object's Properties palette contains an option that lets you enable or disable the object to cast shadows when blocking light that uses the Soft DRT shadows feature.

Enable or Disable Shadow Features

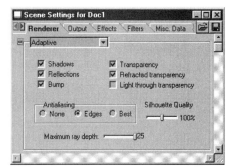

Figure 30. The Renderer tab of the **Current Scene Settings** dialog box contains a setting that includes or excludes shadows from the render.

Enabling and disabling shadows in renders

To enable or disable the creation of shadows during a render:

1. Choose Current Scene Settings from the Render menu.

2. Click the Renderer tab.

3. Expand the rendering engine settings area by clicking the Plus sign (arrow on the Mac).

4. Place or remove a check mark in the Shadows checkbox to enable or disable shadow production during the rendering process **(Figure 30)**.

✔ Tips

■ If a light's shadow feature is set to Ray-traced shadows, then a 3D object will cast shadows even if the Cast Shadows checkbox in the General tab of its Properties palette is not checked.

■ If a light's shadow feature is set to Soft DRT Shadows, then an object will produce shadows only if the Cast Shadows checkbox in the General tab of its Properties palette is checked.

■ Deselecting the Shadows setting in the Renderer tab of the Current Scene Setting dialog box will exclude from the render shadows from any light, regardless of its Shadow feature setting.

■ The Render Area tool, however, will display shadows even if the Shadows checkbox on the Renderer tab of the Current Scene Settings dialog box is unchecked.

■ If a 3D object is contained in a group, it must be ungrouped in order to display the Cast Shadows checkbox in the General tab of its Properties palette.

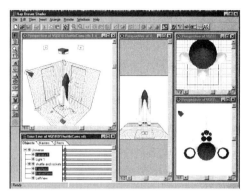

Figure 1. The left, default Perspective window shows the view from the default camera, Camera 1. The middle Perspective window shows the view from a second camera, called LeftView. The top right Perspective window shows the view from a third camera, called "TopView". The bottom right Perspective window shows the view from a fourth camera, called "BottomView". Note that all four cameras are selected in the Objects tab of the Time Line window.

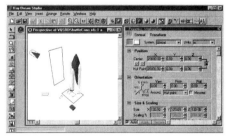

Figure 2. Sending the default Perspective window's working box to a far-off location does not disturb the view of the default camera, Camera 1.

Ray Dream lets you view and render a scene from multiple cameras that can be positioned in different locations. The cameras can also be configured with different lenses and other characteristics **(Figure 1)**.

While it is possible to produce complex scenes with a single camera, you would probably have to waste a great deal of time and effort to reposition the camera repeatedly in order to achieve the desired results.

In such cases, it is far easier to create additional cameras, to position and configure them to perform specific functions, and then to forget about them until they are actually used in the production process.

THE DEFAULT CAMERA

The default camera, identified as Camera 1 in the Time Line window, is perched above the ground plane and between the left and right planes of the Perspective window's working box.

The default camera points directly at the universe's origin. If the working box is selected and sent to some remote location within the universe, the default camera continues its fix on the universe's origin, and the working box will seem to have disappeared **(Figure 2)**.

ADDING NEW CAMERAS TO A SCENE

New cameras can be added to a scene with:

- The Insert/Camera menu command
- The Create Camera tool
- The Windows/New Perspective menu command

Inserting a new camera and opening a new Perspective window

The Insert/Camera menu command lets you easily create and position a new camera and gives you the option of opening a new Perspective window at the same time.

In the steps below you will create a new camera and a new Perspective window that will enable you to visualize the scene's default camera.

To insert a new camera and to open a new Perspective window simultaneously:

1. Make the Perspective window the current window.

2. Choose Camera from the Insert menu **(Figure 3)**.

3. In the Create Camera dialog box, enter a name for the camera.

and

Accept the default camera type of Conical **(Figure 4)**.

and

Click the Wide Angle (24mm) radio button to set the lens type.

and

Click the Open New Perspective Window radio button to open a new Perspective window.

Figure 3. Choose **Camera** from the **Insert** menu.

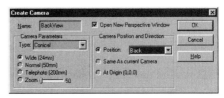

Figure 4. The **Create Camera** dialog box.

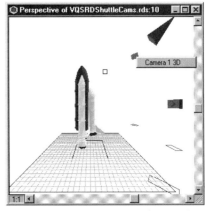

Figure 5. This new Perspective window uses the new camera that was placed behind the working box in the original Perspective window. By virtue of its position, direction, and lens settings, it is possible to "see" the default camera, Camera 1.

Figure 6. The Create Camera tool is located on the Perspective window's Tools toolbar.

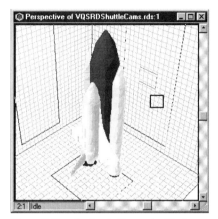

Figure 7. Drag the Create Camera tool to the desired location and release the mouse.

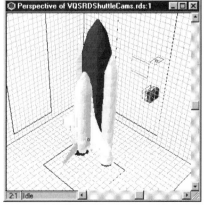

Figure 8. The new camera appears in the scene, but still needs to be positioned and aimed to be useful.

and

Click the Position radio button.

and

Choose Back from the dropdown list box.

and

Click OK.

4. To confirm that the blue object near the top right of the new Perspective window is the default camera, called Camera 1, click it and hold the mouse button down until its name pops up on the screen **(Figure 5)**.

Using the Create Camera tool

New cameras can also be added with the Create Camera tool.

To create a new camera:

1. Pick a Perspective window into which the camera will be placed and make it the current window.

2. Click the Create Camera tool **(Figure 6)**.

3. Drag the Create Camera tool to the desired location in the Perspective window and release the mouse.

or

Click and release the mouse at the desired location in the Perspective window **(Figure 7)**.

✔ Tips

■ To rename the camera something more descriptive than "Camera 2", select the camera in either the Perspective or Hierarchy window, display the General tab of its Properties palette, enter a new name, and click the Apply button or the Auto checkbox.

■ Once a new camera is created **(Figure 8)**, it can be precisely positioned with the camera positioning techniques described later in this chapter.

Creating or selecting a camera when creating a new Perspective window

Just as Ray Dream gives you the option of creating a new Perspective window or using an existing one when you create a new camera, it also gives you the option of creating a new camera or using an existing one when you create a new Perspective window.

To create or select a camera when creating a new Perspective window:

1. Choose New Perspective from the Windows menu **(Figure 9)** to open the New Perspective Window dialog box **(Figure 10)**.

2. To use an existing camera, click the Use Camera radio button.

and

Select the camera that will provide the view for the new Perspective window.

or

2. To create a new camera, click the Create New Camera radio button.

and

Specify the new camera's name, type, lens, and other settings as desired.

The new Perspective window **(Figure 11)** can be used in the same manner as the default Perspective window.

WORKING WITH MULTIPLE CAMERAS AND PERSPECTIVE WINDOWS

You can easily switch between Perspective windows, and between cameras in any Perspective window.

Figure 9. Choose **New Perspective** from the **Windows** menu.

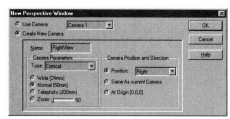

Figure 10. The **New Perspective Window** dialog box.

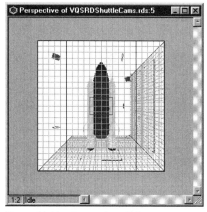

Figure 11. New Perspective windows are numbered sequentially and can be used in the same manner as the original Perspective window.

Figure 12. The **Windows** menu includes a list of available Perspective windows.

Figure 13. The **Camera** submenu of the **View** menu provides a list of available cameras that can be used to compose the current Perspective window.

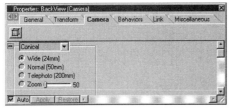

Figure 14. The Camera tab of the Properties palette for the currently selected camera. See the "Positioning and aiming the camera" section later in this chapter to learn how to select a camera and display its Properties palette.

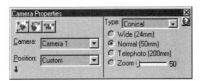

Figure 15. When the Camera Properties window is first opened, it appears in its collapsed state and displays the properties for the first camera in the Scene's hierarchy of objects. In this case, the first camera is the original, default camera, which is still called Camera 1.

To switch between Perspective windows:

1. Click the title bar or other portion of the Perspective window you wish to make the current window.

or

Choose the target Perspective window from the Windows menu **(Figure 12)**.

To change the camera providing the Perspective window's view:

1. Make the Perspective window the current window.

2. Choose Camera from the View menu.

3. Click the desired camera from the submenu **(Figure 13)**.

Using dedicated cameras

Notwithstanding the ease of moving between Perspective windows and cameras, it is easy to get confused as to which camera is supplying the view to which Perspective window.

It is also easy to move a camera from a desirable position that hasn't yet been saved as a preset position with the procedure outlined later in this chapter.

It is therefore a good idea to dedicate a specific camera to each Perspective window in your scene. For example, you might use only the original, default camera and Perspective window together as the changeable "utility view."

SETTING CAMERA PROPERTIES

Like objects and lights, cameras have properties that can easily be inspected and edited with Ray Dream Studio's Properties palette **(Figure 14)**.

But Ray Dream Studio offers a wider range of options and tools in a specialized window called the Camera Properties window **(Figure 15)**. This window also features a dropdown list of all existing cameras that saves the trouble of accessing the Time Line or Perspective window to select the camera you wish to configure.

To set camera properties using the Camera Properties window:

1. Choose Camera Properties from the Windows menu **(Figure 16)**.

2. Select a camera to configure by selecting its name from the dropdown list box.

3. Position the camera by clicking the Position dropdown list and selecting one of the preset positions, a custom position, or a position occupied by another camera.

4. To select a lens type, choose Conical, Isometric, or IVRM Spherical from the Type dropdown list.

5. To configure a Conical lens, click Wide, Normal, Telephoto, or Zoom and, in the last case, adjust the Zoom slider to the desired zoom level.

6. To configure an Isometric lens, adjust the Zoom slider to the desired zoom level **(Figure 17)**.

✔ Tips

■ The Isometric lens provides a view that is traditionally used by draftsmen. In an isometric view, objects are not reduced in size to reflect their distance from the viewer **(Figure 18)**.

■ The IVRM Spherical lens produces a spherical render that can be used only with a virtual reality viewer applet, such as the RealSpace Traveler.

You will return to the Camera Properties window in a moment when you learn how to pan, track, and dolly the camera. But first you need to know how to position the camera and how to point it at other objects in the scene.

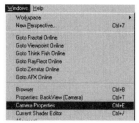

Figure 16. Choose **Camera Properties** from the **Windows** menu to access the Camera Properties window.

Figure 17. The settings area for an Isometric camera.

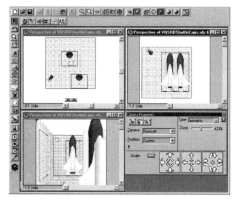

Figure 18. The top-left Perspective window shows a top-down view of a scene that contains two space shuttles, and two cameras that view the shuttles from the left position. The leftmost camera uses a conical lens and results in the Perspective window shown at the bottom left of the screen. Notice that the farther shuttle looks smaller. The rightmost camera uses an Isometric lens and results in the Perspective window shown at the top right of the screen. It settings are shown in the Camera Properties dialog box, shown at the bottom right of the screen. Notice how the camera using the Isometric lens results in a view in which the size of objects does not vary with their distance from the camera.

Figure 19. You can set the currently selected camera's position and orientation with the Transform tab of its Properties palette. You can also increase or decrease the size of the blue camera object that appears in the scene with the Size settings.

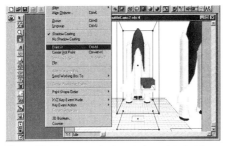

Figure 20. The camera is about to be pointed at the left shuttle.

POSITIONING AND AIMING THE CAMERA

Like 3D objects and lights, cameras can be positioned with reference to a point in the universe, the Perspective window's working box, or the currently selected bounding box of an object or group.

To position a camera:

1. Select the camera in the Perspective window or the Time Line window.

2. Choose Properties from the Windows menu to display the camera's Properties palette.

3. Click the Transform tab.

4. Position the camera relative to the Universe by entering X,Y, and Z values in the Position area **(Figure 19)**.

Pointing and distancing the camera

Two other, more natural ways of positioning and orienting a camera in your scene are pointing and distancing.

You can easily point a camera directly at any 3D object in your scene.

To point a camera:

1. Select the target object by clicking it in either the Perspective window or the Hierarchy window.

2. While holding down the Shift key, click the camera to be pointed.

3. Choose Point At from the Arrange menu **(Figure 20)**.

✔ Tip

■ A camera cannot be aimed directly at a light or at another camera.

A camera can be distanced from any 3D object, light, or camera in the scene. Either the camera or the other object can be moved to accomplish the distancing.

Position a Camera

To set the distance between a camera and any other item in a scene:

1. Select the target object by clicking it in either the Perspective window or the Hierarchy window.

2. While holding down the Shift key, click the camera to be distanced.

3. Choose Properties from the Windows menu to display the Properties palette.

4. Choose the object to be anchored from the dropdown list.

and

Enter the distance and units of measurement.

and

If the Auto checkbox is not checked, click the Apply button **(Figure 21)**.

✔ Tip

■ If the camera is moved in a distancing operation, it may no longer be aimed properly. If so, repeat the aim procedure outlined above to reacquire the visual target.

Moving the camera: dolly, pan, and track

While coarse camera positioning can be accomplished by dragging a camera around the scene or numerically specifying its position and orientation, finer adjustments are frequently required. Similarly, in animations, it is frequently desirable to move the camera's position over time in order to provide a panoramic sweep or to follow the movement of another object.

Ray Dream Studio 5 supports three standard camera movements:

• Dollying is the rotation of a camera around a selected object. Dollying changes the camera's position and orientation, so that an object can be viewed from different positions.

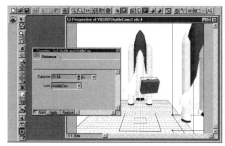

Figure 21. The right shuttle is about to be moved closer to the camera.

Figure 22. The Dolly, Pan, and Track camera movement tools are located in the Perspective window's Tools toolbar.

Figure 23. The **Camera Properties** dialog box contains the same three camera movement tools (dolly, pan, and track) as the Tools toolbar. It also contains a Navigational panel that is located along its bottom-right edge and can be viewed only when the dialog box is expanded, by clicking the key icon. The Navigational panel contains three control clusters. Left to right, they are the pan, track, and dolly remote controls.

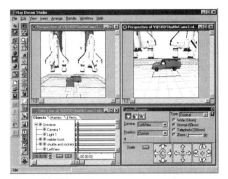

Figure 24. This workspace arrangement is recommended to perform camera movements efficiently. The camera to be moved is called "LeftView", and it produces the view seen through the right-hand Perspective window. A second camera, called "Spy", was added to the scene, above and behind the LeftView Camera. It produces the view seen through the left Perspective window, and lets you select the LeftView to align it to gravity after it has been moved. Alignment of the LeftView camera will, of course, update the view it produces in the right Perspective window. This arrangement is necessary because a camera must be selected in a Perspective window before it can be aligned to gravity. Selecting a camera in the Time Line window does not enable the On Gravity command in the Align command's submenu.

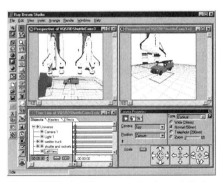

Figure 25. The LeftView camera has been dollied to the left around the service truck. The LeftView camera was then selected in the left Perspective window and aligned to gravity. The end result is visible in the right Perspective window.

- Panning is the rotation of a camera around its own axis. Panning changes the orientation of the camera, but not its position. Panning is used to aim the camera at a different subject.

- Tracking is the translation of a camera's position in 3D space. By moving a camera up, down, left, or right relative to your screen, a camera's position is changed relative to the object.

These movements may be effected with either:

- The tools that are located in both the Perspective window's Tools toolbar **(Figure 22)** and the upper-left portion of the Camera Properties window.

- The Navigational panel that is located in the lower-right portion of the fully expanded Camera Properties window **(Figure 23)**.

Preparing the work space

When learning and using camera movements, it's a good idea to monitor both the camera itself, as observed with one Perspective window that uses another camera, and the view it provides to a second Perspective window **(Figure 24)**. This will make it much easier to visualize and control the movement, and more importantly, to align the moved camera to gravity, if necessary, after the movement has occurred.

Executing the movements

To dolly the camera:

1. Select the object around which you wish to dolly the camera **(Figure 25)**.

or

Deselect all objects to dolly the camera around the universe's point of origin. Then choose Step 2 or Step 3.

2. To dolly with the Dolly tool, click the title bar of the Perspective window that uses the camera you wish to dolly to make it the current window.

and

Click the Dolly tool in the Tools toolbar then drag the Dolly tool in the Perspective window in the desired direction.

or

3. To dolly with the Navigational panel, click the Dolly Up, Dolly Right, Dolly Down, or Dolly Left buttons to rotate the camera in the desired direction.

4. If necessary, align the dollied camera to gravity using the procedure outlined below.

To pan the camera:

1. Choose Step 2 or Step 3.

2. To pan with the Pan Camera tool, click the title bar of the Perspective window that uses the camera you wish to pan to make it the current window **(Figure 26)**.

and

Click the Pan tool in the Tools toolbar then drag the Pan tool in the Perspective window in the desired direction.

3. To pan with the Navigational panel, click the Pan Up, Pan Right, Pan Down, Pan Left, Rotate Counterclockwise, or Rotate Clockwise buttons to rotate the camera in the desired direction.

4. If necessary, align the panned camera to gravity using the procedure outlined below.

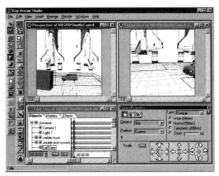

Figure 26. The LeftView camera has been panned to the left around its own vertical axis. The LeftView camera was then selected in the left Perspective window and aligned to gravity. The end result is visible in the right Perspective window.

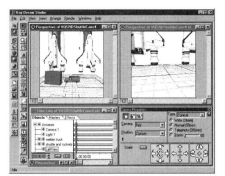

Figure 27. The LeftView camera was tracked straight in toward the left shuttle. The LeftView camera was then selected in the left Perspective window and aligned to gravity. The end result is visible in the right Perspective window.

Figure 28. Choose **Align** from the **Arrange** menu, and select **On Gravity** from the submenu.

To track the camera:

1. Choose Step 2 or Step 3.

2. To track with the Track Camera tool, click the title bar of the Perspective window that uses the camera you wish to track to make it the current window **(Figure 27)**.

and

Click the Track tool in the Tools toolbar. Then drag the Track tool in the Perspective window in the desired direction.

3. To track with the Navigational panel, click the Track Up, Track Right, Track Down, Track Left, Track In, or Track Out buttons to move the camera in the desired direction.

4. If necessary, align the tracked camera to gravity using the procedure outlined below.

Aligning the moved camera on gravity

Aligning the moved camera to gravity is necessary to eliminate any undesired rotation of the camera.

To align the moved camera to gravity:

1. Make the Perspective window with which you can visualize the moved camera the current window.

2. If any other object is selected, deselect all objects by clicking any empty area of the Perspective window.

3. Click the moved camera to select it.

4. Choose Align from the Arrange menu, and then choose On Gravity from the submenu **(Figure 28)**.

5. To inspect the changes to the view produced by the aligned camera, display and inspect the Perspective window whose view is taken from the moved camera.

Calibrating the camera movement tools

The angle and distance increments used by the Navigational panel are calibrated with the Increments dialog box.

To calibrate the camera movement tools:

1. Click the Scale icon on the Navigational panel.

2. In the Increments dialog box, enter the desired values and units of measurement and click OK **(Figure 29)**.

Direct manipulation of camera settings

Like lights, cameras can also be positioned, aimed, and moved with their direct manipulation handles.

To use a camera's direct manipulation handles:

1. Click the camera to be manipulated in the Perspective window to select it.

2. Display the camera's Properties palette by choosing Properties from the Windows menu.

3. Click the Camera tab.

4. Place a check in the Auto checkbox if it is not checked.

5. Click the Show/Hide Direct Manipulation button to display the camera's handles.

6. Drag the handles to pan and track the camera **(Figure 30)**.

SAVING CAMERA SETTINGS

Once a camera is positioned, pointed, distanced, and configured as desired, both its view and its settings can be saved as a preset position.

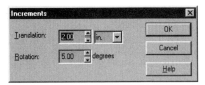

Figure 29. The **Increments** dialog box.

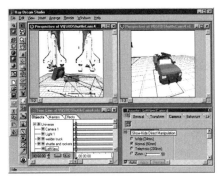

Figure 30. Drag the handles to pan and track the camera, as shown in the left Perspective window.

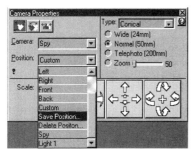

Figure 31. Choose **Save Position** from the Position dropdown list of the Camera Properties window.

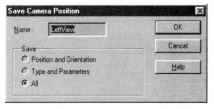

Figure 32. The **Save Camera Position** dialog box.

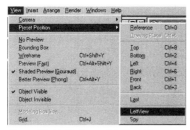

Figure 33. Verify the availability of the saved preset position by choosing **Preset Position** from the **View** menu and scanning the submenu for the new entry.

To save a camera's view as a preset position:

1. Display the Camera Properties window as described above.

2. Choose the camera whose position you wish to save from the Camera dropdown list box of the Camera Properties window.

3. Choose Save Position from the Position dropdown list box **(Figure 31)**.

4. In the Save Camera Position dialog box, enter the name of the position **(Figure 32)**.

5. Click the Position and Orientation radio button to save only the camera's position and orientation.

   or

   Click the Type and Parameters button to save only the camera's type and settings.

   or

   Click All to save the camera's position, orientation, type, and parameter settings.

6. Click OK to save the position as a preset position.

7. To verify the availability of the saved preset position for use by other cameras, choose Preset Position from the View menu and scan the submenu for the new preset position **(Figure 33)**.

✔ Tip

■ You can also store and access camera settings with the Cameras tab of the Browser palette.

ACTION! 14

Once your scene is populated with 3D objects, lights, and cameras, you are ready to add the action, in the form of animation and behaviors.

ACTION TYPES AND DEFINITIONS

Ray Dream supports two different types of action:

- Animation
- Behavior

Animation is any change over time in the position—or any other attribute—of any 3D object, light, or camera in the scene.

Behavior is a movement that is applied to any 3D object, light, or camera in a scene.

Behaviors are similar to shaders and deformers in that they are stored in the Browser palette and can be applied to 3D objects with the drag and drop or Apply button techniques. But behaviors differ from shaders and deformers in that they can be applied to lights and cameras as well as to 3D objects.

Before learning how Ray Dream uses animation and behaviors, it may be helpful for many readers to review the basic principles and techniques of traditional animation and scene production.

TRADITIONAL ANIMATION: PRINCIPLES AND TECHNIQUES

Ray Dream Studio animations use many of the principles and techniques that are used to animate 2D artwork into cartoon movies, and clay models into claymation (movies that feature clay animated characters).

The animation production process usually takes place in five distinct phases:

1. Drawing or, stop-action claymation, modeling the objects, characters, backdrops, backgrounds, and other artwork **(Figure 1)**.

2. Storyboarding scenes in a series of rough sketches.

3. Drawing or positioning the key frames—i.e., the landmark frames at which substantial changes in the scene take place **(Figures 2–3)**.

4. Drawing or positioning the tweeners—i.e., the frames that are positioned between the key frames **(Figure 4)**.

5. Photographing the key frames and tweeners **(Figure 5)**.

Once the animation has been produced, it can be edited, post-produced, and eventually broadcast or otherwise distributed.

More about changes

The changes that take place between two key frames in a traditional animation, can be few or many, limited or substantial, subtle or dramatic.

One, some, or all of the following attributes can be altered in one, some, or all of the tweeners in order to depict the changes that occur between the key frames:

Figure 1. In this production, an alien ship will fire a torpedo on a jet plane. The jet is a stock object called "sr-71" that can be found in the Objects tab of the Browser palette. The alien ship, shown here, is a copy of the jet object to which a stock bend and twist deformer, called "Xbend180", has been applied. The alien ship has also been scaled up in size and shaded with a stock shader called BlueGlow.

Figure 2. Ray Dream lets you combine the storyboarding and key event phases of the animation production process. The first panel in the storyboard is a view through the rendering camera of the first frame in the production. Note that the torpedo has been fired.

Figure 3. The second storyboard panel shows the scene at the next key event, which occurs one second into the movie. Because the frame rate used for this scene is 6 frames per second, this is the sixth frame.

Figure 4. Ray Dream Studio automatically creates a drawing for each frame between any two consecutive key events. This panel shows the third frame, which occurs halfway between the first and second key events.

Figure 5. A Ray Dream Studio production is "filmed" with the lights and cameras that you place in the scene. The final "print" is an AVI or QuickTime movie file and can be viewed with Ray Dream's Movie viewer immediately after it is rendered.

Object Changes:
- Visibility
- Type
- Number
- Position
- Orientation
- Color
- Texture
- Size
- Scale
- Geometry

Light Changes:
- Visibility
- Type
- Number
- Position
- Orientation
- Half angle and falloff angle
- Range
- Gel
- Effects
- Intensity

Camera Changes:
- Type
- Number
- Position
- Orientation
- Lens
- Zoom
- Filter
- Effects
- Depth of Field
- Focus

To be sure, it is no easy task to depict and draw and animate the volume, perspective, lighting, realism, and physics of a 3D world scene with 2D drawing tools and techniques.

Changes Between Key Frames

ADDING ACTION TO A SCENE

Fortunately, Ray Dream makes it possible for those of us who cannot afford to hire an army of skilled artists and animators to produce first-rate models, scenes, still renders, and animated renders, all from within the integrated Ray Dream Studio environment. Even better, Ray Dream affords creative possibilities that are simply not available with traditional animation techniques.

Animating the space shuttle

To illustrate how Ray Dream makes short work of the traditional animation process, consider a simple movie that shows the space shuttle lifting off and rising into the air. This movie:

- Has a running time of 3 seconds.
- Has a frame rate of 6 fps (frames per second).
- Uses the stock space shuttle object that is located in the Land&Sea family in the Objects tab of the Browser palette.

The traditional animator would have to spend a fair amount of time to render or arrange the scene and photograph it repeatedly.

But with Ray Dream Studio 5, the complete animation process is reduced to a handful of steps that can be performed in roughly five minutes.

To animate a space shuttle liftoff:

1. Create a new, empty scene.

2. Choose Workspace from the Windows menu.

and

Select 800x600 Animation or 1024x768 Animation from the submenu to set up the workspace for the animation.

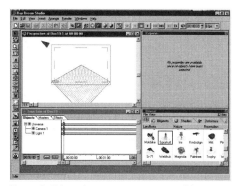

Figure 6. This workspace arrangement provides access to the Perspective window, the Time Line window, the Properties and Browser palettes, and the Time Controller toolbar.

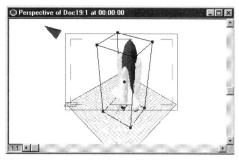

Figure 7. The space shuttle 3D object.

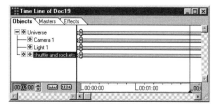

Figure 8. The Time Line window.

Animate the Space Shuttle

Figure 9. The Time Controller toolbar.

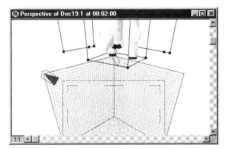

Figure 10. Drag the shuttle's projection on the active, right plane so that its engines clear the top border of the Production Frame, and release the mouse.

Figure 11. The diagonal stripe in the center of the shuttle's transition Track indicates that this segment of the Track is located between two key events. Double-click any portion of the segment to open the **Transition Options** dialog box.

3. Click the Perspective window to make it the current window.

and

Choose Production Frame from the View menu to identify the area of the screen that will be rendered **(Figure 6)**.

4. Click the Spcshutl icon from the Land&Sea family in the Objects tab of the Browser palette.

and

Drag the icon into the Perspective window and release the mouse.

5. Click and drag the shuttle object into the center of the Production Frame **(Figure 7)**.

6. Place the current time indicator in the Time Line window at the 2-second point by dragging its bulb-like bottom portion with the mouse to the right and releasing the mouse when it is over the 2-second mark.

or

Click and enter "02" in the seconds field (i.e., the middle pair of digits) in the Time Edit Controller in either the Time Line window **(Figure 8)** or the Time Controller toolbar **(Figure 9)**.

7. Display the working box's right plane by clicking the right plane region of the Display Planes tool.

and

Make the right plane the active plane by holding the Alt/Option key and clicking the right plane region again.

8. While holding down the Shift key, click and drag the shuttle object's projection on the right plane upward so that its engines are placed just beyond the top of the Production Frame **(Figure 10)**.

9. To apply a transition effect that simulates the shuttle's gradual acceleration during liftoff, make the Time Line the current window **(Figure 11)**.

and

Double-click the track that is directly to the right of the shuttle to open the Transition Options dialog box **(Figure 12)**.

and

Choose Linear from the dropdown list box of transition types.

and

Drag the Ease In/Out Slider to the extreme right (100%) position.

and

Click OK to apply these settings to the 10 "tweener" frames that will be automatically rendered between the first key frame at time 0-second mark and the second one at the 2-second mark.

10. To continue the movie for 1 second after the shuttle has left the Production Frame, move the Current Time Bar away from the 2-second mark.

and

Position the mouse over the right edge of the render range so that it becomes a crosshair.

and

Click and drag the crosshair cursor to the right and release it when it is over the 3-second mark on the Time Axis **(Figure 13)**.

11. To render a low res movie, choose Anim - Fast Preview from the Render menu **(Figure 14)**.

12. When the movie has been rendered, review it in the Ray Dream Movie viewer **(Figure 15)**.

and

If you wish to save the movie in a disk file, choose Save from the File menu to specify a file name and path in the Save dialog box **(Figure 16)**.

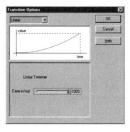

Figure 12. The Transition Options dialog box. The slider has been adjusted to accelerate the transition of the shuttle from its initial position in the first key event at the 0-second frame to its eventual position in the second key event at the 2-second frame.

Figure 13. By extending the render range for an additional period of one second, the movie will not end too abruptly after the shuttle has left the frame.

Figure 14. Choose **Anim–Fast Preview** from the **Render** menu.

Figure 15. Play, stop, loop, or scrub the movie with the Movie viewer controls.

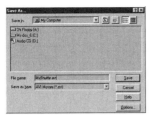

Figure 16. Saving the rendered movie.

Figure 17. Expanding the Objects hierarchy reveals many tracks that can be transitioned over time.

Figure 18. The Masters tracks that can be animated.

Figure 19. The Effects tracks that can be animated.

 Tip

■ The next chapter contains detailed information about selecting and configuring Ray Dream Studio's many render options and settings.

WORKING WITH THE TIME LINE WINDOW

In the first chapter of this book, you learned that the Perspective window excels at depicting the spatial relationships between the objects of a scene, while the hierarchy area of the Time Line window excels at depicting their logical relationships.

The Time Line window also excels at depicting the temporal relationships between key events—i.e., the order of their occurrence, and the amount of time that separates their occurrence.

Exploring the Time Line window

The Time Line window features three main tabs:

- The **Objects tab** shows the logical relationship between groups and the objects, cameras, lights, and other groups that comprise their members **(Figure 17)**.

- The **Masters tab** lists the master copy of each object. One master object is created for every geometrically unique object **(Figure 18)**.

- The **Effects tab** displays the Render settings for the current scene **(Figure 19)**.

The Time Line window also contains a timeline settings area. This area holds the following controls for editing any animatable events that can be accessed in the Objects, Masters, or Effects tabs **(Figure 20)**:

- The **Time Axis** is a scrollable gray ruler-like region at the bottom of the Time Line window that contains the timeline for the scene.

- The **Current Time Bar** indicates the time and frame that is currently selected and displayed in the Perspective window. When this bar is dragged to a specific time/frame position, the Perspective window updates to show that scene at the new time and frame.

- The **Render Range** is a white segment of the Time Axis that defines the sequence of frames that would be animated if you launched an animation render or preview using the scene's current render settings.

- The **Animatable Property Bars**, also known as the tracks, indicate by their presence which objects, properties, and settings can be animated.

- The **key event marker** shows the time and frame position of a key event, which, in turn, is a particular arrangement of the scene's objects, lights, cameras, and render settings. key event markers can be copied, deleted, moved, and mirrored.

- The **tweener indicator** discloses that segment of a track which falls between two key event markers. Double-clicking any part of the indicated segment opens the Transition Options dialog box, in which the tweener's type and settings can be specified, as described below.

- The **Time Edit Controller** is used to display and edit the current time/frame position. The first pair of

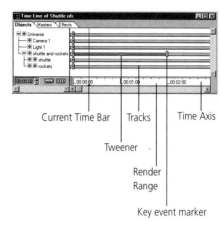

Figure 20. The Time Line window controls.

Figure 21. The **Set Time Axis** dialog box.

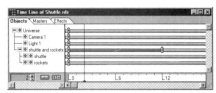

Figure 22. Clicking the right button of the Set Time Axis controls toggles the units of measurement used by the Time Axis between hours, minutes, and frame numbers and, as shown here, only frame numbers.

Figure 23. The "Current Frame" referred to in the **Scene Settings** dialog box is the frame that is specified as the current frame in the Time Line window and the Time Controller toolbar.

Figure 24. The Render Range, which provides the numbers of the first and last frames to be rendered, can also be set in the Scene Settings dialog box.

Figure 25. The Time Edit Controller that is located on the Time Controller toolbar is always synchronized with the Time Edit Controller in the Time Line window.

digits represents hours. The second pair represents seconds. The third pair represents frame numbers.

- The left Time Axis control button displays the Set Time Axis dialog box **(Figure 21)**, which contains three settings:

- The Division setting controls whether the division marks are drawn every 1/3, 1, 2, 4, 10, or 20 seconds or every 1 or 2 minutes.

- The Frame Rate setting lets you specify a frame-per-second rate of 1, 2, 3, 6, 12, 15, 18, 24, 25, 30, 50, or 60 frames per second.

- The Snap to Frame Boundary checkbox controls whether the Key Event markers and the Current Time Bar will snap to frame markers during creation or movement.

- The right Time Axis control button toggles the division markings on the Time Axis and the Time Edit Controller fields in the Time Line window between a time/frame number display and a frame number display **(Figure 22)**.

✔ Tips

- ■ When you render a still image, the image is composed using the scene configuration and the render effects that exist at the Current Frame **(Figure 23)**.

- ■ When you render a movie, the render range provides the starting and ending frame numbers **(Figure 24)**.

- ■ If the Time Controller toolbar is displayed, a Time Edit Controller is also displayed in that toolbar **(Figure 25)**. Its values and units of measurement are synchronized with the Time Edit Controller located at the bottom-left corner of the Time Line window.

Editing the timeline

Key events can be selected, copied, pasted, moved, and deleted.

To select and edit single or multiple key events:

1. Click the first key event marker.

2. To add other key event markers to the selection, hold down the Shift key and click the markers **(Figure 26)**.

or

1. Click the Selection tool.

2. Click and drag the mouse to draw a marquee around the marker or markers to be selected

and

Release the mouse button.

The appearance of a plus sign on a key event marker indicates that two or more key event markers overlap each other **(Figure 27)**.

To visualize overlapping key event markers:

1. Click the Zoom tool in the Tools tool-bar.

2. Click the marker repeatedly to expand the scale of the Time axis until the two markers are displayed separately.

or

Expand the scale of the Time axis with the Time Axis control and the Set Time Axis dialog box, as described above.

4. Move either marker or both, if desired.

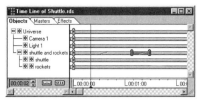

Figure 26. Two key event markers have been selected.

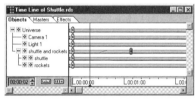

Figure 27. Overlapping key event markers are indicated by a plus sign.

Editing the Timeline

To edit a key event marker selection:

1. To delete the selection, press the Delete or Backspace key.

or

Choose Cut from the Edit menu.

2. To move the selection, click and drag it to another position on its track.

3. To move a marker while maintaining its position between the markers immediately before and after it, hold down the Shift key while dragging the marker.

4. To nudge the selection, hold the Shift key while pressing the Left or Right Arrow key to move the marker one frame at a time.

5. To copy the selection and paste the copy to a new location on the same track, hold down the Alt/Option key while Right-clicking/Ctrl-clicking the selection.

and

Without releasing the mouse, drag the now selected copy to the desired location.

6. To paste a marker selection that has been copied to the clipboard to another item that can accept the events contained in the selected markers, select the target item in the Hierarchy area.

and

Choose Paste from the Edit menu to insert the copy at the same time/frame position of the original selection.

7. To stretch the selection of three or more markers to increase or decrease the number of tweener frames proportionally, hold the Ctrl/Command key while dragging one of the markers.

8. To undo the most recent edits to the Time Line window, make the Time Line window the current window and Choose Undo from the Edit menu.

Edit a Key Event Marker Selection

Selecting and configuring tweeners

The tweener setting specifies how the transition between two key frames will occur.

To edit and configure a tweener:

1. Display, expand, and scroll the Time Line window to display part or all of the segment within which the tweener is located.

2. Double-click the tweener segment to open the Transition Options dialog box.

3. Click the dropdown list button to display a list of available tweeners.

4. Select one of the following tweeners from the list:

- Bezier **(Figure 28)**
- Discrete **(Figure 29)**
- Formula **(Figure 30)**
- Linear **(Figure 31)**
- Oscillate **(Figure 32)**

5. While viewing the preview area for visual feedback, adjust the slider controls in the settings area to configure the transition as desired.

6. Click OK to apply the tweener type and settings.

or

Click cancel to abort the process.

Animating other properties

In addition to animating transformations—that is, changes in the position and orientation of 3D objects, cameras and lights, and in the size of 3D objects—you can perform the Animation, timeline-editing, and tweener configuration operations outlined above on any object, property, effect, or other setting that has a track displayed next to it in the timeline area of the Time Line window.

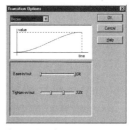

Figure 28. The Bezier transition options.

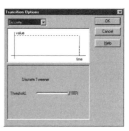

Figure 29. The Discrete transition options.

Figure 30. The Formula transition options.

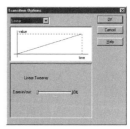

Figure 31. The Linear transition options.

Edit and Configure a Tweener

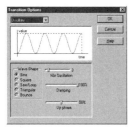

Figure 32. The Oscillate transition options.

Figure 33. The Animate checkbox in General tab of the Properties palette controls whether an object's animation Tracks are displayed in the Time Line window.

✔ Tips

■ Some tracks contain other, nested Tracks that are hidden if they are not expanded. If a plus sign is displayed to the left of any item listed in the Objects, Masters, or Effects tab, click the plus sign to expand the item and display the nested tracks. Repeat the expansion process until all tracks have been expanded.

■ You can enable or disable the "animatability" of most objects by checking or unchecking the Animate checkbox in the General tab of their Properties palette **(Figure 33)**.

■ The XYZ Event mode can affect the appearance of your animation. When the default setting, "Mark XYZ Together", is used, transforming an object in one dimension causes key events to be placed on the X, Y, and Z tracks. The other mode, Only Mark Changed, places a key event marker only on the track or tracks that correspond to axes whose values have changed. The mode is set by choosing the XYZ Event Mode command from the Arrange menu.

BEHAVIORS

In the very first chapter, you added a spin behavior to an object and rendered a movie using the scene's default render range of 2 seconds.

In the next few pages, you will learn how to select, configure, and blend a variety of behaviors.

Stock behaviors

Ray Dream Studio offers a wide variety of stock behaviors:

• **Point At** causes a camera or light to aim itself toward another object.

• **Bounce** causes the object to bounce up and down.

Behaviors

- **Inverse Kinematics** causes linked objects to move together.

- **Spin** causes an object to spin around an axis.

- **Track** causes an object to follow the movements of another, unlinked object. It can be used to make a camera or light track a moving object.

- **Initial Velocity** sets an item's inertia at frame 1 and cannot be reset with key event markers in later frames.

- **Directional Force**, **Point Force**, **Flow Force**, **Damping Force**, and **Rotational Force** are all physical forces that you can apply to your objects.

- **Apply Physical Effects** instructs the object to obey the Initial Velocity and the various Force behaviors.

Applying, ordering, and removing behaviors

Behaviors are applied with the Behavior tab of the Properties palette.

To apply a behavior to a 3D object, camera, or light:

1. Select the object, camera, or light.

2. If the Properties palette is not displayed, choose Properties from the Windows menu.

3. Click the Behaviors tab.

4. Click the pink plus sign.

5. Chose the behavior from the Add dialog box and click OK **(Figure 34)**.

6. Configure the behavior's settings.

7. If the Auto checkbox does not contain a check mark, click it to enter Auto apply mode.

or

Click the Apply button.

The relative positions of behaviors determine their order of precedence.

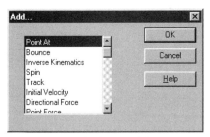

Figure 34. The **Add Behaviors** dialog box.

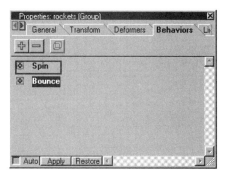

Figure 35. Reorder behaviors by dragging and dropping them in the desired order.

To reorder behaviors:

1. Collapse all expanded behavior setting areas by clicking the minus sign (arrow on the Mac) that appears to the left of their names.

2. Click and drag the name of the behavior to be moved to its new relative position **(Figure 35)**.

✔ Tip

■ Multiple behaviors can be applied to an object unless they are contradictory, in which case the last to be added will take precedence.

Behaviors are applied with the Behavior tab of the Properties palette.

To remove a behavior from an object, camera, or light:

1. Select the host object.

2. Select the behavior in the Behavior tab of the Properties palette by clicking its name.

3. Press the Delete or Backspace key.

Applying physics behaviors to objects and enforcing their effects on other objects

A special procedure must be followed to apply the Initial Velocity and various Force behaviors to an object.

To apply physical forces to an object:

1. Position the current time to the first frame.

2. Select the object.

3. Using the procedure described above for adding behaviors, add the Apply Physical Effects behavior to the first behavior position.

4. Add one or more of the Initial Velocity and various Force behaviors in any order, and adjust their settings **(Figure 36)**.

Likewise, a special procedure must be followed to ensure that an object that has been given a physics behavior can exert that behavior on other objects in transactions such as collisions.

To cause the physical behaviors of one object to influence another object:

1. Select the other object.

2. Click the Miscellaneous tab of its Properties palette.

3. Click the pink plus sign to open the Add dialog box.

and

Double-click the Physical Effects Solid property **(Figure 37)**.

✔ Tip

■ Physical force behaviors and the Physical Effects Solid property should not be confused with collision tracking. Collision tracking, which is enabled or disabled with a toggle button that appears on the Rendering toolbar **(Figure 38)**, helps you place objects against each other when you are arranging them in the Perspective window. If enabled, collision tracking temporarily "stops" you from dragging one solid object through another, to give you the opportunity to leave them against each other.

VISUALIZING AND PREVIEWING ANIMATIONS

Before investing the time to produce a final render or even a draft one, it is a good idea to check your work with two simple procedures:

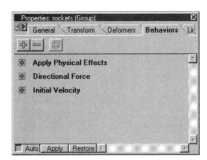

Figure 36. Physical forces can be used only if they are ordered in a proper sequence.

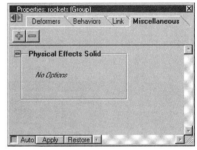

Figure 37. An object that has physical forces will not influence other objects unless the Physical Effects Solid property is enabled in the Miscellaneous tab of its Properties palette.

Figure 38. Collision tracking, which is unrelated to physics behaviors, is enabled or disabled through the Collision Tracking tool on the Rendering toolbar.

Physical Behaviors

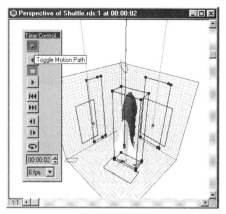

Figure 39. The shuttle's motion path is displayed because the View Motion Path button is depressed.

- Visualize the individual motion path of each animated 3D object, light, and camera.

- Preview the animation in the Perspective window.

To perform these steps, you should first display both the Rendering toolbar and the Time Controller toolbar. Using the stock work space settings for animation will display both of these toolbars.

Viewing an object's motion path

The first step is to view the motion path for individual objects. The motion path is a 3D curve that runs through the Perspective window to show you how the currently selected object moves throughout the course of the animation.

To toggle the visibility of an object's motion path:

1. Select the object in either the Time Line or Perspective window, whichever is more convenient.

2. Make the Perspective window the current window.

3. Click the Toggle Motion Path button in the Time Controller toolbar to the in position to display the path.

and

Click the button to the out position to hide the motion path **(Figure 39)**.

✔ Tips

■ You cannot manipulate the motion path to set or adjust an object's animation path.

■ Only one object's motion path can be displayed at a time.

The next step is to preview the dynamics of the animation in the Perspective window.

View Object's Motion Path

To preview an animation in the Perspective window:

1. Make the Perspective window the current window.

2. To maximize performance, verify that the current preview quality that is specified in the View menu is the lowest level of quality that is consistent with the purpose of the preview.

3. If the Shaded or Better preview mode is used, click the Interactivity button on the Rendering toolbar to enable objects to move during the preview **(Figure 40)**.

4. If desired, click the Loop button to the in position to enable the playback to loop until you press the stop button.

5. Click the Play button to play the animation forward.

or

Click the Play Backward button to run the animation backwards.

6. Click the Previous Frame button to move to the frame right before the current frame.

7. Click the Next Frame button to move to the frame right after the current frame.

8. Click the Rewind button to move to the first frame.

9. Click the Fast Forward button to move to the last frame in the render range.

10. Press the Stop button to end the preview **(Figure 41)**.

In the next and final chapter, you will learn how to configure the many different render options and other scene settings to generate professional still and movie renders.

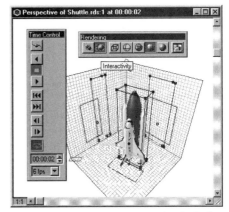

Figure 40. Preparing to preview an animation in the Perspective window using the Shaded level of preview quality.

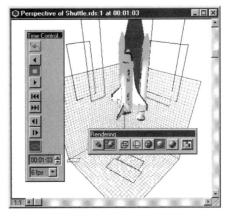

Figure 41. Previewing the shuttle.

Preview an Animation

Figure 1. This trophy is a stock object taken from the Browser palette. It was rendered as a still, using the ThinkFish Natural Media Rendering Engine's silk screen drawing option.

Figure 2. This is the last frame of a rendered movie, in which the same trophy is rotated to give the appearance of shaking. Note that the bottom and top of the trophy move out of the production frame at this particular point in the action and are therefore outside of the rendered frame.

Figure 3. The first trophy image was opened in Windows 95 Paint and revised to include a block of text.

Rendering is the process of capturing and outputting a 2D view of a 3D scene. A still is a rendering of a single image that is captured by a single camera **(Figure 1)**. A movie is a rendering of a series of images that reflect changes to objects and lights over time **(Figure 2)**.

The ultimate goal of building and refining a 3D scene is to produce one or more renderings that can be used with other applications. For example, a rendered still can be enhanced, composited, or otherwise manipulated with image editing programs **(Figure 3)**, and rendered animations can be incorporated into movies that are produced with desktop video editing programs.

The five phases of rendering

Renders are performed and managed in five phases:

- Planning the render.
- Setting up the render.
- Performing the render.
- Reviewing the render.
- Managing the render.

Performing test renders

Scenes frequently undergo multiple renderings that help you spot problems before investing the time to produce a final rendering. Each such "test" render and the final render should be put through each of the five phases.

The remainder of this chapter will teach you how to progress through these phases, step by step.

Five Phases of Rendering

PLANNING THE RENDER

Preparing the render involves two major steps:

- Identifying how the render will be used.
- Selecting the frame or frames to be rendered.

Identifying how the render will be used

Stills and movies can be used in a variety of ways, such as publication in print-based publications, HTML pages on the World Wide Web, and broadcast-quality video productions. Render settings dictate the aesthetics, the logistics, and the statistics of the final render—that is, the quality of the output file, the memory and storage required for the job, and the amount of time it will take. Thus, the first goal should be to develop a specification for the final render.

Selecting the frame or frames to be rendered

To render a still image, you need to select the view from the scene that will be rendered, and to frame that view with the Production Frame.

A still can, of course, be rendered from a single frame taken from a sequence of frames that were created to form a movie. In such a case, it is helpful to navigate the timeline in the Time Line window to preview the scene at the position of the target frame.

To select and frame a view to be rendered as a still:

1. Open the scene by choosing Open from the File menu **(Figure 4)**.

2. Select the scene file in the Open File dialog box **(Figure 5)**.

Figure 4. Open a scene with the **Open** command under the **File** menu.

Figure 5. Select the scene to open from the **Open File** dialog box.

Planning the Render

Figure 6. Set up the Perspective window and, if desired, the Time Line window, as shown.

Figure 7. The **Production Frame** command in the **View** menu causes the production frame to be displayed in the Perspective window.

Figure 8. Once selected, the production frame can moved and resized.

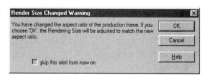

Figure 9. Ray Dream warns you if you change the aspect ratio of the production frame.

3. Display the Perspective window and make it the current window.

4. Choose Preset Position from the View menu and select Reference in the submenu.

or

Select a custom camera by choosing Camera from the View menu and selecting a camera from the submenu.

5. To use a frame other than the first frame, open and scroll the Time Line window, and navigate to the point in time at which the frame occurs.

or

Use the controls on the Time Controller toolbar to navigate to the point in time at which the desired frame occurs.

6. Adjust your view of the window contents with Zoom, Hand, and Camera Dolly tools if desired **(Figure 6)**.

7. Choose production frame from the View menu to display the production frame **(Figure 7)**.

8. Click the Production Frame to select it **(Figure 8)**.

9. To resize the production frame without changing the aspect ration, hold down the Shift key and drag any corner handle toward or away from the center of the frame.

or

To resize the production frame and change its aspect ratio, drag any corner handle toward or away from the center of the frame and confirm the operation in the Render Size Changed Warning dialog box **(Figure 9)**.

To render a movie, you must designate the sequence of frames by referencing the starting frame's time and the ending frame's time. In the next section, you will learn how to use the movie options of the Scene Settings window's Output tab to perform this task.

Render a View as a Still

✔ **Tips**

■ The production frame acts like the viewfinder of a camera. Reducing the size of the production frame has the same effect as zooming into a scene with a zoom lens.

■ The Zoom tools, however, do not resize or otherwise affect the production frame's size or scope.

■ If an object or camera moves, then part or all of the subject may fall outside of the production frame. Care must therefore be taken when sizing and positioning the production frame.

Figure 10. Ray Dream's stock renders for stills and animations can be selected and launched from the **Render** menu.

SETTING UP THE RENDER

Ray Dream Studio provides multiple render options. How you configure these options will determine what the render will look like and how much time, memory, and storage it will consume.

Figure 11. To interrupt or abort the render process, click the Close WIndow button on the Render Document window.

Using stock renders

Before investing time in creating a custom render, it makes sense to determine whether one of Ray Dream's 14 stock renders would achieve the goals of the current render session. These stock renders can satisfy a wide range of goals, from quick and dirty renders to fully detailed animation renders.

To render with a stock render command:

1. Make the Perspective window the current window.

2. Select and launch the desired stock render by choosing its command from the Render menu **(Figure 10)**.

Figure 12. Click the Continue or Abort button.

To abort or interrupt the rendering process:

1. Press the Escape key.

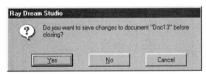

Figure 13. When closing a Render Document window, you are prompted to save or discard the document.

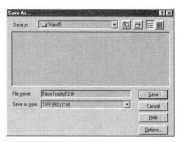

Figure 14. Enter a file name to save the render document to disk.

Figure 15. The Renderer tab of the Scene Settings window.

Figure 16. The **Current Scene Settings** command is accessed via the **Render** menu.

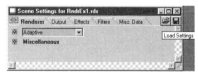

Figure 17. The Open File button is located at top right corner the Rendering Settings window.

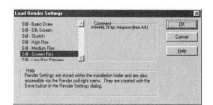

Figure 18. The **Load Render Settings** dialog box.

or

Close the window in which the render is being performed **(Figure 11)**, and click the Continue Rendering or Abort Rendering button **(Figure 12)**.

To save or discard the render:

1. Click the render document's close window button.

2. Click Yes or No in the warning dialog box that appears **(Figure 13)**.

3. If you click Yes, enter a file name in the Save As dialog box **(Figure 14)**.

✔ Tip

■ When you perform a stock render, the render begins immediately.

Customizing renders

Render options are set in the Rendering Settings window **(Figure 15)**.

To open the Rendering Settings window:

1. Choose Current Scene Settings from the Render menu **(Figure 16)**.

Loading a saved render

You can create a custom render from scratch. Or, you can load and customize a saved render. A saved render is a group of settings that are stored in a disk file. Instructions for managing saved renders are set forth at the end of this chapter.

To open a saved render:

1. Click the Open File button on the Rendering Settings window **(Figure 17)**.

2. In the Load Render Settings dialog box, click the saved render setting and click OK **(Figure 18)**.

Render options

The Rendering Settings window contains five tabs. The tabs and the options they contain are listed here:

- The Renderer tab lets you specify and configure one of four rendering engines **(Figure 19)**.
- The Output tab lets you specify the render's image size, camera, file name, file size, file format, and file G-Buffer contents **(Figure 20)**.
- The Effects tab lets you specify the render's ambient light, atmosphere, background, and backdrop **(Figure 21)**.
- The Filters tab lets you set one or more filters for the render from a list of 11 stock filters **(Figure 22)**.
- The Miscellaneous Data tab lets you specify the use and fidelity level of physical effects **(Figure 23)**.

✔ Tip

- ■ When configuring a render engine or any other tab of the Rendering Settings window, be sure to expand any area of the tab that is collapsed by clicking its plus sign (arrow on the Mac).

Choosing and configuring a rendering engine

The rendering engine has a major impact on both the appearance and the speed of the render.

Ray Dream Studio provides four rendering engines:

- The Draft Z-Buffer engine is best suited to quick and dirty renders.
- The NaturalMedia ThinkFish engine produces renders that appear to be drawn or sketched by hand.

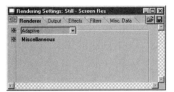

Figure 19. The Renderer tab contains settings for the rendering engine.

Figure 20. The Output tab contains settings for the data that will be used to create the render output file, and the format and specifications for that file.

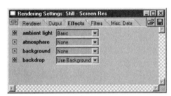

Figure 21. The Effects tab contains settings for the render's lighting, atmosphere, backdrop, and background.

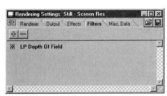

Figure 22. The Filters tab contains settings for the filters that will be used to enhance or distort the render.

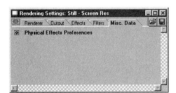

Figure 23. The Miscellaneous Data tab contains settings for the render's physical effects.

Figure 24. Select a rendering engine.

Figure 25. The Draft Z-Buffer rendering engine.

Figure 26. The NaturalMedia ThinkFish rendering engine .

- The Ray Tracer engine is used to produce final, highly detailed renders. It literally traces rays of light as they interact with the objects in the scene.

- The Adaptive engine is a variation of the Ray Tracer engine. To save time, this engine renders objects with ray tracing and empty regions with an estimating algorithm.

To set the rendering engine:

1. Click the Render tab of the Current Scene Settings window.

2. Click the dropdown list of rendering engines.

3. Click the desired engine (**Figure 24**).

To configure the Draft Z-Buffer engine:

1. Set the Reflected color by double-clicking its preview swatch (**Figure 25**), and select a new color from the color picker dialog box.

2. Set the Transparency color by double-clicking its preview swatch and select a new color from the color picker dialog box.

3. Click the desired preview quality (Wireframe, Preview, Shaded Preview, or Better preview) in the Quality section.

To configure the NaturalMedia ThinkFish engine:

1. Place a check in the Preview Scene checkbox to preview configuration changes using your scene (**Figure 26**).

or

Remove the check to use the default cube preview.

2. Place a check in the Auto Preview checkbox to cause the preview to update instantly.

or

Remove the check in the Auto Preview checkbox and press the Refresh Preview button to update the preview manually.

3. Select the drawing type (Basic Draw, Crystal, Inkwash, Multilevel Shading, Silk Screen, Sketch 1, or Sketch 2) from the dropdown list of drawing types.

4. Place or remove a check in the Default Lighting checkbox to enable or disable default lighting in the preview.

5. Adjust the Line Thickness slider to a value between 0 and 300%.

6. Adjust the Sketchiness slider to a value between 0 and 100% to increase or decrease the hand-drawn effect.

To configure the Ray Tracer engine:

1. Enable or disable each of the following features: Shadows, Reflections, Bump, Transparency, Refracted Transparency, and Light Through Transparency **(Figure 27)**.

2. Set the Adaptive Oversampling level to None, Fast, or Best.

3. Set the Maximum Ray Depth from 1 to 25.

To configure the Adaptive engine:

1. Enable or disable each of the following features: Shadows, Reflections, Bump, Transparency, Refracted Transparency, and Light Through Transparency **(Figure 28)**.

2. Set the Antialiasing feature to None, Edges, or Best.

3. Adjust the Silhouette Quality slider between 0 and 200%.

4. Set the Maximum Ray Depth from 1 to 25.

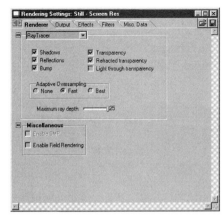

Figure 27. The RayTracer rendering engine.

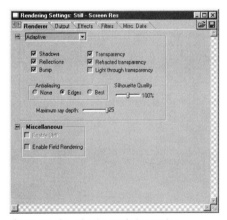

Figure 28. The Adaptive rendering engine.

Figure 29. Configuring the Image Size settings for the render's Output options.

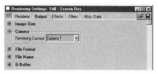

Figure 30. Configuring the Camera settings for the render's Output options.

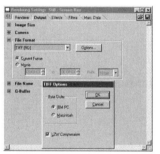

Figure 31. Configure the File Format settings for a still render's Output options, and the TIFF options available for the currently selected file format.

Figure 32. Configuring the File Format settings for a movie render's Output options, and the Video Compression options that are available for the currently selected file format.

Configuring the output options

Some of the output options vary according to whether the render is a still or a movie and according to the file type that you select.

To configure the render's output options:

1. Configure the Image Size settings in the following order **(Figure 29)**:

   • Place or remove a check in the Keep Proportions checkbox to maintain or discard proportions while resizing the render's dimensions in the next step.

   • Enter values and select units of measurement for the render's height and width.

   • Enter a Resolution value between 1 and 2400 dots per inch.

   • Enter a Pixel Aspect Ratio.

2. Configure the Camera setting by selecting the camera that will capture the render from the dropdown list of available cameras **(Figure 30)**.

3. If the render is a still, click the Current Frame radio button.

   and

   Configure the File Format settings in the following order **(Figure 31)**:

   • Select one of the following file formats from the File Format dropdown list: BMP, PhotoPaint, Painter Riff, GIF, JPEG, Photoshop 2.5, TIFF, PCX, or Targa.

   • Click the Options button to display and set any options that are available for the specific file type.

4. If the render is a movie, click the Movie radio button.

   and

   Configure the File Format settings in the following order **(Figure 32)**:

- Select one of the following file formats: AVI Movies, Sequenced BMP, Sequenced PhotoPaint, Sequenced Painter Riff, Sequenced GIF, Sequenced JPEG, Sequenced Photoshop 2.5, Sequenced TIFF, Sequenced PCX, or Sequenced Targa.

- Set the frames per second in the Rate dropdown list.

- Click the Options button to display and set any options that are available for the specific file type.

5. Configure the File Name settings as follows **(Figure 33)**:

- Click the Using Default File Name radio button to use a system-supplied file name.

or

- Click the In Named File radio button.

  and

  Click the Set button to specify a file name.

  and

  Enter a file name in the Save As dialog box, and click the Save button.

6. If the selected file format supports G-Buffer data, configure the File Format settings by specifying which of the following items should be placed in the file in addition to the RGB data: Pixel Color, Mask, Distance, Object Index, Normal Vector, 3D Position, and Surface Coordinates **(Figure 34)**.

Estimating render time and resolution

Because rendering can take a great deal of time, it is a good idea to get a time estimate before performing a render.

It is also helpful to know the maximum resolution render that could be produced within a specified period of time.

The Image Size settings of the Output options provide you with the means of estimating both numbers.

Figure 33. Configuring the File Name settings for the render's Output options.

Figure 34. Configuring the G-Buffer settings for the render's Output options.

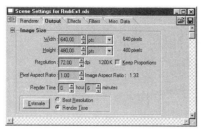

Figure 35. Estimating render time using the current settings.

Figure 36. Estimating highest possible render resolution within a specific amount of time using current settings.

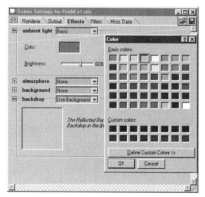

Figure 37. Configuring the render's Effects options, and the system's **Color Picker** dialog box, which is opened by double-clicking the ambient light's preview color swatch.

To estimate render time using the current settings:

1. If it is not already displayed, display the Output options tab of the Current Scenes Settings window and expand the Image Size settings area as described above **(Figure 35)**.

2. Click the Render Time radio button.

3. Click the Estimate button.

4. Read the estimated render time in the Render Time field.

To estimate best render resolution within a specified time:

1. Click the Best Resolution radio button in the Image Size area of the Output options tab **(Figure 36)**.

2. Enter a time period in the Render Time fields.

3. Click the Estimate button.

Configuring special effects

To configure a render's Effects options:

1. Select the ambient light type from the dropdown list box (if types other than Basic are available on your installation) **(Figure 37)**.

2. Set the ambient light's color by double-clicking its preview swatch and selecting a color from the Color Picker dialog box.

3. Adjust the Brightness slider to a value between 0 and 100%.

4. Select an atmosphere type (None, Cloudy Fog, or Distance Fox) from the atmosphere type dropdown list.

5. Select a background type (None, Bi-Gradient, Color, Formula, Map, or Movie) from the background type dropdown list.

Estimate Render Time and Best Resolution

6. Specify a backdrop type (use Background, Bi-Gradient, Color, Formula, Map, or Movie) from the backdrop type dropdown list.

7. Specify any subsidiary settings.

Configuring the filters

To configure the render's Filter options:

1. Click the pink plus sign to add a filter **(Figure 38)**.

2. In the filter type dropdown list, choose one of the following: LP Depth of Field, LP Lens Flare, LP Cross Screen, LP Glow, LP Nebula, LP Pulsator, LP Stars, LP Vario Cross, VL 3D Light Cone, VL Light Sphere, VL Aura.

3. If it is collapsed, expand the Filter area of the tab by clicking its yellow plus sign (arrow on the Mac).

4. Adjust the filter's settings **(Figure 39)**.

5. To remove a filter, click its name to select it and click the pink Minus sign.

6. To change the order of filters, select one or more filters by clicking them (while holding Shift for multiple filters) and drag the selection to the desired level in the tab **(Figure 40)**.

To configure a render's Miscellaneous Data options:

1. Enable or disable the render's Physical Effects option **(Figure 41)**.

2. Specify the fidelity level.

Working with render preferences and individual object overrides

Render preferences include the default rendering engine, shadow, reflection, and transparency settings. Changes to these preferences do not affect existing scenes. These settings become the default settings for all new scenes.

Figure 38. Configuring the render's Filter options.

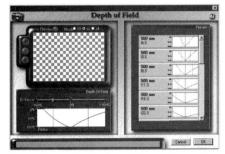

Figure 39. Configuring the additional, filter-specific options.

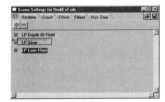

Figure 40. Changing the filter order with a drag and drop operation.

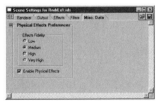

Figure 41. Configuring the render's Miscellaneous Data options.

Configure Render's Filter Options

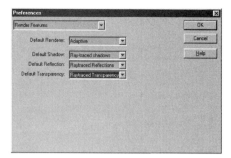

Figure 42. Setting default render preferences.

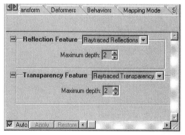

Figure 43. Default render preferences can be overridden for any object in a scene by editing the Rendering tab of its Properties palette.

To edit render preferences:

1. Choose Preferences from the File menu.

2. Choose Render Features from the dropdown list **(Figure 42)**.

3. Choose a default render engine from the Default Render dropdown list.

4. Choose a default shadow type (No shadows, Ray-traced shadows or Soft DRT shadows) from the Default Shadow dropdown list.

5. Choose a default reflection type (No reflections or Ray-traced reflections) from the Default Reflection dropdown list.

6. Choose a default transparency type (No transparency or Raytraced transparency) from the Default Transparency dropdown list.

Overriding render options for individual objects

Two render options—reflection and refraction—can be overridden for any individual object in a scene with the Rendering tab of its Properties palette. These options are useful in the creation of transparent objects, like window glass, and refractive objects, like prisms and fluids.

To override render options for a specific object:

1. Select the object in the Perspective or Time Line window.

2. Display the Properties palette by choosing Properties from the Windows menu.

3. Click the Rendering tab.

4. Set the Reflection Feature and Transparency Feature settings as desired **(Figure 43)**.

5. If the Auto checkbox is not checked, click the Apply button to apply the new property settings.

Edit Render Preferences

✔ Tip

■ If an object has been combined with other objects in a group, you must select the object individually by clicking and holding the mouse and selecting it from the pop-up of group members, or by clicking its name in the Time Line window.

Figure 44. The Rendering toolbar. The Render tool at the extreme right launches a render using the scene's current render settings.

PERFORMING THE RENDER

Renders can be performed individually or together in a batch queue.

Performing a single render

A single render is performed with a simple menu command.

To perform a render:

1. If it is not already displayed, display the Rendering toolbar by choosing Toolbars from the View menu and clicking Rendering in the toolbar list.

and

Click the render tool **(Figure 44)**.

or

1. Choose Use Current Settings from the Render menu **(Figure 45)**.

✔ Tip

■ To interrupt or abort a render before it is completed, use the procedures described earlier in this chapter in the section dealing with stock renders.

Performing multiple renders with the batch queue

A batch queue renders a series of scene files, one after the other, during a single render session. This process can put your computer to productive use in the background or while you are away from your desk.

Figure 45. The **Use Current Settings** command in the **Render** menu also launches a render using the current scene settings.

Perform a Render

Figure 46. Choose **Batch Queue** from the **Render** menu.

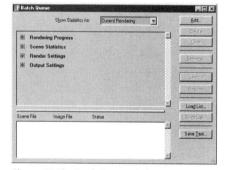

Figure 47. The Batch Queue window.

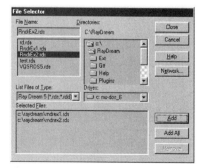

Figure 48. The **File Selector** dialog box is used to add files to the batch queue.

Separate scene files vs separate scene file instances

It is frequently necessary to create multiple renders from the same scene. For example, you may wish to render with different cameras, or from different points on the timeline.

Only one set of scene settings can be associated with a scene at any given time. Thus, to batch-queue multiple renders of the same scene, you could save multiple copies of the scene by using the File/Save As command and then customizing the render camera, timeline position, and other options for each desired render. These separate scene files could then be rendered together in a batch queue.

An easier but less flexible approach is to add the same scene file several times to a batch queue, and to use the temporary setting override features provided by the batch queue interface.

Defining the batch queue

The procedure for defining and launching a batch queue is basically the same for both of the strategies outlined above (saving multiple scene files or using multiple instances of the same file with temporary overrides).

To define, launch, and save a batch queue:

1. Choose Batch Queue from the Render menu **(Figure 46)**.

2. Size and position the Batch Queue window as desired **(Figure 47)**.

3. To add different scene files to the queue, click the Add button.

and

Select one, several, or all of the files in a directory in the File Selector dialog box **(Figure 48)**.

4. To add multiple instances of the same file, click the Add button and select the file as many times as desired.

5. To make temporary changes to the render settings for any scene file in the queue, click the Settings button.

and

Change the settings in the Override Render Settings dialog box, either manually **(Figure 49)**, or by clicking the Load Settings button and loading a saved settings file **(Figure 50)**.

and

Click OK to return to the Batch Queue dialog box.

6. Perform the batch queue render immediately by clicking the Launch button.

or

Save the batch queue to a disk file for later loading and launching by clicking the Save List button and naming and saving a batch queue file with the Save As dialog box **(Figure 51)**.

✔ **Tips**

■ To load and launch a previously saved batch queue file from the Batch Queue dialog box, click the Load List button, select the file with the Open dialog box, and press the Launch button.

■ Setting changes made in the Override Render Settings dialog box affect only the render performed by the batch queue and do not affect the scene file's settings.

■ You can, however, save the settings you specify in the Override Render Settings dialog box to a new file. To do so, click the Save Settings button, and name and save the new file with the Save Scene Settings dialog box.

Monitoring batch queue status

You can monitor the progress, statistics, and settings for either the currently executing render or any other render in the queue.

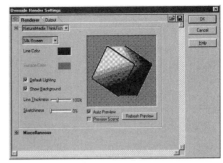

Figure 49. The **Override Settings** dialog box is used to temporarily override render settings for different scene files and different instances of the same scene file.

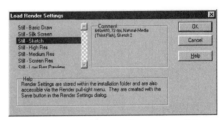

Figure 50. Use the **Load Render Settings** dialog box to select and load a saved render setting file to override a scene file's render settings temporarily.

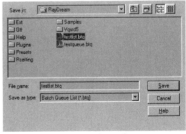

Figure 51. Batch queue lists can be saved by pressing the Save List button in the Batch Queue window and entering a file name in the **Save As** dialog box.

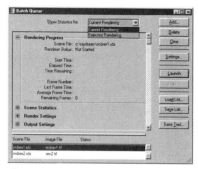

Figure 52. Specifying and examining a batch queue render.

Figure 53. To review batch queue renders, drag them with your system's file-finding applet and place them into the Ray Dream Studio window.

Figure 54. Ray Dream opens still renders in Image windows and movie renders in Movie windows.

To monitor the progress of a batch queue:

1. Choose Current Rendering from the "Show Statistics for" dropdown list box **(Figure 52)**.

or

Select a render in the Scene File list, and choose Selected Rendering from the dropdown list.

2. Expand and examine the statistics for the Rendering Process, Scene Statistics, Render Settings, and Output Settings.

REVIEWING THE RENDER

When a single render (i.e., a render that is launched with the Render button or command and is not in a batch queue) is complete, Ray Dream automatically presents the resulting file in either an Image window or a Movie window.

But when multiple renders are performed in a batch queue, you must manually open those files.

To review render files produced by a batch queue:

1. Choose Open from the File menu.

and

Choose Movie Files in the "Files of type" dropdown list box.

and

Open the movie file.

or

1. Launch your system's file-finding applet (Windows 95 Explorer or Macintosh Finder).

2. Locate the files you wish to review.

3. Select and drag the files onto the Ray Dream Studio window **(Figure 53)**.

4. To use the Image window or Movie window **(Figure 54)** that opens for each file, follow the directions below.

To use the Image window:

1. Position the Zoom pointer (the magnifying glass with a plus sign in its lens) on the part of the image you wish to examine.

2. To zoom in, click the Zoom tool.

3. To zoom out, click the Zoom tool while pressing the Alt/Option key.

To use the Movie window:

You can use the Movie window to view QuickTime and AVI movies.

- Click the Play button to play the movie.

- Click the Pause button to pause the movie.

- Click the Frame Forward or Frame Back button to advance or rewind the movie one frame at a time.

- Click the Loop button to replay the movie continuously until you click another button.

- Drag the slider to scrub through to a specific point of the movie.

In the case of a single render, you can, of course, save or discard the render output file as described earlier in this chapter. Batch renders, however, are different. Clicking their Close Window buttons does not discard them because they have already been saved to disk.

You have to use your system's file management application to delete any render file that has been saved to disk.

MANAGING THE RENDER

It has already been noted that render settings can be saved to disk and used at a later time. It has also been noted that a render setting differs from the render output file in that the former is a specification for the latter, and the latter is the byproduct of the former.

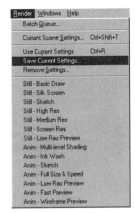

Figure 55. Render settings can be saved with the **Save Current Settings** command in the **Render** menu.

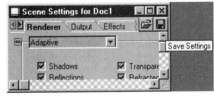

Figure 56. Render settings can also be saved with the Save Current Settings button in the **Current Scene Settings** dialog box.

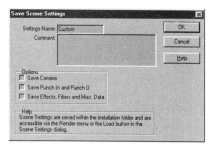

Figure 57. The **Save Scene Settings** dialog box.

Figure 58. Saved scene settings can be removed with the **Remove Settings** command in the **Render** menu.

Ray Dream Studio lets you manage renders by:

- Saving the render settings.
- Removing the render settings.

Saving render settings

To save the current render settings to disk:

1. Choose Save Current Settings from the Render menu **(Figure 55)**.

   or

   Click the Save Settings button in the top right corner of the Rendering Settings window **(Figure 56)**.

2. In the Save Scene Settings dialog box, enter a name and comment for the render.

   and

   Check or uncheck the Save Camera, Save Punch, and Save Filters, Effects, and Miscellaneous Data options as desired **(Figure 57)**.

Removing renders

To remove a render from your disk:

1. Choose Remove Settings from the Render menu **(Figure 58)**.

2. In the Remove Render Settings dialog box, select the settings to remove and click OK **(Figure 59)**.

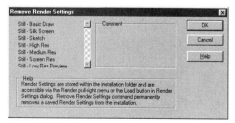

Figure 59. The **Remove Render Settings** dialog box.

Save Current Render Settings

APPENDIX: List of Keyboard Shortcuts by Menu

PERSPECTIVE WINDOW MENUS

(i.e., menus available when Perspective window is active)

	Windows	Mac
File Menu		
New	Ctrl+N	Command-N
Open	Ctrl+O	Command-O
Close	Ctrl+F4	Command-W
Save	Ctrl+S	Command-S
Print	Ctrl+P	Command-P
Preferences	Ctrl+Shift+P	Command-Shift-P
Exit	Alt+F4	Command-Q
Edit Menu		
Undo	Ctrl+Z	Command-Z
Redo	Ctrl+Y	Command-Y
Cut	Ctrl+X	Command-X
Copy	Ctrl+C	Command-C
Paste	Ctrl+V	Command-V
Duplicate	Ctrl+D	Command-D
Duplicate with symmetry	Ctrl+Alt+D	Command-D
Select All	Ctrl+Alt+C	Command-A
Select All Objects	Ctrl+Alt+A	Command-Option-A
Find	Ctrl+F	Command-F
View Menu		
Preset Position		
Reference	Ctrl+0	Command-0
Drawing Plane	Ctrl+5	Command-5
Top	Ctrl+5	Command-5
Bottom	Ctrl+2	Command-2
Left	Ctrl+4	Command-4
Right	Ctrl+6	Command-6
Front	Ctrl+1	Command-1
Back	Ctrl+3	Command-3
Wireframe	Ctrl+Shift+Y	Command-Shift-Y

	Windows	**Mac**
Preview (Fast)	.Ctrl+Alt+Shift+Y	.Command-Option-Shift-Y
Better Preview (Phong)	.Ctrl+Alt+Y	.Command-Option-Y
Grid	.Ctrl+J	.Command-J
Production Frame	.Ctrl+Alt+F	.Command-Option-F

Insert Menu

Camera	.Ctrl+Alt+C	.Command-Option-C
Light	.Ctrl+Alt+L	.Command-Option-L

Arrange Menu

Align Objects	.Ctrl+K	.Command-K
Group .:	.Ctrl+G	.Command-G
Ungroup	.Ctrl+U	.Command-U
Point At	.Ctrl+M	.Command-M
Center Hot Point	.Ctrl+Alt+H	.Command-Option-H
Send To Origin	.Ctrl+Shift+O	.Command-Shift-O
Send Working Box To		
Global Universe	.Ctrl+Alt+B	.Command-Option-B
Local Universe	.Ctrl+B	.Command-B
Selection	.Ctrl+Alt+Shift+B	.Command-Option-Shift-B

Render Menu

Current Scene Settings	.Ctrl+Shift+T	.Command-Shift-T
Use Current Scene		
Settings	.Ctrl+R	.Command-R

Windows Menu

New Perspective	.Ctrl+7	.Command-7
Browser	.Ctrl+B	.Command-B
Properties	.Ctrl+E	.Command-E
Current Shader Editor	.Ctrl+/	.Command-/

FREE FORM MODELER MENUS

Windows   Mac

File Menu
(See Perspective File menu)

Edit Menu
(See Perspective Edit menu)

View Menu
(See Perspective View menu)

Sections Menu
Center . . . . .Ctrl+Shift+C . . . . .Command-Shift-C
Show Shapes Numbers . . . . . . .Ctrl+Shift+N . . . . .Command-Shift-N
Cross Section Options . . . . .Ctrl+Alt+N . . . . .Command-Option-N

Arrange Menu
Group . . . . .Ctrl+G . . . . .Command-G
Ungroup . . . . .Ctrl+U . . . . .Command-U
Combine as Compound . . . . . .Ctrl+Alt+G . . . . .Command-Option-G

Render Menu
(See Perspective Render menu)

Windows
(See Perspective Windows menu)

Keyboard Shortcuts

MESH FORM MODELER MENUS

Windows   Mac

File Menu
(See Perspective File menu)

Edit Menu
(See Perspective Edit menu)

View Menu
Preset Position

	Windows	Mac
Reference	Ctrl+0	Command-0
Drawing Plane	Ctrl+5	Command-5
Top	Ctrl+8	Command-8
Bottom	Ctrl+2	Command-2
Left	Ctrl+4	Command-4
Right	Ctrl+6	Command-6
Front	Ctrl+1	Command-1
Back	Ctrl+3	Command-3
Reset Drawing Plane	Ctrl+Alt+0	Command-Option-0

Send Drawing Plane to

	Windows	Mac
Selection	Ctrl+Alt+5	Command-Option-5
Screen	Ctrl+Alt+7	Command-Option-7
Position	Ctrl+Alt+9	Command-Option-9
Top	Ctrl+Alt+8	Command-Option-8
Bottom	Ctrl+Alt+2	Command-Option-2
Left	Ctrl+Alt+4	Command-Option-4
Right	Ctrl+Alt+6	Command-Option-6
Front	Ctrl+Alt+1	Command-Option-1
Back	Ctrl+Alt+3	Command-Option-3
Wireframe	Ctrl+Shift+Y	Command-Shift-Y
Preview (Fast)	Ctrl+Alt+Shift+Y	Command-Option-Shift-Y
Grid	Ctrl+J	Command-J

Selection Menu

	Windows	Mac
Weld	Ctrl+Shift+W	Command-Shift-W
Link	Ctrl+L	Command-L
Unlink	Ctrl+U	Command-U

Render Menu
(see Perspective Render menu)

Windows
(See Perspective Windows menu)

INDEX

Index

Index

Index